THE WARLO_

US EIGHTH AIR FORCE FIGHTER COLOURS OF WORLD WAR II

VOLUME 1
THE 4TH, 20TH & 55TH FIGHTER GROUPS

Barry & Ann Money

FLIGHT RECORDER PUBLICATIONS

A passion for accuracy

First published in Great Britain in 2003 by
Flight Recorder Publications Ltd
Ashtree House, Station Road, Ottringham,
East Yorkshire, HU12 0BJ
Tel: 01964 624223 Fax: 01964 624666
E-mail: beketley@dircon.co.uk
Website: www.flight-recorder.com
© 2003 Flight Recorder Publications Ltd

ISBN 0 9545605 1 5

Edited by Barry Ketley
Design by Flight Recorder Publications Ltd
Printed in Italy by Eurolitho S.p.A.

ALSO AVAILABLE

A Civilian Affair
A Brief History of the Civilian Aircraft Company of Hedon
by
Eduard F. Winkler
ISBN 0 9545605 0 7

FORTHCOMING

Checkerboard Hunters
The Croatian Volunteers of 15./JG 52 on the Eastern Front
by
Marko Jeras, Dragisa Brăsnović
& Zdenko Kinjerovac
ISBN 0 9545605 2 3

Caption to title page:
Lockheed P-38J-10-LO 42-67757 of the 38th Fighter Squadron, 55th Fighter Group, in January 1944. Flown by an unidentified pilot, it shows the typically non-descript camouflage and markings worn by the type when it first arrived in Britain. This particular aircraft may be the replacement for 42-67064, also coded CG-C, which was lost in an accident in January 1944. If it was, it did not survive for long as it was shot down over Venlo, Holland, on 31 January, Lt. David P. Fisher being killed.

INTRODUCTION
A world in monochrome

Having lived through World War 2, I know that it was not fought in black and white, but you would not realize this from the huge majority of contemporary photographs published on the subject to date.

Interested mainly in the United States Eighth Air Force, I gradually realized that this was probably the largest aerial force the world will ever see. As I learned more about its units, it dawned on me: it was also the most colourful.

Colour photography was in its infancy at the start of the 1940s, particularly among amateurs. In wartime England, there were other priorities. Only a few, very few, really keen and enthusiastic snap-takers were able to secure colour film from the States, and make good use of it.

About a decade ago, some of these wartime colour shots began to appear in print, thanks to the works of Roger Freeman, Jeff Ethell, Thomas Ivie, and Warren Bodie, the greats among those who were writing on the subject. But colour remains comparatively scarce.

I wanted to see this wonderful armada in colour. Two things happened, to make a beginning possible. First came retirement, which gave me time. Second, I discovered computers, which meant I could produce the work at a reasonable rate. All that was needed now was information! For this I have scoured any and every published source of photographs I could acquire, my first and only criteria being that every reproduction must be based on photographic evidence. I have in every case ignored written descriptions, and other people's artwork, and worked only from my own interpretation of available photos.

Where are the pictures? Some are here thanks to Mike Bailey, Bruce Robertson and Philip Jarrett, but for most, see the bibliography. There are a few more on the Internet these days too, but for every aircraft for which photos are available, there are three that have never had their portraits published. It is difficult to imagine that American pilots in particular flew combat missions and risked their lives time and time again in an assigned machine, and a ground crew devoted all their waking hours to maintaining it, without ever recording it on film! If the photos were taken, they have remained hidden in personal archives, which in so many cases have been destroyed upon the demise of the owner, or for many other reasons.

Then there are the multitude of 'teasers', those photographs that show part of the aircraft, but manage to mask vital detail such as codes and serials, or are taken from the 'other side', with no other photographic coverage available. Sheer frustration!

This book is aimed unashamedly straight at fellow model-makers and also, possibly, at those manufacturing decals. There are lots of decals for Eighth Air Force aircraft available, but many of the well-known aces' aircraft are repeated on sheet after sheet, whereas the less-known aircraft have never been covered, at least in decal form.

The aircraft drawings are not presented as definitive scale drawings; they are simply the canvas on which to place the aircraft's unique artwork and colours. Great care has been taken with style and placement of artwork. Some interpretation of colours has been necessary, this being done by comparison to other known colours in the photograph, and other pictures of the same Group's aircraft. They are as accurate as I could possibly make them, but all errors are mine, and if you have any photographic proof which might correct any of these, I would be delighted to see it, via the publisher.

This will hopefully be the first of a series, eventually to cover all of the Mighty Eighth's Fighter Groups. Any and all photographic help would be most welcome. Updates and additions would be possible to the units already covered, possibly as a separate volume to finish the series.

Barry Money
Somerset
2003

Glossary

Amr.	Armourer
Asst.	Assistant
Capt.	Captain
CO	Commanding Officer
Col.	Colonel
ETO	European Theatre of Operations
FG	Fighter Group
FS	Fighter Squadron
HQ	Headquarters
KIA	Killed in Action
Lt.	Lieutenant
Lt. Col.	Lieutenant Colonel
Maj.	Major
MIA	Missing in Action
NG	Neutral Gray 43
NMF	Natural metal finish
OD	Olive Drab 41
POW	Prisoner of War
Sgt.	Sergeant
S/Sgt.	Staff Sergeant
T/Sgt.	Technical Sergeant

Below: Type recognition or European Theatre of Operations (ETO) bands as applied to Thunderbolts from February 1943. White on camouflaged aircraft, black on those in natural metal finish. Horizontal tail band in lower position of 36 inches below fin tip on all aircraft after P-47D-3-RA, and all P-47D-RE models.

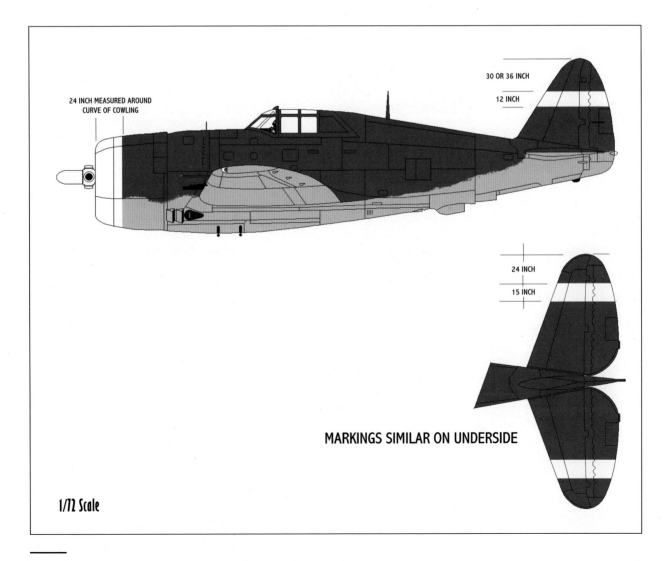

24 INCH MEASURED AROUND CURVE OF COWLING

30 OR 36 INCH

12 INCH

24 INCH

15 INCH

MARKINGS SIMILAR ON UNDERSIDE

1/72 Scale

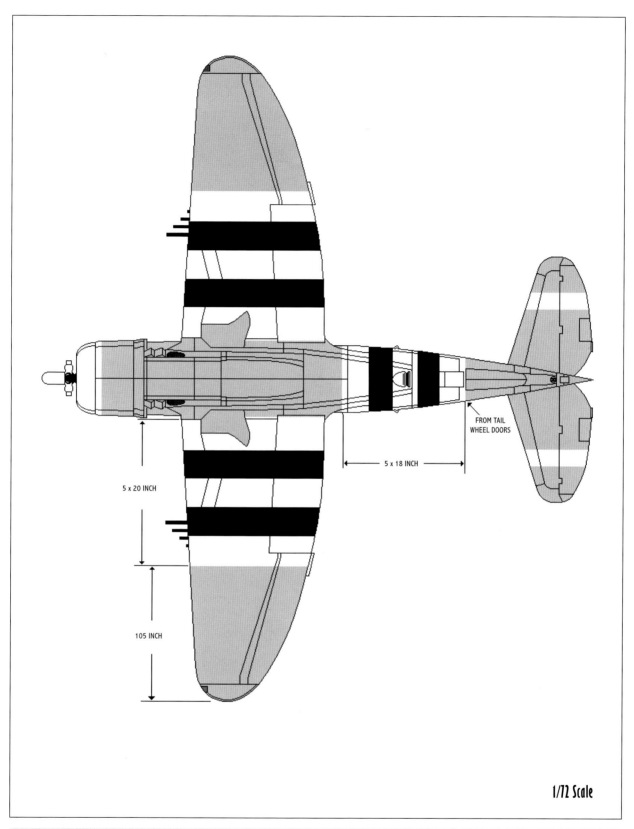

FROM TAIL
WHEEL DOORS

5 x 18 INCH

5 x 20 INCH

105 INCH

1/72 Scale

D-Day stripes as applied to P-47s from 5th June 1944. Upper and lower surfaces the same. Removed from upper surfaces from July 1944, and completely from wings in September.

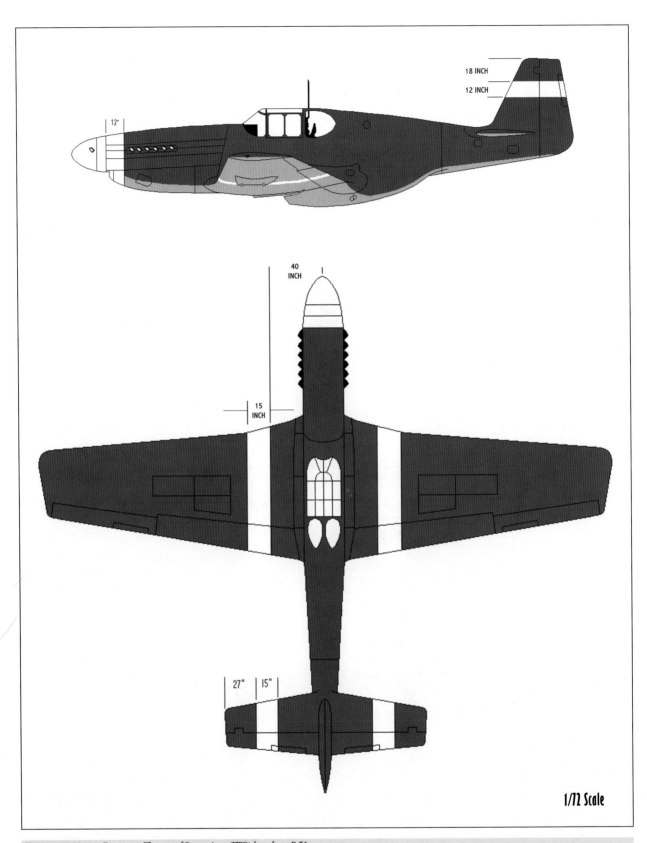

18 INCH
12 INCH

12"

40 INCH

15 INCH

27"   15"

1/72 Scale

Type recognition or European Theatre of Operations (ETO) bands on P-51s, as applied from 20 December 1943. Band across fin and rudder ordered removed from camouflaged aircraft from 23 March 1944, as it broke up the outline of this distinctive feature. Not consistently removed from NMF aircraft.

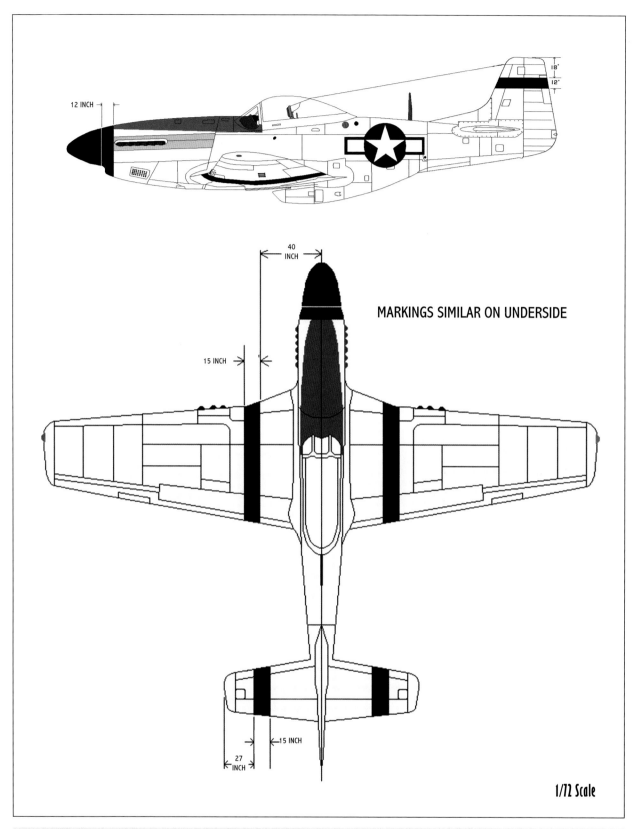

12 INCH

18"
12"

40 INCH

MARKINGS SIMILAR ON UNDERSIDE

15 INCH

15 INCH

27 INCH

1/72 Scale

Type recognition or European Theatre of Operations (ETO) bands on P-51s, as applied from 20 December 1943. Band across fin and rudder, ordered removed from 23 March 1944, not consistently removed from NMF aircraft.

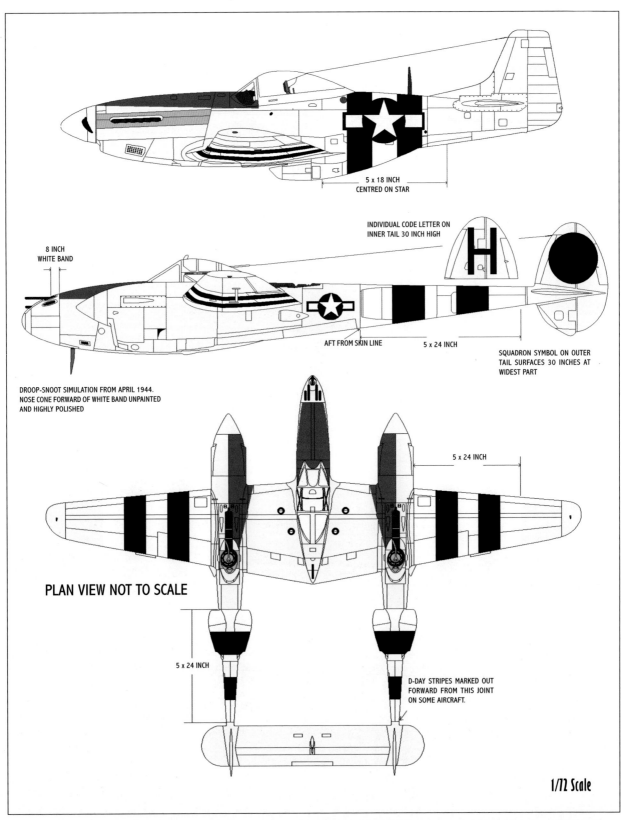

5 x 18 INCH
CENTRED ON STAR

INDIVIDUAL CODE LETTER ON
INNER TAIL 30 INCH HIGH

8 INCH
WHITE BAND

H

AFT FROM SKIN LINE

5 x 24 INCH

SQUADRON SYMBOL ON OUTER
TAIL SURFACES 30 INCHES AT
WIDEST PART

DROOP-SNOOT SIMULATION FROM APRIL 1944.
NOSE CONE FORWARD OF WHITE BAND UNPAINTED
AND HIGHLY POLISHED

5 x 24 INCH

PLAN VIEW NOT TO SCALE

5 x 24 INCH

D-DAY STRIPES MARKED OUT
FORWARD FROM THIS JOINT
ON SOME AIRCRAFT.

1/72 Scale

D-Day stripes as applied to Mustangs from 5 June 1944. Removed from upper surfaces in July 1944, and from wing undersides by October.

No type recognition bands were necessary for the Lightning owing to its distinctive planform. D-Day stripes applied from 5 June 1944, removed from upper surfaces in July, and completely from wings by October 1944. Droopsnoot simulation applied from April 1944, discontinued late summer 1944.

THE 4TH FIGHTER GROUP
The sons of Eagles

The three existing RAF 'Eagle' squadrons, numbered 71, 121 and 133, became the 4th Fighter Group of the United States Army Air Force on 22 August 1942.

They were then flying Spitfire Mark Vbs which they initially kept in American service. These aircraft were camouflaged in the then current Royal Air Force Temperate day fighter scheme, consisting of a disruptive pattern in Dark Green and Ocean Grey on all upper surfaces, and Medium Sea Grey undersides. Spinners were Sky or Night black, and there was an 18 inch wide band of Sky around the rear fuselage. Wing leading edges, outboard of the cannon, were Yellow, to provide head-on recognition.

The RAF roundels were over-painted on the fuselage sides, port upper and starboard lower wings by US star insignia. The roundels on the starboard upper and port lower wings were painted out, as were the fin flashes.

At this time the US star insignia then in use consisted only of the white star on a blue circle. These were 36 inch diameter on fuselage, including a 2 inch yellow border, 32 inch on lower wing and 56 inch on upper wing surfaces. Serial numbers were in black on rear fuselage. Code letters were Sky, with the squadron codes ahead of the star and the individual aircraft letter aft, 18 inches high, though there may have been examples with 24 inch high codes.

The ex-Eagle squadron codes were retained, the 334th being XR, the 335th using AV and the 336th, MD.

The 4th Fighter Group flew over 1,200 sorties in their Spitfires, and gained 11·5 confirmed victories. In January 1943 the group received their first P-47 Thunderbolts. The 334th FS went non-operational and acted as an Operational Training Unit to allow pilots to convert to the new aircraft. Their Spitfires were distributed to the other two squadrons.

P-47s were delivered in the standard USAAF colour scheme of Olive Drab 41 on all upper surfaces, with Neutral Gray 43 undersides. Serial numbers were on the fin, in yellow, 7½ inch high digits.

National insignia was the star-on-circle type in four positions. Fuselage stars were 32 inches diameter with a 2 inch yellow circle surround, making the total diameter 36 inches. Those on the wings were 45 inch diameter and did not have the yellow surround.

Before the Thunderbolts ever went into action, there were instances of their being mistaken for Focke-Wulf FW 190s. To help overcome this, white bands were painted on the nose and on the tail surfaces. That on the nose was 24 inches wide, this being measured around the curve of the cowling. On the tail, the bands were a 12 inch wide one around the fin and rudder, centred 26 inches from the top, while those on the horizontal surfaces were 18 inches wide, centred 33 inches from the tip of each tail plane. Also a larger national insignia was added under both wings, this being 59 inches in diameter.

These markings were common throughout the P-47 groups, and were not peculiar to the 4th. However, the 4th appear to have been better at conforming than some units, and the writer has found no photographs of their Thunderbolts without the large underwing stars, appropriate to the period in style.

At first, the aircraft were marked with the last two digits of the serial number, ahead of the fuselage insignia, as individual identifications, in white 18 inch figures. On 3 April 1943 the Group were issued with a new set of codes. These were QP for the 334 Squadron, WD for the 335th, and VF for the 336th. These they kept for the duration. They were applied as on the Spitfires, but 24 inches high, in white.

The codes were not always applied in the standard block form of lettering; the 334th in particular used a more rounded style, probably from locally produced stencils.

On 29 June 1943, bars were added to the star insignia, and the whole thing given a red 2 inch wide surround. This red surround lasted only six weeks and on 14 August it was ordered to be replaced by Insignia Blue. This was the only major change in markings while the group operated Thunderbolts.

All in all, the Spitfires and Thunderbolts of the 4th were more or less standard as regards colours and markings, the only individual items being examples of nose art.

In early 1944 the group began to receive P-51 Mustangs, flying their first all-Mustang operation on 28 February.

These early P-51s were the B and C models, and were received in the standard colours of Olive Drab top surfaces and Neutral Gray undersides. The national insignia appeared in the usual four positions; the large underwing stars were never applied to Mustangs. Serial numbers were applied to fin and rudder in yellow.

Almost immediately there were instances of the P-51 being mistaken for the Bf 109 and attacked by P-47s and P-38s. To overcome this, white recognition bands were painted on the nose and around the wings and tail surfaces. The orders for this were issued in December 1943 and so all the 4th group Mustangs were so marked from the start.

The markings consisted of a white spinner and the first 12 inches of the cowling, a 12 inch wide band around the fin and rudder, upper edge to be 18 inches from the tip. A 15 inch band around each horizontal tail surface, 33 inches from the tip and a 15 inch band around each wing, starting 15 feet from the tip. These markings were applied to all P-51s operating out of the UK and became known as ETO bands.

It was found that the bands on the vertical tail broke up the outline of this distinctive feature, and so on 23 March 1944 the bands were ordered removed from the vertical tail. On 13 March 1944 the coloured noses were ordered to identify the various Mustang groups. The 4th FG's famous red was applied to most aircraft over the period 15th to 18th, as the P-51s were grounded for mechanical reasons during that time. It covered the spinner and first 12 inches of the cowling, the same area previously painted white.

After 770 B-models and 200 C-models had been delivered, the Mustang was delivered in natural metal finish (NMF) from then on.

Codes and serials, and ETO bands were in black on the NMF finish and strangely, the tail bands reappeared. No official reason for this has been found.

On 5 June the D-Day stripes were applied overnight to all aircraft, these varying slightly in position from aircraft to aircraft. These were subsequently removed from upper surfaces in July 1944, then from wing under-surfaces in September, and from the underside of the fuselage early in 1945.

In October 1944, coloured rudders were introduced to identify the squadrons; these were red for the 334th, white for the 335th, and blue for the 336th. The 335th's white rudder was outlined red, after one aircraft had an experimental black outline applied, but red was the colour settled upon.

In December 1944 the red nose was extended back to 24 inches, to differentiate them from the red-nosed Fifteenth Air Force groups then starting to appear over the Continent more frequently. In January 1945 this nose colour was swept down and to the rear in a curve, ending roughly in line with the wing leading edge underside.

In late 1944 and early 1945 the 335th FS painted some of their canopy frames red. The 336th were said to have painted their's OD but all the colour pictures seen by the author show them to be black.

Modellers should be aware, however, that the ETO bands, D-Day bands, canopy frames and other elements such as letters and numerals could vary greatly. With regard to officially ordered markings, however, the 4th FG were better than most for conformity.

As always, for modelling purposes, photo references are really indispensable.

Above: This P-47D-1-RE, 42-7922 poses for type recognition photos somewhere over England in early 1943. The white type recognition markings have been applied but as yet no unit markings. The notoriously unstable character of the Olive Drab camouflage is already evident.

Right: Some of the earliest members of the 4th Fighter Group, 336th Fighter Squadron, pose in front of John Godfrey's P-51B-5-NA, 43-6765, VF-P, in April 1944. The aircraft wears well-worn Olive Drab and Neutral Gray paintwork with eleven kill markings just below the windscreen. The pilots are, from left: Donald Emerson, R. Hughes, Don Gentile, Kendal Carlson and D. Patchen. See colour profiles 149, 180, 183, 197.

Lower right: This is the wreck of Don Gentile's P-51B-5, 43-6913, after he spectacularly crashed it in front of the press at Debden on 13 April 1944, much to the embarrassment of his CO, Col. Don Blakeslee. Gentile had just completed his tour which probably saved him from major punishment, but the aircraft never flew again. See colour profile 183.

Left: *Don Gentile's P-51B, Shangri-La, in happier circumstances. Finished in full Olive Drab and Neutral Gray camouflage, it has the white type recognition markings on the nose and wings, with Gentile's personal red and white checks under the exhaust. The flamboyant nose art features the pugnacious eagle specially created by Walt Disney for the Eagle Squadrons of the RAF, of which Gentile was a founder member. Eventually wartime ownership of the eagle emblem settled with the 336th Fighter Squadron.*

Centre left: *This 'officially interfered with' photo of Spitfire Vb EN783 at Debden shows the markings used by the 334th FS in October 1942. See colour profile 2.*

Below: *P-51D-15-NA 44-15326, Sizzlin' Liz, was the aircraft of Maj. Gerald E. Montgomery of the 334th FS in December 1944. The red nose Group marking has been extended back to the breather plate and the aircraft has acquired a red rudder. See colour profile 59.*

334th Fighter Squadron

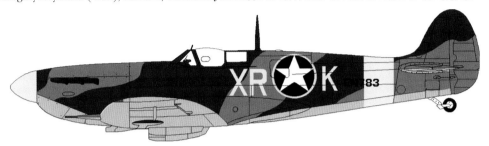

1 Maj. Gregory Daymond ('Gus'), Burbank, California. Joined 334 FS 29/9/42 as CO. Left to return to USA 3/3/43.

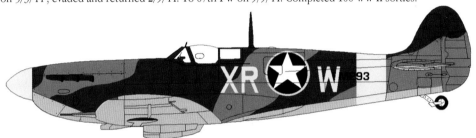

2 Capt. Steve N Pisanos ('The Greek'), Plainfield, New Jersey. Joined 334 FS 24/10/42 from 71 (Eagle) Squadron. Shot down in a P-51B on 5/3/44 , evaded and returned 2/9/44. To 67th FW on 9/9/44. Completed 106 WW II sorties.

3 Lt. Col. James A. Clark Jr, Westbury, New York. Joined 334 FS 15/9/42 until 15/3/43, then joined HQ Squadron. Squadron Operations officer 22/5/43, 'C' Flt CO 2/6/43, 'B' Flt CO 11/7/43, 'A' Flt CO 10/9/43. Squadron CO 1/3/44. Ex-71 (Eagle) Squadron.

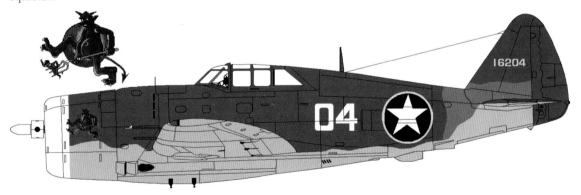

4 Capt. Richard D. McMinn, Salt Lake City, Utah. Joined 334 FS 16/9/42. 'B' Flt. CO from 28/11/42 until KIA 15/4/43.

1/72 Scale

1: Daymond's assigned Spitfire Vb BM510. It carries RAF camouflage in Ocean Grey and Dark Green on upper surfaces and Medium Sea Grey on the undersides. Sky spinner, codes and tail band , Yellow wing leading edges, outboard of cannons. Damaged in a landing accident on 25/10/42. Repaired and transferred to 335th FS 18/1/43, possibly being coded AV-F. See 7.
2: Pisanos flew this Spitfire Vb with 71 Eagle Squadron, then with 334th FS.
3: Spitfire VB BM293, Clark's first assigned aircraft with the 4th, November 1942. Later transferred to 335th FS and coded AV-L. RAF camouflage and

colours, US stars in 4 positions, only those on fuselage with yellow surround. Clark shared one victory in Spitfires. See 29, 30, 48, 49, 81.
4: P-47C-2-RE, 41-6204, showing the earliest markings applied to the Group's Thunderbolts. The fuselage insignia had yellow circle surrounds, these being removed when the bars were added in July 1943. Last 2 of the serial used as fuselage code, repeated under lip of cowling in yellow with black outline. Standard USAAF camouflage of Olive Drab 41 (OD) and Neutral Gray 43 (NG). See 22.

334th Fighter Squadron

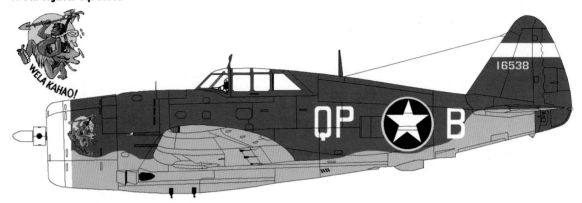

5   Capt. Stanley M. Anderson, Indianapolis, Indiana. From 71 Eagle Sqn to 334th FS 15/9/42 until KIA 15/9/43. Shot down by FW 190 into sea off Ostend. Also Capt. Walter J. Hollander ('Lulu'), Honolulu, Hawaii. To 334th FS 15/9/42 from 71 Eagle Sqn. 18/5/43 transferred to 65th Fighter Wing. Was Squadron Operations Officer from 16/12/42.

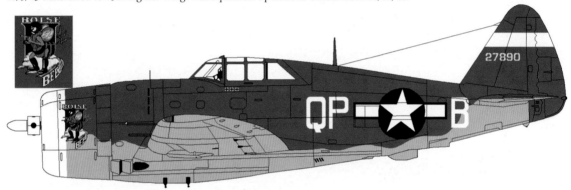

6   Capt. Duane Willard Beeson ('Bee'), Boise, Idaho. Joined 334th FS 13/10/42. Was Squadron Gunnery Officer until 25/9/43 when he became Group Gunnery Officer until 15/11/43. 'C' Flight CO until 28/12/43, then Squadron Operations Officer until 7/3/44, Squadron CO 15/3/44 until he was lost.

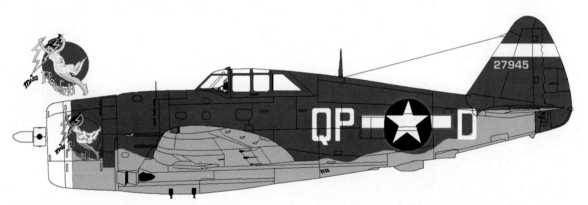

7   Capt. Steve N Pisanos ('The Greek'), Plainfield, New Jersey. Joined 334th FS 24/10/42 from 71 (Eagle) Squadron. Shot down in a P-51B on 5/3/44 , evaded and returned 2/9/44. To 67th FW on 9/9/44. Completed 106 WW II sorties.

1/72 Scale

5: *This P-47C-1-RE was shared by Anderson and Hollander early in 1943. It was crash-landed, on fire, by Anderson near Langham, UK, and written off on 15/4/43. Later that day he was KIA in QP-E 41-6407. Aircraft in standard Olive Drab 41 and Neutral Gray 43,white nose & tail bands, yellow circle around fuselage insignia. Don Allen artwork.*

6: *Beeson's assigned Thunderbolt was this P-47D-I-RE 42-7890. Standard OD and NG scheme, white ETO bands, nose and all tail surfaces. Three white-outlined black victory marks, as in July 1943. Beeson scored 12 victories in*

the Thunderbolt, 11 in this aircraft. See 33.

7: *The P-47D-1-RE 42-7945 flown by Steve Pisanos during August 1943. It is in the usual OD and NG with white nose and tail bands, and carries the Red surround to national insignia used during July and August 1943. 'Miss Plainfield' artwork by Don Allen. Crew Chief P.Fox. See 2.*

334th Fighter Squadron

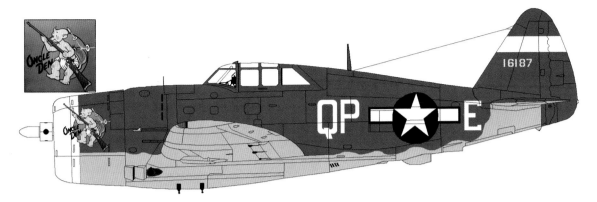

8 Capt. Herbert J. Blanchfield. Joined 334th FS 18/8/43. Went MIA 9/5/44, became POW.

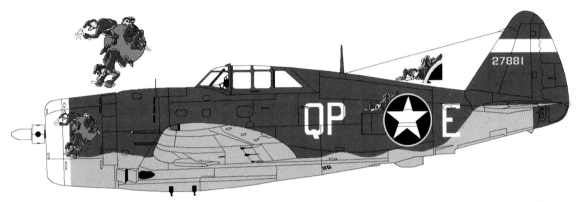

9 1st Lt. Vincent R. Castle ('Bud'), Bluffs, Illinois. Joined 334th FS 19/2/43, and was killed in a flying accident 19/6/43 at Debden. Flew 17 operations.

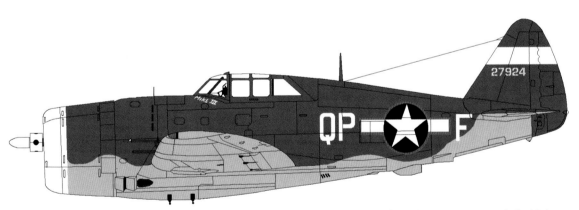

10 Maj. Winslow M. Sobanski ('Mike'), New York City, New York. To 334th FS 25/5/43 until KIA on D-Day. 'A' Flight CO from 29/11/43, Squadron CO April 1944.

1/72 Scale

8: Blanchfield's P-47-C-2RE was Robert Priser's 'Quack', re-coded 'E' and with new art work. Standard ETO white bands on nose and all tail surfaces. See 20, 35, 36, 37.

9: P-47D-1-RE 42-7881 flown by Castle when he was killed in a flying accident when he stalled and dived into the ground off the end of the runway. Aircraft is OD and NG, white bands on tail and cowling. Yellow surround to fuselage insignia only. Don Allen artwork shows Gremlins — who seem to have succeeded in their activities. Crew Chief Robert Kellett.

10: 'Mike III', P-47D-1-RE 42-7924. Flown by Sobanski, July 1943, on the first drop-tank mission. It has the usual OD and NG scheme with white tail and nose identification bands and the short-lived Red surround to national insignia. See 11.

334th Fighter Squadron

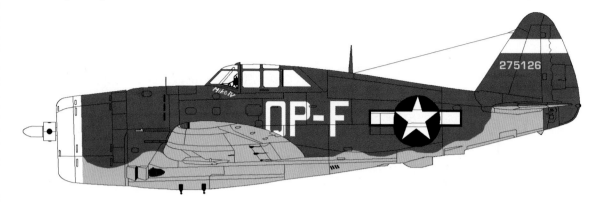

11 Maj. Winslow M. Sobanski ('Mike'). Late 1943.

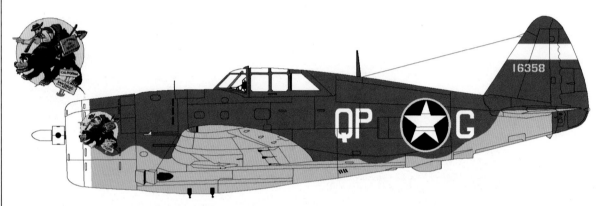

12 Capt. Archie W. Chatterley, San Diego, California. Joined 334th FS 20/1/43. Served until became POW on 27/3/44. 'C' Flight CO from 1/3/44. Assistant Squadron Operations and Gunnery Officer from 21/3/44.

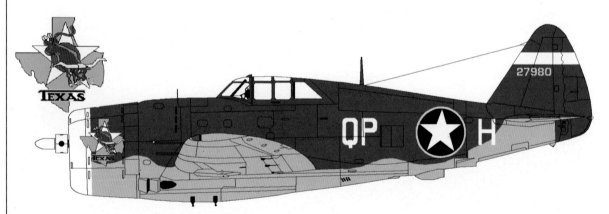

13 Maj. Gerald E. Montgomery ('Monty'), Dallas, Texas. With 334th FS from 15/5/43 to end of war. 'A' Flt. CO until 2/6/44. Squadron Operations Officer until 9/11/44.

1/72 Scale

11: Mike Sobanski flew this P-47-D-10-RE, 42-75126, in late 1943. Standard OD and NG finish. White identification bands on nose and tail surfaces. Code QP-F unusually applied forward of star, would be sorted out when time allowed. This was caused by the addition of the bars to the star insignia, leaving no room aft for the code letter 'F'. The name in front of the canopy is 'Mike IV'. See 10.

12: This was 'Cal or Bust', Chatterley's assigned P-47C-5-RE from 2/43. OD and NG scheme with white nose and tail bands. Artwork on port side only.

13: This P-47D-2-RE was Montgomery's only known Thunderbolt. Standard colours and white bands. C/Chief E. Nelson. See 59, 60.

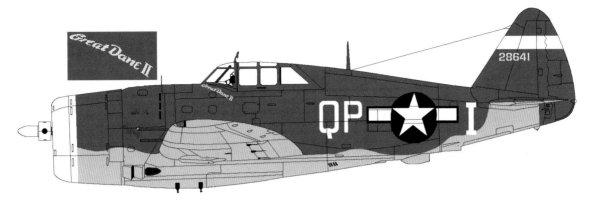

14 Capt. David A. Van Epps, Williams Bay, Wisconsin. Joined 334th FS 26/9/43 until 9/4/44 when he became POW. 'D' Flt. CO 22/3/44.

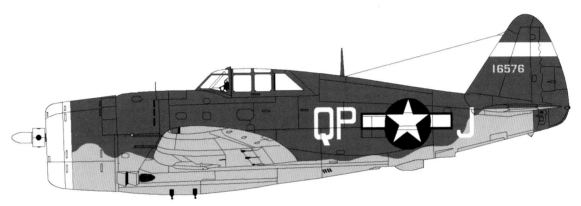

15 Maj. Howard D. Hively ('Deacon'), Norman, California. Joined 334th FS 17/9/42, until 29/1/45, then to 4th FG HQ Squadron. Was Squadron CO 6/6/44. Deputy Group CO 9/8/44. Ex-71 'Eagle' Squadron.

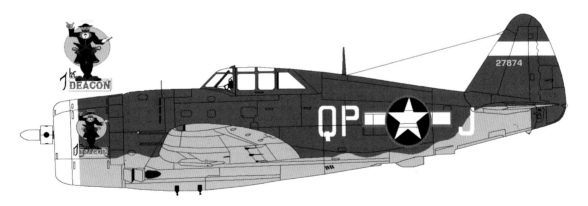

16 Maj. Howard D. Hively ('Deacon'), Norman, California.

1/72 Scale

14: *Van Epps flew this P-47D-5-RE 42-8641 in late 1943 and January 1944. OD and NG, white tail bands. Name 'Great Dane II' under the windscreen.*
15: *Hiveley baled out of this P-47C-5-RE into the English Channel on 15 June 1943, after being shot-up by fighters over St. Nazaire U-Boat pens. He was picked up by ASR launch. OD and NG with white bands on all tail surfaces. No artwork on aircraft. It was assigned jointly to him and Duane Beeson at the time. See 16, 17, 40, 61, 62.*
16: *P-47D, 42-7874, QP-J, flown by Hively, August 1943. OD and NG with white recognition bands on all tail surfaces. Insignia has the red surround used for 6 weeks July/August 1943. Don Allen artwork. See 15, 17, 40, 61, 62.*

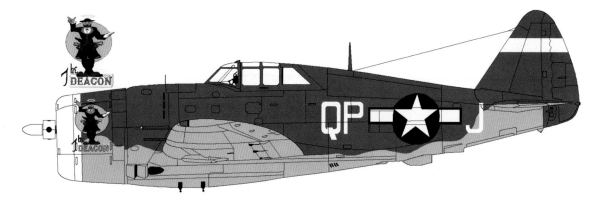

17 Maj. Howard D. Hively ('Deacon'), Norman, California.

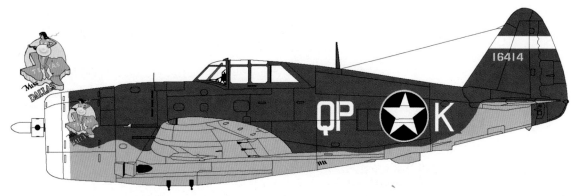

18 Capt. Victor J. France ('Vic'), Dallas, Texas. Joined 334th FS 13/10/42. KIA 18/4/44. 'C' Flt CO from 21/3/44.

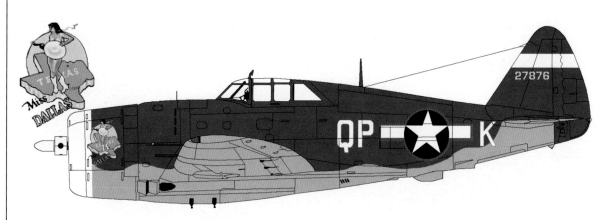

19 Capt. Victor J. France ('Vic'), Dallas, Texas.

1/72 Scale

17: Another D-model with 'Deacon' artwork. The serial is unknown, but it is definitely not the same aircraft as 42-7874. See 15, 16, 40, 61, 62.

18: This P-47C-5-RE 41-6414 was assigned jointly to Vic France and Steve Pisanos in April 1943. It was lost 15 April 1943, when Col. Peterson baled out into the Channel. Standard OD and NG, with white bands on tail surfaces. Yellow surround to fuselage insignia. Crew Chief Don Allen, Asst.C/C P. Fox. See 19, 41.

19: Vic France flew this P-47D-1-RE in July/August 1943. Again in the stand-ard OD and NG scheme with white bands on all tail surfaces. It also has the Red surround to the national insignia which was ordered from 29/6/43, but lasted only until 14/8/43, when it was replaced by Insignia Blue. Codes are thinly outlined Red. See 18, 41.

334th Fighter Squadron

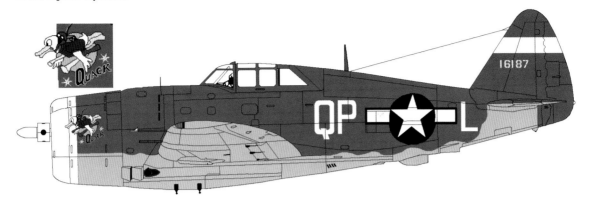

20 Capt. Robert L. Priser ('Junior'). Joined 334th FS 15/9/42. Left 23/11/43 for Ninth Air Force. Was 'A' Flight CO from 13/9/43.

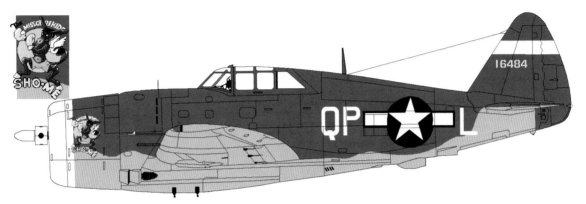

21 Lt. Ralph Kidd Hofer ('Kid'), Salem, Missouri. Joined 334th FS 22/9/43, served until KIA 2/7/44. 'A' Flight CO from 2/6/44.

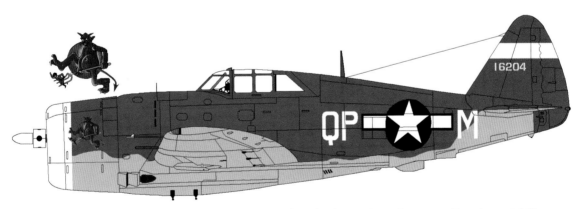

22 Capt. Richard D. McMinn, Salt Lake City, Utah. Joined 334 FS 16/9/42. 'B' Flt. CO from 28/11/42 until KIA 15/4/43.

1/72 Scale

20: *This was Priser's only assigned aircraft. P-47C-2-RE 41-6187, 'Quack'. White bands on horizontal and vertical tail surfaces and nose. Art work port side only. Ralph Hofer scored his first victory on his first mission while flying this aircraft. See 8, 21, 43.*

21: *This P-47C-5-RE was Hofer's first assigned aircraft with the 4th. He scored only a single victory in a P-47 (not this aircraft) OD and NG, white nose and tail bands. Artwork port side only. This aircraft was written off 2/12/43 when it burst into flames at 13.22 hrs. and dived into the ground near Kenton, UK.*

The wreckage was spread over 4 acres and F/O John P. McNabb was killed. See 43, 50.

22: *P-47C-2-RE 41-6204 was McMinn's only assigned aircraft with the 4th. He was killed in it on 15 April 1943, being shot down by an FW190. Went into the sea in flames 5 miles off the Belgian coast, near Ostend, at 17.00 hrs. Aircraft has standard OD and NG finish and white bands on nose and all tail surfaces. Artwork is a red devil carrying Hitler on a fork, port side only. This aircraft was previously assigned to Gus Daymond during February 1943.*

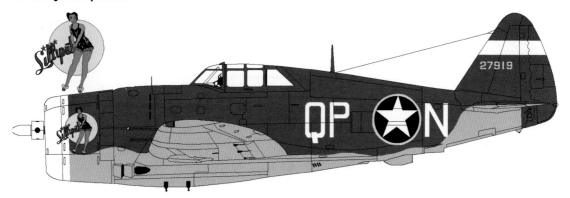

23 1st Lt. William Brewster Morgan ('Brew'), Honolulu, Hawaii. To 334th FS 15/9/42 from 71 'Eagle' Squadron. MIA 21/5/43, when shot down into North Sea off Ostend by enemy fighters. Became POW.

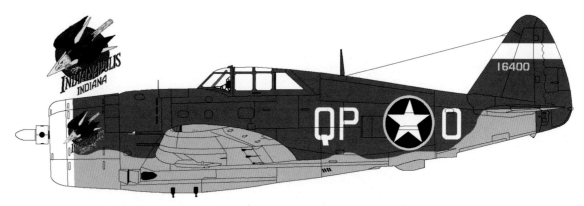

24 Capt. Vernon A. Boehle, Indianapolis, Indiana. Joined 334th FS 13/10/42 until 23/11/43 when transferred to Ninth Air Force.

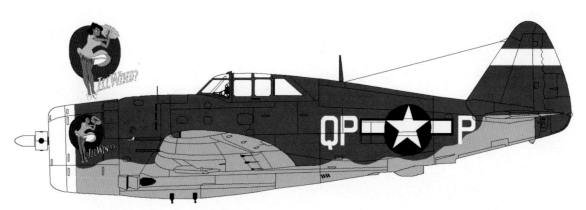

25 Capt. Nicholas Megura ('Cowboy'), Ansonia, Connecticut. Joined 334th FS 3/7/43, served until 22/5/44 when shot up by a P-38, but made it to Sweden, where he was interned. Did not return to operations after his release on 28/6/44.

1/72 Scale

23: P-47D-1-RE 42-7919 was Morgan's aircraft in spring 1943. Completely standard colours and markings for the period. Artwork by Don Allen.
24: P-47C-5-RE of Vernon Boehle, April 1943. Standard colour scheme, yellow circle around fuselage insignia only.
25: This P-47C was Megura's first assigned aircraft and carried standard markings. Unfortunately the serial is not known. Note the artwork differences between this and that on his P-51B. Crew Chief P. Fox, Asst. Crew Chief J. Byrge. See 38, 45.

334th Fighter Squadron

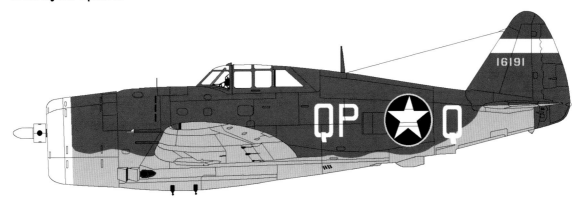

26 Maj. Henry L. Mills ('Hank'), New York City, New York. Joined 334th FS 23/10/42 until 6/3/44 when he baled out west of Brandenburg, Germany, after engine trouble and became POW.

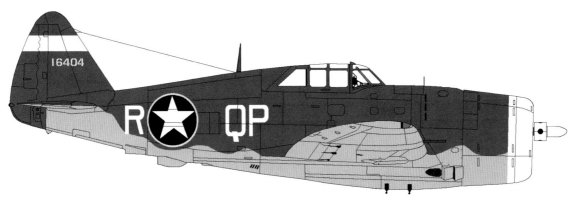

27 This P-47C-5-RE was belly-landed after undercarriage failure on 9/4/43 by 1st Lt. Richard V. Douglass.

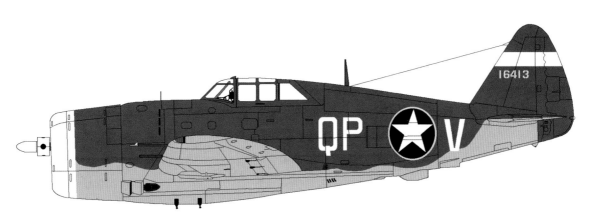

28 Lt. Col. Oscar H. Coen, Marion, Illinois. Joined 334th FS as CO 3/3/43 until 26/10/43 when he went to 356th FG. Maj. Thomas J. Andrews, Costa Mesa, California. With 334th FS 16/9/42 until 11/9/43 when his tour ended. 'A' Flight CO from 16/4/43. Squadron Operations Officer from 2/6/43. Acting CO 13/4/43.

1/72 Scale

26: This P-47C-2-RE was Mill's aircraft in May/June 1943. It was slightly damaged in a belly-landing, but quickly repaired. 41-6191 carries the standard OD and NG finish with white bands on nose and tail surfaces, and has the yellow circle around fuselage insignia only.

27: This P-47C-5-RE was belly-landed owing to undercarriage failure on 9/4/43 by 1st Lt. Richard V. Douglass. Standard colours and markings scheme.

28: P-47C-2-RE 41-6413 was jointly assigned to Andrews and Coen from April 1943. Re-coded 'W' and assigned to J. Clark autumn 1943. Standard col-

ours and markings, with a 'V' on inner wheel in red or black.

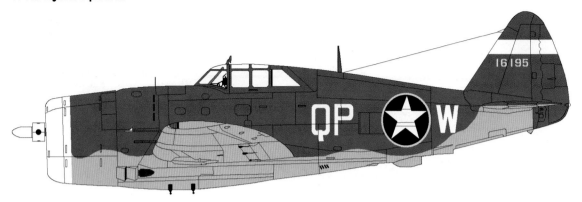

29 Lt. Col. James A. Clark Jr, Westbury, New York. Joined 334th FS 15/9/42 until 15/3/43, then joined HQ Squadron. Squadron Operations Officer 22/5/43, 'C' Flt CO 2/6/43, 'B' Flt CO 11/7/43, 'A' Flt CO 10/9/43. Squadron CO 1/3/44. Ex-71 (Eagle) Squadron.

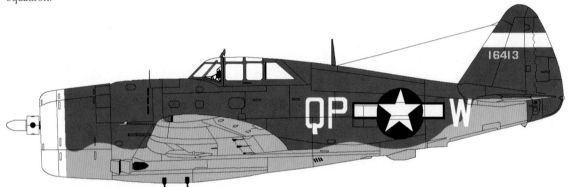

30 Lt. Col. James A. Clark Jr, Westbury, New York.

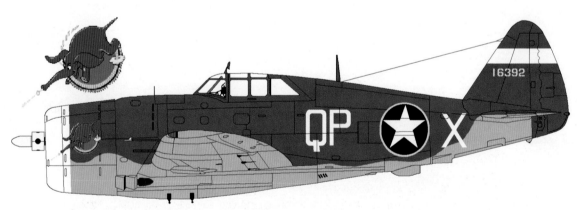

31 Capt. William T. O'Reagan, Los Angeles, California. To 334th FS 16/9/42 until end of tour 27/9/43. 'B' Flt. CO 16/4/43, Squadron Operations Officer 10/9/43. Ex-71 (Eagle) Squadron.

1/72 Scale

29: *This P-47C-2-RE was jointly assigned to Clark and Capt. Alexander Rafalovich during March/April 1943. OD and NG, white nose and tail bands. Yellow circle surround on fuselage insignia only. See 30, 48, 49, 81.*

30: *This was Clark's P-47C-5-RE in Autumn 1943. This aircraft was previously flown by Oscar Coen and Thomas Andrews as QP-V. Standard colours and markings for the period. Clark scored 4 kills in Thunderbolts. See 29, 48, 49, 81.*

31: *P-47C-5-RE 41-6392 assigned to O'Reagan in April 1944. Standard OD and NG scheme with white bands on nose and tail. Yellow circle around fuselage insignia only. Artwork by Don Allen.*

334th Fighter Squadron

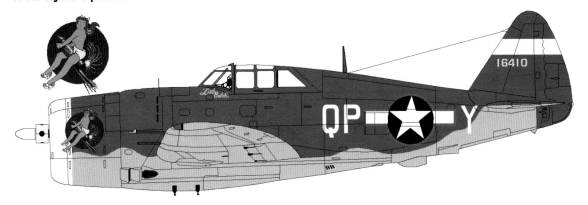

32 Capt. William B. Smith, Bluefield, Virginia. To 334th FS 23/5/43 until KIA 13/9/44. 'B 'Flight CO June 1944.

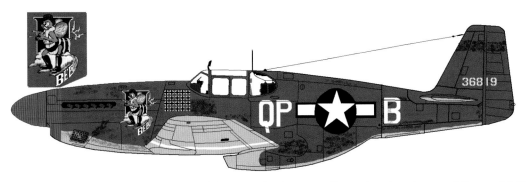

33 Capt. Duane Willard Beeson ('Bee'). Boise, Idaho. Joined 334 FS 13/10/42. Was Squadron Gunnery Officer until 25/9/43 when he became Group Gunnery Officer until 15/11/43. 'C' Flight CO until 28/12/43, then Squadron Operations Officer until 7/3/44, Squadron CO 15/3/44 until he was lost.

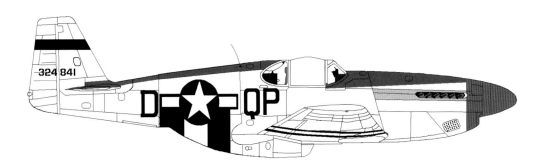

34 2nd Lt. C.G. Howard, Tulsa, Oklahoma. With 334th FS from 11/6/44 until KIA 18/8/44. Bounced by 15 Bf 109s. Shot down and killed near Beauvais, France.

1/72 Scale

31: P-47C-5-RE 41-6410 was Smith's aircraft in July/August 1943. Standard colours and markings, with the red surround to national insignia. Name 'Little Butch' under windshield. Artwork by Don Allen, who was also the Crew Chief.

33: 43-6819, P-51-B-5-NA was Beeson's assigned Mustang. Very blotchy, touched-up OD and NG scheme. White ETO bands on wings only. 20 white outlined black crosses. Shot down in this aircraft 5/4/44. Became POW. Crew Chief W. Wahl. See 6.

34: This was Howard's P-51B-15-NA, 43-24841, August 1944, and the aircraft in which he was killed. Top surfaces are OD, including wings and tail. Undersides natural metal finish. D-Day stripes on undersides of wings and fuselage. Black ETO bands on all tail surfaces.

334th Fighter Squadron

35 Capt. Herbert J. Blanchfield. Joined 334th FS 18/8/43. Went MIA 9/5/44, became POW.

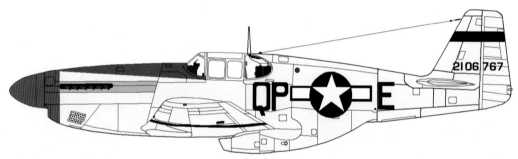

36 Capt. Herbert J. Blanchfield.

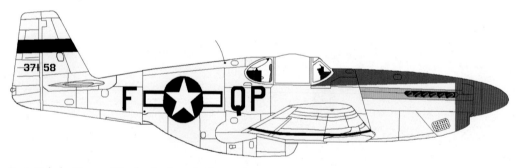

37 Capt. Herbert J. Blanchfield.

38 Capt. Nicholas Megura ('Cowboy'), Ansonia, Connecticut.

1/72 Scale

35: *Blanchfield's first P-51 was this brand new B-7-NA, 43-6746, as it appeared February 1944. OD and NG, white bands on nose, all tail surfaces and on wings. See 36, 37, 50.*

36: *Same aircraft late March 1944. White bands removed from all tail surfaces, red nose added. Later re-coded QP-X. See 35, 37, 50.*

37: *Blanchfield's second and last P-51 was this B-15-NA, 42-106767, which he flew during May 1944 until he and the aircraft were shot down by flak, while attacking St. Dizier airfield on 9/5/44. He became a POW. This was one of*

the first natural metal finish aircraft to join the group. It has the red Group nose marking and black bands on wings and all tail surfaces. See 35, 36.

38: *P-51B-10-NA 43-7158 was the aircraft Megura was flying when be was shot up by a P-38, but made it to internment in Sweden. Black bands on wings and all tail surfaces. Natural metal finish overall. See 45.*

334th Fighter Squadron

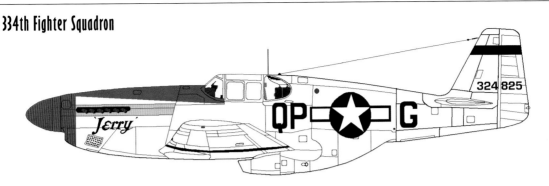

39 2nd Lt. Thomas E. Fraser, Atlanta, Georgia. To 334th FS 1/5/44 until he became POW, 6/6/44, D-Day.

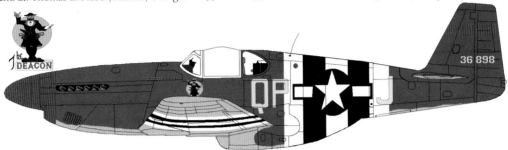

40 Maj. Howard D. Hively ('Deacon'), Norman, California.

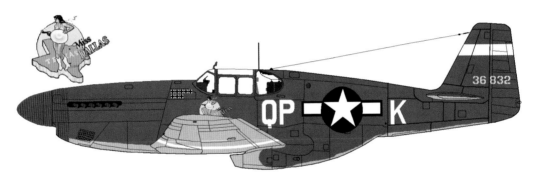

41 Capt. Victor J. France ('Vic'), Dallas, Texas.

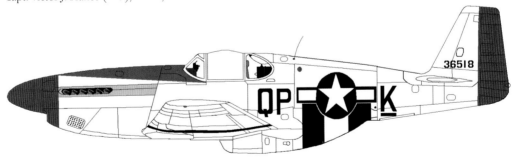

42 1st Lt. James W. Ayers, Tulsa, Oklahoma. Joined 334th FS 11/6/44 until end of war. Was 'C' Flight CO from 27/3/45.

1/72 Scale

39: P-51B-15-NA 43-24825 was Fraser's aircraft in May/June 1944. NMF overall with black bands on wings and all tail surfaces. It was lost on D-Day, Fraser becoming POW.

40: Hively's P-51B-5-NA 43-6898 in June 1944. OD and NG. Full D-Day stripes, red band round fin and rudder. No bands on horizontal tail. Codes outlined red. 9 white outlined black crosses ahead of windshield. C/Chief V. Andea, Armourer G. Roen. Aircraft lost the evening of D-Day. Maj. Mike Sobanski shot down by fighters and killed. See 15, 16, 61, 62.

41: This P-51B-5-NA was the aircraft Vic France was lost in on 18 April 1944, near Stendal, Germany. He flew into the ground while chasing a Bf 109 at low level, aircraft exploded in flames. OD and NG, white bands on wings and tail. Red outlined codes. Eight black kill crosses. See 18, 19.

42: This was Ayer's P-51B-5-NA, 43-6518 in November 1944. It was NMF with D-Day bands on lower fuselage only and black ETO bands on wings and horizontal tail. Aircraft had been retro-fitted with fin fillet and Malcolm hood.

334th Fighter Squadron

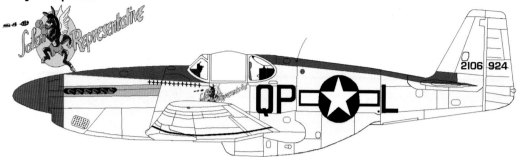

43 Lt. Ralph Kidd Hofer, ('Kid'), Salem, Missouri. Joined 334th FS 22/9/43, served until KIA 2/7/44. 'A' Flight CO from 2/6/44.

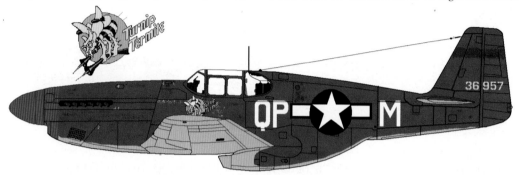

44 Capt. Donald M. Malmsten, Burwell, Nebraska. Joined 334th FS 4/4/44, stayed until end of war. 'B' Flight CO 31/1/45.

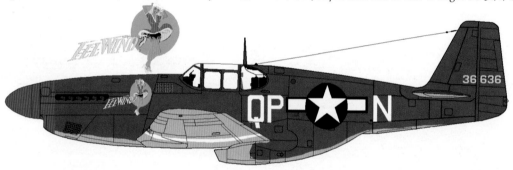

45 Capt. Nicholas Megura ('Cowboy'), Ansonia, Connecticut.

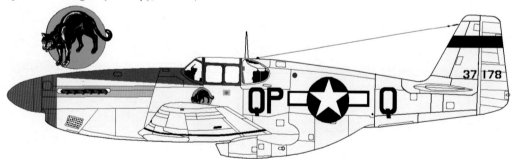

46 2nd Lt. Mark H. Kolter, Lima, Ohio. Joined 334th FS 4/4/44. Killed in action 30/5/44 — disappeared south-west of Brandenburg, Germany.

1/72 Scale

43: Hofer's assigned Mustang was 'Salem Representative', P-51B-15-NA, 42-106924. NMF aircraft, top surfaces of wing and tail, also fuselage in OD. Black bands on wings, top and bottom. None on horizontal tail. Note red bands around fin and rudder. Whitewall tyres. Nicknamed 'Kidd' on black band on left undercarriage door. 13 kill crosses plus a train and 2 sail boats under windscreen. Crew Chief R. Kellet. See 21, 50.

44: P-51B-7-NA 43-6957. OD and NG, no white bands on tail. Re-assigned May 1944 to Lt. Frank E. Speer. Lost on D-Day, 6/6/44, with Lt. Edward J.

Steppe who was KIA near Dreux, France.

45: Megura's P-51B-5-NA 43-6636, has OD and NG finish, white bands on wings only. 15 black cross victory marks ahead of windscreen. He scored 4 plus 2 shared victories in this aircraft. See also 25, 38.

46: P-51B-10-NA 43-7178 was Kolter's only assigned aircraft. He was flying it when he disappeared. NMF overall, full black ETO bands on wings and tail. Canopy framing OD. Nose art by Don Allen.

334th Fighter Squadron

47 Capt. David W. Howe, East Hickory, Philadelphia. With 334th FS from 22/9/43 until 30/3/45 when returned to USA. 500 combat hours in two tours without an abort.

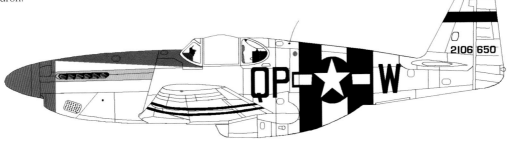

48 Lt. Col James A. Clark Jr, Westbury, New York. Joined 334 FS 15/9/42 until 15/3/43, then joined HQ Squadron. Squadron Operations Officer 22/5/43, 'C' Flt CO 2/6/43, 'B' Flt CO 11/7/43, 'A' Flt CO 10/9/43. Squadron CO 1/3/44. Ex-71 (Eagle) Squadron.

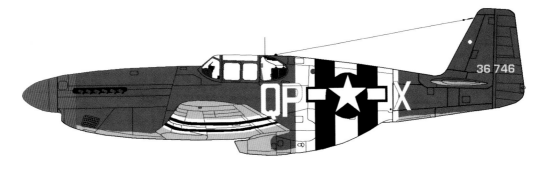

49 Lt. Col James A. Clark Jr, Westbury, New York.

50 Lt. Ralph Kidd Hofer, ('Kid'), Salem, Missouri.

1/72 Scale

47: *This P-51B-5-NA was flown by Howe in May 1944. Standard OD and NG, with white ETO bands on wings only. See 58.*

48: *Jim Clark flew this P-51B-5-NA in March/April 1944. OD and NG, white bands on wings only. 14¹/₂ white outlined black swastikas under cockpit. Tail bands painted out with fresh OD paint. See 30, 49, 51.*

49: *Clark's aircraft at the beginning of June 1944 was this P-51B-10-NA 42-106650. NMF overall, full D-Day stripes plus ETO bands on tail surfaces. Aircraft lost on 2/7/44 near Budapest, Hungary, at about 10.45 hours. Last*

seen having trouble releasing tanks, Lt. Thomas S. Sharp was KIA. See 30, 48, 51.

50: *43-6746 again, coded QP-X and marked with full invasion stripes in June 1944. On 2 July 1944 Lt. Ralph 'Kid' Hofer was KIA in this aircraft near Mostar, Hungary. Victim of Bf 109, possibly flown by Erich Hartmann of JG 52. 4th FG was flying with the 325th FG from Italy, en-route home from first Russian shuttle mission. See 21, 35 and 43.*

334th Fighter Squadron

51 Lt. Col. Claiborne H. Kinnard Jr, Franklin, Tennessee. With HQ Squadron from 8/9/44 until 29/11/44, then to 355th FG. He was Acting Group CO, and then CO.

52 1st Lt. Robert S. Voyles, Delmont, South Dakota. To 334th FS 18/9/44 until POW 27/2/45.

53 Lt. Col. Sidney S. Woods ('Sid'), Somerton, Arizona. Joined 4th HQ Squadron on 26/2/45. Previous service with 8th FG in Pacific, 479th and 355th FGs in ETO. Deputy Group CO from date he joined. Shot down 16/4/45 on his 180th mission. POW for last 13 days of the war.

54 This P-51D-10-NA was with the 334th FS in early 1945. It was lost on 27/2/45 when Lt. Robert Voyles had to bale out after it was hit by 20mm flak at Weimar airfield, Germany.

1/72 Scale

51: Kinnard's aircraft with the 4th. P-51D-10-NA 44-14292, in NMF with D-Day stripes lower fuselage only. Black ETO bands on wings and horizontal tail. Upper surfaces had wavy bands of OD on wings, tail and fuselage. There was an oblique red stripe on anti-glare panel. Name 'Man O' War' red with black outline. Codes outlined red. 18 kill marks around canopy, with pilot's name above. Aircraft had two mirrors. Crew Chief R. Lonier, Asst. Crew Chief B. Anderson, Armr. R. Easly. To Voyles as 'Old Witch' in January 1945. See 52.
52: 44-14292, passed on to Lt. Voyles in January 1945. NMF overall, black

bands on wings and horizontal tail. D-Day stripes removed. Crew Chief E. Pfankuche.
53: This P-51D-20-NA was Wood's assigned aircraft. Shot down in it on 16/4/45 by flak at Praha Airfield, Czechoslovakia. NMF overall, red nose and rudder, red outlined codes. No ETO bands. 2 Japanese, 6 German kills on canopy rail. Scored 5 FW 190s on 22/3/45 over Furstenwalde and Eggersdorf.
54: 44-14537. Aircraft NMF overall, black bands on wings and horizontal tail surfaces. Codes outlined red, twin mirrors.

334th Fighter Squadron

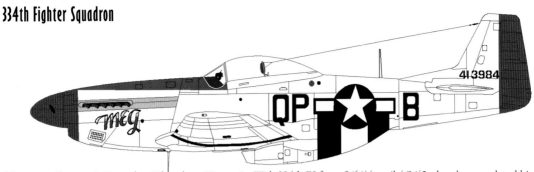

55 1st Lt. Clarence L. Boretsky, Milwaukee, Wisconsin. With 334th FS from 2/6/44 until 4/3/45 when he completed his tour. Was 'D' Flight CO from 21/12/44.

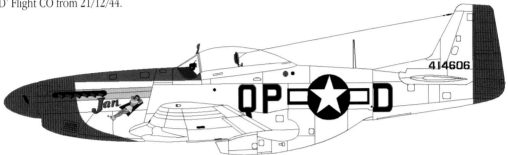

56 1st Lt. Robert A. Dickmeyer, Ada, Ohio. To 334th FS 2/6/44 until tour expired 26/12/44. 'D' Flight CO from 20/11/44.

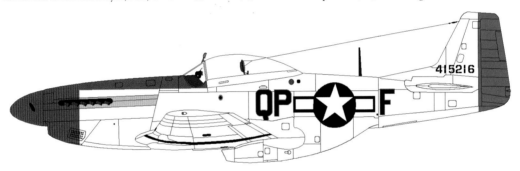

57 This P-51D-15-NA, 44-15216, was with the 334th FS in winter of 1944-1945.

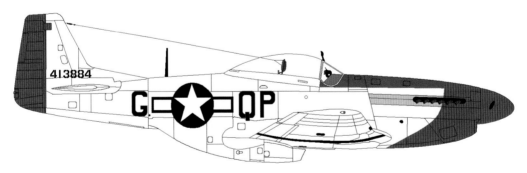

58 Capt. David W. Howe, East Hickory, Philadelphia. With 334th FS from 22/9/43 until 30/3/45 when returned to USA. 500 combat hours in two tours without an abort.

1/72 Scale

55: P-51D-5-NA 44-13984 flown by Boretsky in late 1944. NMF with D-Day stripes on lower fuselage and black ETO bands on wings and horizontal tail. Later re-coded QP-U and renamed 'Davey Lee' by 2nd Lt. Marvin Arthur. Crew Chief Don Allen. Asst. Crew Chief Jerry Byrge. See 77.

56: This P-51D-10-NA was Dickmeyer's assigned machine in late 1944. No ETO bands or D-Day stripes. Codes outlined red, nose colour in 1945 swept style. Not known who the pilot was after Dickmeyer went home, but if he left in December 1944, then he did not fly it in this colour scheme. Crew Chief

for Lt. Dickmeyer was G. Russel.

57: This P-51D-15-NA 44-15216 was with the 334th FS winter of 1945. It has ETO bands on wings and horizontal tail and the 24 inch wide red nose colour as in December 1944.

58: Howe's P-51D-5-NA, January 1945. Has black ETO bands on horizontal tail and wings, but not on fin and rudder. NMF overall, red nose and rudder. Codes thinly outlined in red. Single mirror. Fin fillet has been retro-fitted. See 47.

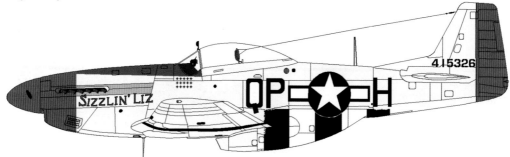

59 Maj. Gerald E. Montgomery ('Monty'), Dallas, Texas.

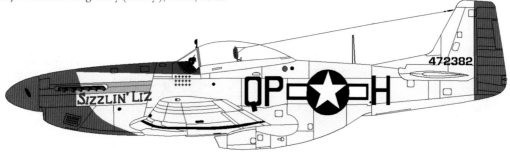

60 Maj. Gerald E. Montgomery ('Monty'), Dallas, Texas.

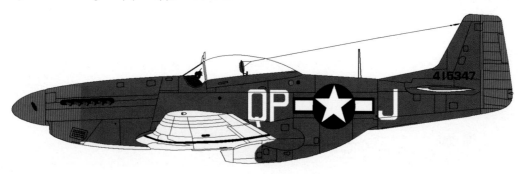

61 Maj. Howard D. Hively ('Deacon'), Norman, California.

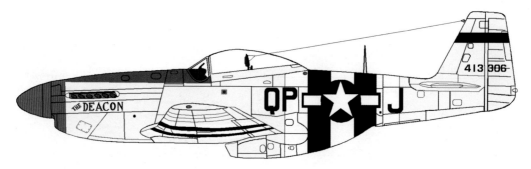

62 Maj. Howard D. Hively ('Deacon'), Norman, California.

1/72 Scale

59: *This P-51D-15-NA 44-15326 was Montgomery's aircraft in December 1944. Nose colour extended back to 3rd exhaust in December D-Day stripes under fuselage only. ETO bands on wings and horizontal tail. Crew Chief E Nelson. See 13, 60.*

60: *P-51D-20-NA flown by Montgomery during spring of 1945. ETO bands on wings and horizontal tail. No D-Day stripes. Crew Chief E. Nelson. See 13, 59.*

61: *Deacon flew this P-51D-15-NA as 334th FS CO at the end of 1944. It was OD on top, NMF underneath, but note the OD wrapped around under rear fuselage. Black ETO bands on wings and horizontal tail. Aircraft re-coded QP-O and flown by Louis Norley, from end of January 1945. This was the only 'D' model in the Group to be painted Olive Drab. See 15-17, 40, 62.*

62: *This P-51D-5-NA 44-13306 was Hively's aircraft at the time of the Russia shuttle mission. NMF overall, with full D-Day stripes on wings and fuselage, and black ETO bands on tail surfaces. Name under exhausts 'The Deacon' is black with yellow outline. Codes black with red outline. See 15-17, 40, 61.*

334th Fighter Squadron

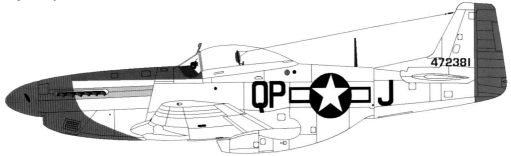

63 Lt. Carl G. Payne, San Antonio, Texas. Joined 334th FS 22/9/44 until 21/9/45

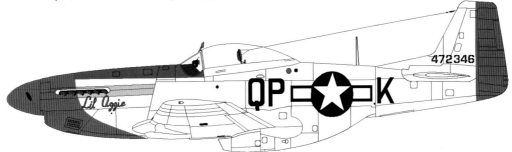

64 P-51D-20NA 44-72346 was assigned to the 4th FG late in the war. Assigned pilot not known.

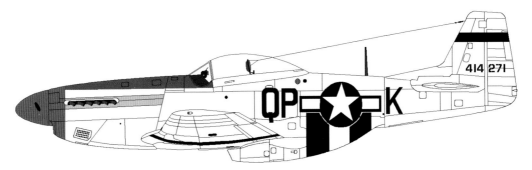

65 Capt. Thomas E. Joyce, Ulysses, Kansas. Joined 334th FS 1/5/44 until 12/9/44 when he became a POW.

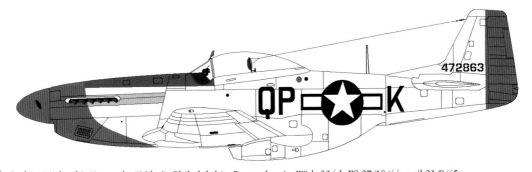

66 2nd Lt. Michael J. Kennedy ('Mike'), Philadelphia, Pennsylvania. With 334th FS 27/10/44 until 21/9/45.

1/72 Scale

63: Payne flew this P-51D-20-NA, 44-72381, in March 1945. No bands or stripes.
64: P-51D-20-NA 44-72346 was assigned to the Group late in the war. NMF without bands or stripes. Name 'Lil Aggie' is red with black outline. Assigned pilot not known.
65: The P-51D-10-NA, 44-14271, Joyce was flying when he was shot down to become a POW, near Darmstadt, Germany. NMF with full ETO bands and D-Day stripes under rear fuselage.
66: P-51D-25-NA 44-72863 arrived in the Group near the end of the war and
was assigned to Lt. Kennedy. It was NMF overall, no bands or stripes, codes were not outlined.

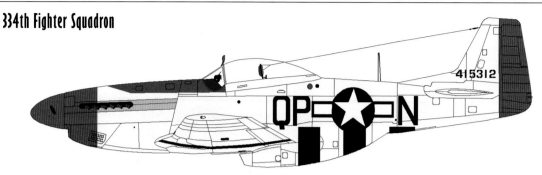

67 Maj. Shelton W. Monroe ('Shel'), Waycross, Georgia. To 334th FS 23/1/44 until 26/1/45, then to 335th FS. 'A' Flt. CO 2/7/44, Assistant Squadron Gunnery and Operations Officer 9/11/44. With 335th FS from 25/1/45 to 8/4/45, then to HQ Sqn. 335th FS Operations Officer 25/1/45. Later KIA in Korean War.

68 Lt. Grover C. Siems Jr, Wantagh, Long Island, New York. To 334th FS 4/4/44. Returned to USA after he was seriously wounded on the return leg of the Russia shuttle mission, July 1944. He made it to Italy and woke up in an Italian mortuary. He never returned to operations.

69 Maj Louis H. Norley Jr. ('Red Dog') Conrad, Montana. Joined 336th FS 10/7/43, then to 335th FS 30/8/43, until he went to 334th FS 25/1/45 as CO, serving until 9/1945. Thus he served with all three 4th FG Squadrons in a long and eventful career. He was credited with 10.33 air and 5 ground victories.

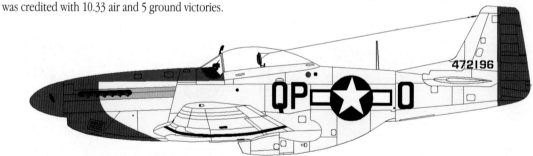

70 Maj Louis H. Norley Jr. ('Red Dog') Conrad, Montana.   **1/72 Scale**

67: This P-51D-15-NA, 44-15312, was crash-landed near Gruitrode, Belgium, by Monroe on 18/12/44. Note unusual anti-glare panel shape, and black and white of D-Day stripes reversed. Black ETO bands on wings and horizontal tail.

68: This P-51-D-5-NA was the aircraft Siems flew on the Russia mission, it was his assigned A/C and one of the earliest D-models to arrive with the 4th F.G. It is NMF overall with full D-Day stripes, also black bands on all tail surfaces. Name 'Gloria III' is black. Nine white-outlined black kill crosses

and 6 black brooms representing fighter sweeps, under windshield.

69: Louis Norley took over Hively's OD painted P-51D-15NA, 44-15347, when he relieved him as CO of the 334th FS in January 1945. He kept it only briefly, re-coded QP-O. It now has the 1945-style nose colouring, black ETO bands on wings and horizontal tail. It was later re-coded QP-V. See 70-71, 129, 178..

70: Louis Norley's aircraft in March 1945 as CO of the 334th FS was P-51D-20-NA 44-72196. It has no D-Day stripes, single mirror, black ETO bands on wing and horizontal tail surfaces. See 69, 71, 129, 178.

334th Fighter Squadron

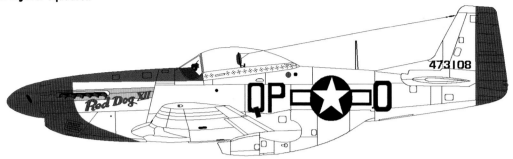

71 Maj. Louis H. Norley Jr ('Red Dog'), Conrad, Montana.

72 2nd Lt. Andrew C. Lacy, Sullivan, Ohio. To 334th FS 18/9/44 until 21/2/45 when he was hit by flak and baled out near Nereshiem, Germany, to become POW.

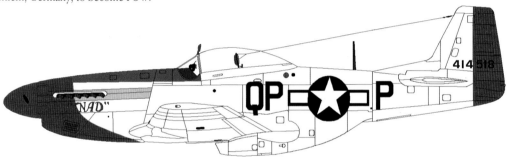

73 2nd Lt. Calvin H. Beason, Anderson, Indiana. With 334th FS from 16/11/44 until end of war.

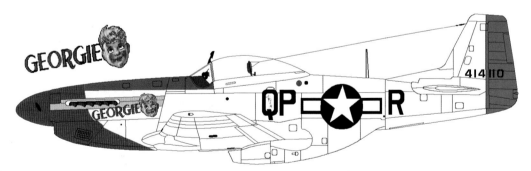

74 1st Lt. Kenneth G. Helfrecht, Madison, Wisconsin. Joined 334th FS 27/10/44, until 21/9/45.

1/72 Scale

71: Norley's P-51D-25-NA at the end of the war. 15 kill swastikas round canopy frame. Codes outlined red, name 'Red Dog XII' in red with black outline. Crew Chief V. Andra. See 69, 70, 129, 178.

72: This was Lacy's assigned aircraft in February 1945, and the one in which he was lost. P-51K-5-NT 44-11677 'Lynette Sue' is NMF with black ETO bands on wings and horizontal tail surfaces.

73: This P-51D-10-NA 44-14518 was Beason's aircraft in early 1945. Named for his wife Nadaline. No stripes or bands, codes outlined red.

74: This was Helfrecht's P-51D-10-NA in early 1945. It has no bands or stripes, and has the 1945 style nose colouring and blue rudder. 'Georgie' was his son. Crew Chief R.Lewis.

334th Fighter Squadron

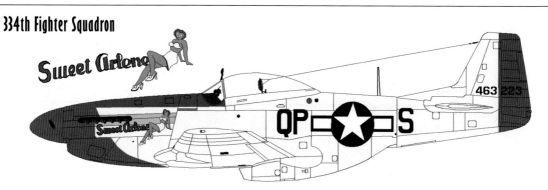

75 2nd Lt. Arthur Reed Bowers, Tiskilwa, Illinois. Joined 334th FS 16/11/44 until end of war. Flak hit on canopy caused neck wound on 26/3/45, north-east of Erlangen, Germany.

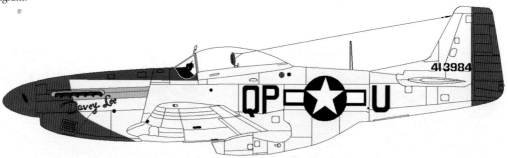

76 Lt. Edward J. Wosniak ('Flak'), Girard, Ohio. Joined 334th FS 12/7/44 until 15/4/44 when he was wounded in a crashlanding in Belgium.

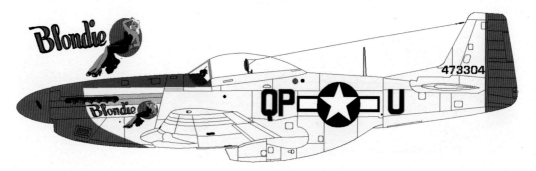

77 2nd Lt. Marvin W. Arthur, Indianapolis, Indiana. To 334th FS 16/11/44 until end of war.

78 2nd Lt. Marvin W. Arthur, Indianapolis, Indiana.

1/72 Scale

75: P-51D-20-NA 44-63223, NMF overall, late war red markings on nose and rudder. No black bands on wings or tail. Single mirror. This was Bower's aircraft in January 1945.

76: Wozniak's aircraft in March 1945 was P-51D-20-NA 44-63583, named 'Helen'. It carries 1945-style markings with bands on wings and horizontal tail. 3 black/white/red kill marks on canopy frame. Aircraft was written off 15/4/45 when crash-landed in Belgium.

77: 'Davey Lee' was Boretsky's 'Meg' passed on to Lt. Arthur and re-coded

QP-U. It was re-named for Lt. Arthur's baby son. Note 1945 swept back red on nose D-Day and ETO bands have been removed. See 55, 78.

78: P-51D-25-NA was Lt. Arthur's last aircraft, in April/May 1945. 'Blondie' was his wife, as interpreted by Don Allen. NMF overall no D-Day or ETO stripes, no mirror. Codes outlined red. Crew Chief Don Allen, Asst. Crew Chief Jerry Byrge. See 77.

334th Fighter Squadron

79 Lt. Raymond A. Dyer, Glassport, Pennsylvania. To 334th FS 2/9/44 until 21/9/45.

80 1st Lt. Ralph H. Buchanan ('Buck'), Los Angeles, California. To 334th FS 27/7/44 until end of war.

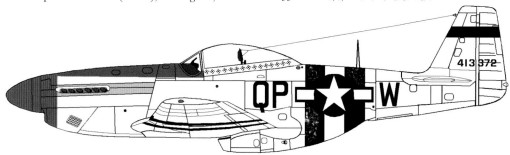

81 Lt. Col. James A. Clark Jr, Westbury, New York. Joined 334 FS 15/9/42 until 15/3/43, then joined HQ Squadron. Squadron Operations Officer 22/5/43, 'C' Flt CO 2/6/43, 'B' Flt CO 11/7/43, 'A' Flt CO 10/9/43. Squadron CO 1/3/44. Ex-71 (Eagle) Squadron.

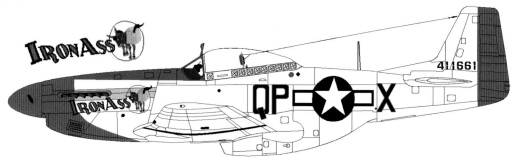

82 Lt. Col. Jack J. Oberhansley, Spanish Fork, Utah. To Group 4/12/44 as Acting CO. Was Deputy CO of 78th FG **1/72 Scale** prior to service with 4th FG.

79: Dyer flew this P-51D-10-NA 44-14323 in early 1945. It has ETO bands on wings and horizontal tail. Red outlined codes include second letter 'V' instead of bar. Name 'Lazy Daisy' is black and red. Aircraft had previously carried name 'Dyer-Ria, The Pointer'.

80: Buchanan's P-51D-20-NA in spring 1945. No ETO bands or D-Day stripes. Codes outlined in red. Black canopy frame and mirror, 334th FS red rudder and 1945-style swept-back nose colour. Artwork by Don Allen.

81: Clark's P-51D-5-NA in August 1944 was 44-13372. NMF overall, full (worn) D-Day stripes, black ETO bands on tail. 15 swastikas on canopy. Crew Chief R. Lonier. Clark had 6 Mustang kills, for a total of 10.5 air and 4.5 ground. See 29-30, 48-49.

82: Oberhansley flew this P-51D-30-NT, 44-11661, while with the 4th. It has the 1945 red nose and rudder, black ETO bands on wings and horizontal tail. 10 black swastika on red flag kill marks on canopy frame. It was lost on 24/2/45, Flight Officer Alvin L. Hand being hit by flak near Emmen, Holland, to become POW. Crew Chief R. Lonier, Armr. R. Easley.

334th Fighter Squadron

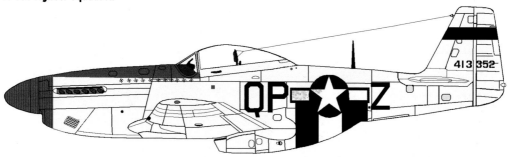

83 Capt. Joseph L. Lang, Boston, Massachusetts. Joined 334th FS 28/12/43 until he was KIA 14/10/44. 'B' Flight CO 2/6/44. Ex-RAF pilot. Shot down by Bf 109s near Kaiserlautern, Germany. He shot down 2 out of 10 before his death.

335th Fighter Squadron

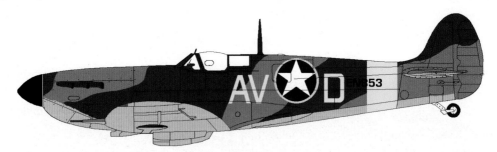

84 Maj. William J. Daley, Amarillo, Texas. Joined Squadron 24/9/42 as CO, having been CO of 121 (Eagle) Squadron, 334th Squadron's previous identity. Left for the USA 22/1/42.

85 Spitfire Vb AD 511, AV-E, of 335th FS, February 1943. Pilot unknown.

1/72 Scale

83: This P-51D -5-NA was Lang's aircraft in July 1944. It is NMF overall and carries black ETO bands on all tail surfaces but none on wings. D-Day stripes on lower fuselage only. 11 black swastika kill marks on cowl. Crew Chief E. Eisler, Asst. Crew Chief W. Rushing.

84: Spitfire Vb EN 853 was Daley's only assigned aircraft while with the 4th FG. Standard RAF colour scheme with US insignia in 4 positions. Note black spinner.

85: Spitfire Vb AD 511, AV-E, of 335th FS, February 1943. Standard RAF colour scheme for the period, with US insignia in four positions. The yellow circle around fuselage insignia only.

335th Fighter Squadron

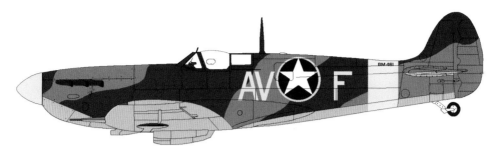

86 Spitfire Vb BM461 with the 335th FS, spring 1943. Previously with 336th FS. Pilot not known.

87 Spitfire Vb EN768 AV-W of the 335 FS in spring 1943. Assigned pilot not known.

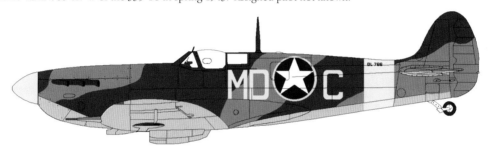

88 Spitfire Vb BL766

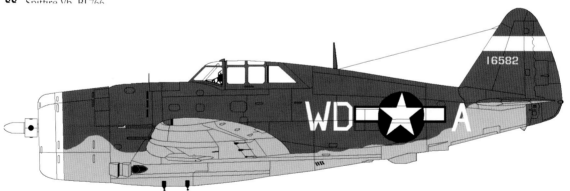

89 Maj. Pierce Winningham McKennon, Clarksville, Arkansas. Joined 335th FS 22/2/43. 'A' Flight CO 22/3/44, Squadron Operations Officer 18/4/44, Squadron CO 18/8/44. Left 21/9/45, went to 368th FG.

1/72 Scale

86: *Spitfire Vb BM461 with the 335th FS spring 1943. Previously with 336th FS Pilot not known. Standard RAF colour scheme with US insignia in 4 positions. Serial on Sky band in very small digits.*

87: *Spitfire Vb EN768 AV-W of the 335th FS in spring 1943. Assigned pilot not known. Standard RAF camouflage.*

88: *Spitfire Vb BL766. Despite the 336th FS codes, the aircraft was possibly assigned to Don Blakeslee during October/November 1942, as it was certainly flown frequently by him at that time. Standard RAF colour scheme,* *but note serial repainted on Sky band in very small (2 inch?) figures. See 103-104, 110, 119-120.*

89: *McKennon flew this P-47C, 41-6582, from March 1943. He scored three victories in Thunderbolts before the Group was re-equipped with the Mustang in March 1944. The aircraft carried white ETO bands on top and bottom sufaces of horizontal tail, as well as on vertical tail. Standard Olive Drab and Neutral Gray camouflage scheme. See 101-102, 112-116.*

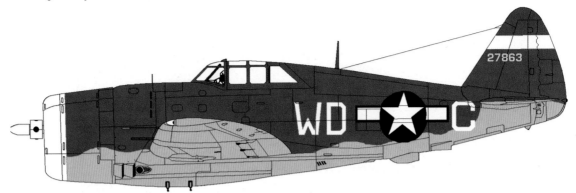

90 Donald James Mathew Blakeslee, Fairport Harbor, Ohio. Joined 335th FS as CO 29/9/42, with rank of captain. He became major 12/1/43. Left squadron 19/5/43, became 4th Group Executive and Operations Officer and Lt. Col. on this date. Became Col. 8/3/44. Group CO from 1/1/44.

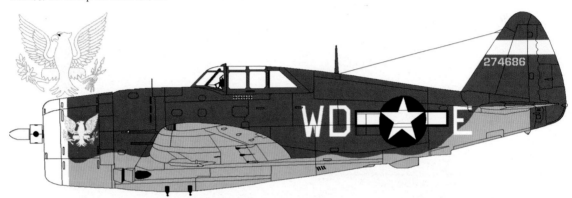

91 Maj. Roy W. Evans, San Bernadino, California. Joined 335th FS 14/10/42. Returned to USA 5/2/44. Squadron CO from 13/8/43. Flew 2nd tour with 359th FG. Became POW.

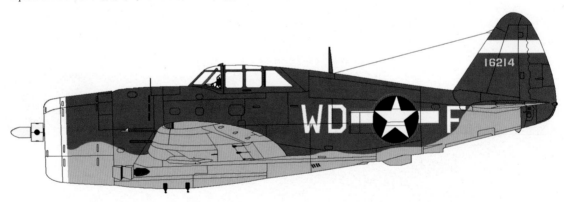

92 Capt. Paul M. Ellington, Tulsa, Oklahoma. With 336th FS from 14/10/42 until 4/3/44. Went down off Dutch coast after engine trouble, became POW.

1/72 Scale

90: *42-7863 P47-D-1-RE. This was Blakeslee's assigned aircraft in September 1943. Standard white ETO recognition bands on nose, vertical and horizontal tail surfaces. All Blakeslee's aircraft were coded WD-C, none carried any personal markings. Shot up in this machine 7/1/44, made forced landing at Manston. Aircraft previously assigned as WD-E to Maj. Roy Evans. See 88, 103-104, 110, 119-120.*

91: Evan's assigned P-47D-1-RE from September 1943. Standard OD and NG, white ETO bands on nose and tail. Eagle Squadron badge on cowl denotes his previous service with 121 (Eagle) Squadron. Aircraft later re-coded WD-M. See 93.

92: Ellington's assigned aircraft in August 1943 was P-47C-2-RE 41-6214, in OD and NG with white nose and tail bands, and the red surround to the national insignia.

335th Fighter Squadron

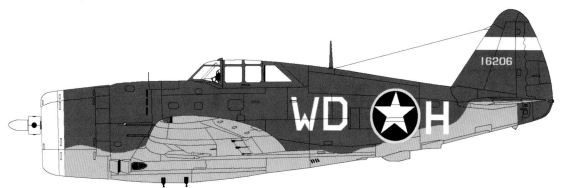

93 Maj. Roy W. Evans, San Bernadino, California.

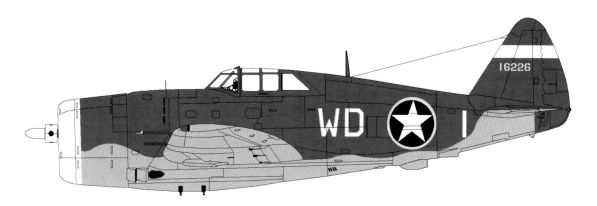

94 Maj. George Carpenter, Oil City, Pennsylvania. To 335th FS 14/10/42 until he became POW 18/4/44. Squadron Operations Officer 6/12/43. Squadron CO 5/2/44.

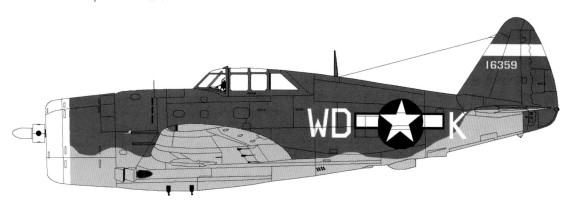

95: Lt. Donald H. Ross, Carson City, Nevada. With 335th FS from 9/10/42 until 27/11/43, then to Ninth Air Force.

1/72 Scale

93: This P-47C-2-RE was assigned to Roy Evans from May 1943. It was previously with the 334th FS coded QP-M. See 91.

94: This P-47C-2-RE was Carpenter's aircraft in May 1943, and he scored the first of his 18 victories in it. OD and NG aircraft with white bands on nose and tail surfaces. Yellow surround to fuselage insignia only.

95: Ross's P-47C-5-RE 41-6359 was written off when it was hit in dispersal by VF-R which suffered a locked rudder during takeoff on 5/1/44. OD and NG scheme with white nose and tail bands.

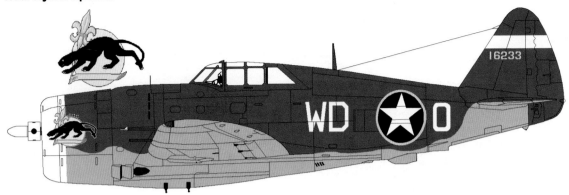

96 Lt. Aubrey C. Stanhope, Bristol, Maine. Joined 335th FS 14/10/42 and served until he became POW 7/9/43.

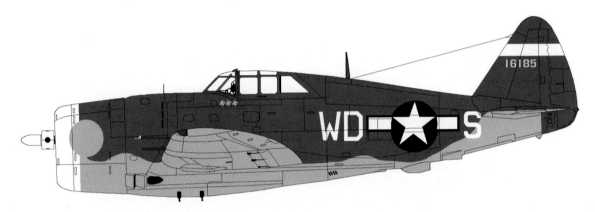

97 Maj. Donald A. Young, Chanute, Kansas. From 121 (Eagle) Squadron to 335th FS 16/9/42 until 9/10/43, then CO of HQ Squadron. Was Squadron Operations Officer from 25/4/43.

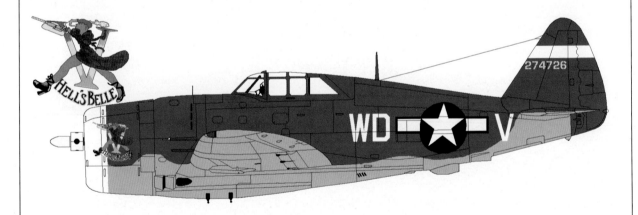

98 Capt. Charles F. Anderson, Gary, Indiana. To 335th FS 11/8/43 until he was KIA 19/4/44.

1/72 Scale

92: This P-47C-2-RE was Stanhope's assigned aircraft with the 4th FG. He was lost in 41-6207, another C-2-RE. This aircraft has the OD and NG scheme, with standard white markings. The artwork was one of Don Allen's earliest.
93: P-47C-2-RE 41-6185 flown by Young at the end of August 1943. OD and NG. White bands on tail. Insignia freshly converted from red to blue outline. 3 swastikas under windshield. White star on blue inner wheel covers.
94: P-47D-6-RE 42-74726 flown by Anderson at the beginning of 1944. Standard colours and markings of the period.

335th Fighter Squadron

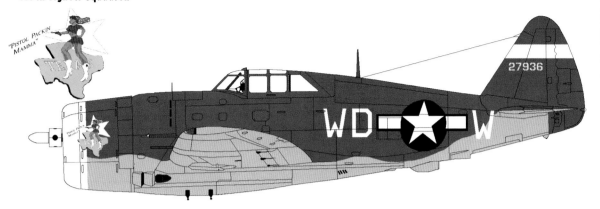

99 Maj. Fonzo D. Smith, Molockoff, Texas. Joined 335th FS 15/9/42, became POW 3/8/44. Squadron Operations Officer 4/10/43. Flew two tours. Assigned to HQ Squadron when he was lost.

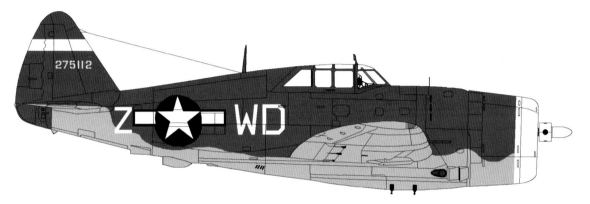

100 Lt. William P. Rowles, McKeesport, Pennsylvania. To 335th FS 26/1/44 until transferred out 22/6/44. Rejoined Squadron 13/5/45 until 1/6/45 then returned to USA.

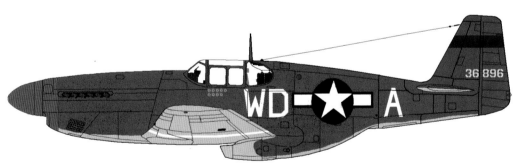

101 Maj. Pierce Winningham McKennon, Clarksville, Arkansas.

1/72 Scale

99: *This P47D-1-RE was Fonzo Smith's assigned aircraft in September 1943. Standard OD and NG with white theatre bands, nose and tail. Aircraft re-coded WD-D in February 1944.*

100: *Rowles flew this P-47D-10-RE 42-75112 in February 1944. During a Ramrod to Marienburg, it was badly damaged by cannon fire and transferred out of the Group as a result. OD and NG, white nose and tail bands.*

101: *This P-51B-7-NA 43-6896 was McKennon's assigned aircraft in March/April 1944, and he scored 6 of his eventual 11 airborne kills in it. White ETO bands on wings only, red Group nose colour from mid March onwards. Aircraft was re-coded WD-F and assigned to Lt. George Stanford 12/5/44. It was lost on 19/6/44, Lt. D. Hill KIA. See 89, 102, 112-116.*

102 Maj. Pierce Winningham McKennon, Clarksville, Arkansas.

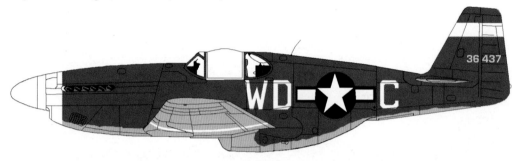

103 Col. Donald James Mathew Blakeslee, Fairport Harbor, Ohio.

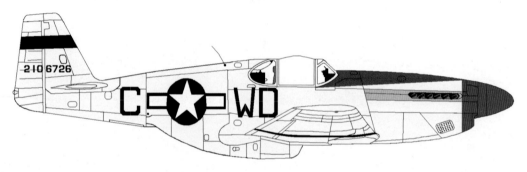

104 Col. Donald James Mathew Blakeslee, Fairport Harbor, Ohio.

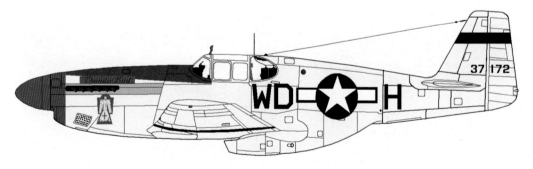

105 Capt. Ted E. Lines, Mesa, Arizona. To 335th FS 4/4/44 until completion of tour 30/11/44, then returned to USA. 'A' Flight CO from 16/9/44.

1/72 Scale

102: McKennon flew this P-51-B 42-106911 from April 1944. He was a Western history buff, hence the artwork of a cowboy on a bucking Mustang. NMF overall with black ETO bands on wing and tail. The red Group nose marking was introduced from March 1944. 13 white-outlined black cross kill marks below cockpit. Nose art and kill marks port side only. See 89, 101, 112-116.

103: P-51-B 43-6437 was his assigned aircraft in March 1944. He was flying this aircraft when he led the first fighter escort over Berlin on 4 March 1944. Full set of white ETO bands. Aircraft later re-coded WD-V, and lost on 7/8/44,

Lt. Sydney V. Wadsworth, POW. See 88, 90, 104, 110, 119-120.

104: P-51-B 42-106726 Blakeslee's assigned aircraft in summer 1944. Black bands on wings and horizontal tail. Re-coded WD-S August 1944. See above,

105: Lines's P-51B-10-NA 43-7172 'Thunder Bird', May 1944. It is NMF overall and carries full black ETO bands on wings and all tail surfaces. Single red mirror. Aircraft lost on D-Day with Flight Officer W. Smith (KIA) when the 335th's entire Blue section was shot down after enemy fighters bounced them under low cloud at 18.40 hours. See 128.

335th Fighter Squadron

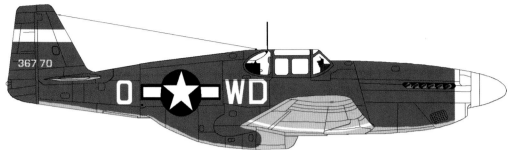

106 Capt. Albert L. Schlegel, Cleveland, Ohio. Joined 335th FS 3/7/43, was KIA 28/8/44. 'B' Flight CO 5/3/44. Squadron Operations Officer 18/8/44.

107 Capt. Albert L. Schlegel, Cleveland, Ohio.

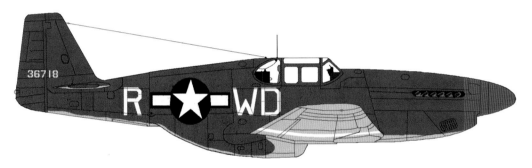

108 Capt. John W. Goodwyn, Saginaw, Michigan. To 336th FS 20/2/44 until 30/9/44 when he completed his tour. 'C' Flight CO 26/5/44, Squadron Operations Officer 9/44.

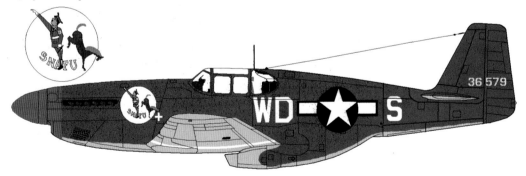

109 1st Lt. Clemens E. Feidler, Fredericksburg, Texas. To 335th FS 18/8/43 until KIA 10/4/44. Hit by flak at Romorontan airfield, attempted to bale out, but crashed before he could do so.

1/72 Scale

106: Schlegel flew this P-51B-5-NA in February/March 1944 and on his return from the first escort over Berlin, 4/3/44, it suffered a collapsed undercarriage. OD and NG with full white ETO bands on nose, wings and all tail surfaces. Later coded WD-O-bar and finally WD-G. Lost 18/6/44 with Lt. Robert W. Little who had arrived on the squadron only 13 days before. See 107.

107: Schlegel's P-51B-10-NA 42-106464 in April/May 1944 showing 10 of his eventual 15 kills, as white-outlined black crosses, on red squares. Aircraft NMF, full black ETO bands on wings and tail. It was previously coded WD-U

and was lost on 27/5/44. Lt. Eliot H. Shapleigh became an evader. See 106.

108: P-51B-5-NA 43-6718 flown by Goodwyn in March/April 1944. OD and NG with white ETO bands on wings only. Red nose added from 13/3/44, most 4th FG aircraft were painted 15-18 August 1944. White tail bands removed at same time.

109: P-51B-5-NA 43-6579 was Feidler's aircraft in March/April 1944. OD and NG, white bands on wings only. It was lost on 18/4/44 with Lt. Lloyd F. Henry, KIA near Rhine Canal area, Berlin.

335th Fighter Squadron

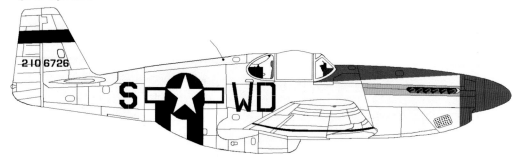

110 Blakeslee's 'B' model re-coded 'S' and flown by Lt. John Goodwyn, August 1944. Not known if it was his assigned aircraft.

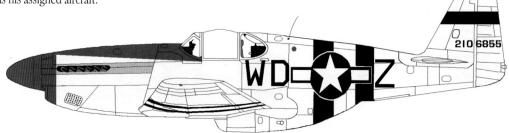

111 This P-51B-15-NA was with the 335th FS from 20/5/44 until it went missing on 18/8/44 with Lt. Robert Cooper, in the Les Andelys area, France, during a fight with 50 Bf 109s.

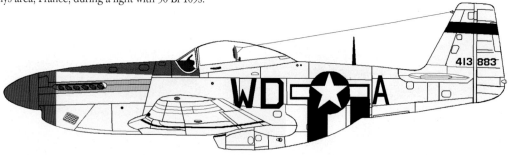

112 Maj. Pierce Winningham McKennon, Clarksville, Arkansas.

113 Maj. Pierce Winningham McKennon, Clarksville, Arkansas.

1/72 Scale

110: 42-106726 in standard finish and markings for August 1944. See 104.
111: This P-51B-15-NA was with the 335th FS from 20/5/44 until it went missing on 18/8/44 with Lt. Robert Cooper, in the Les Andelys area, France. NMF overall with full D-Day stripes, and ETO bands on all tail surfaces. It was flown on the Russia shuttle mission in July by Capt. John Goodwyn.
112: This P-51D-5 was McKennon's assigned aircraft during July-August 1944. Shot down by flak in this aircraft on 28/8/44 while strafing a rail yard. He evaded capture and fought with the Maquis, before returning to Debden in
just over a month. Aircraft is NMF overall with D-Day stripes on lower fuselage only. Black ETO bands on wing and tail surfaces. No kill marks or artwork. See 89, 101-102, 113-116.
113: First machine to carry the 'Ridge Runner' emblem was this P-51D-10-NA, assigned to McKennon in September 1944, on his return from evading. 11 black cross victory marks below exhausts, red nose, canopy frame and mirror. NMF overall with black ETO bands on wing and tail surfaces. Crew Chief, as on all McKennon's aircraft while with the 4th FG, was S/Sgt. Joe Sills.

335th Fighter Squadron

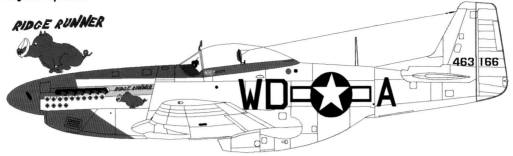

114 Maj. Pierce Winningham McKennon, Clarksville, Arkansas. This is the second 'Ridge Runner'.

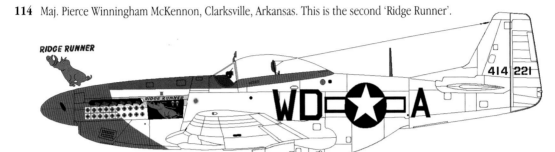

115 Maj. Pierce Winningham McKennon, Clarksville, Arkansas. This is the third 'Ridge Runner'.

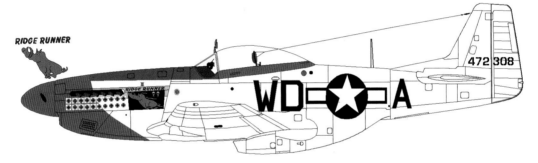

116 Maj. Pierce Winningham McKennon, Clarksville, Arkansas. Fourth and last 'Ridge Runner'. Nose art and kill markings on port side only on all his aircraft.

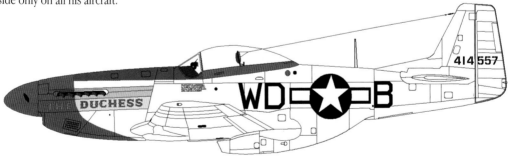

117 Maj. William J. O'Donnell ('Bill'), Philadelphia. Joined 335th FS 8/10/44, until 8/4/45 when he went to 4th FG HQ Squadron. Was 'A' Flight CO from 20/1/45. O'Donnell's aircraft in April 1945 was this P-51D-10-NA, 44-1455. **1/72 Scale**

114: P-51D-20-NA. Artwork is different in detail, it has the late, post-January 1945 swept-under nose colour, white rudder outlined in red. No ETO bands. McKennon was shot down near Neubrandenburg in this aircraft 18/3/45, but rescued by Lt. George Green. 14 crosses, showing ground and air kills.
115: P-51D-10-NA, flown from 19/3/45 until 17/4/45, when it was crash-landed on a French airfield by another pilot. Aircraft was later repaired and re-coded WD-I. Again with different artwork, now with the final total of 20 kill markings. These were 11 air and 9 strafing, all scored in P-47s or P-51Bs,

except a ·5 claim for a FW 190 in a P-51D on Christmas Day 1944.
116: P-51D-20NA, 44-72308, flown from April 1945 until after the war ended. Markings identical to previous, but twin mirrors fitted to canopy. Note 2 white parachutes on artwork, noting his 2 bailouts on 28/8/44 and 18/3/45.
117: 'The Duchess', April 1945. ETO bands on wings and horizontal tail surfaces, not on fin. White rudder with red outline. Name red with orange shadow shading and blue outline, on a yellow background aft of the red nose colouring. Crew Chief W. Gerth, Asst. C/Chief M. Isaac, Amr D.Lambert.

335th Fighter Squadron

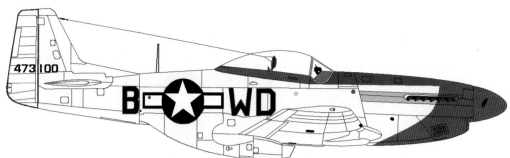

118 P-51D-25-NA, 44-73100, with the 335th FS in April 1945.

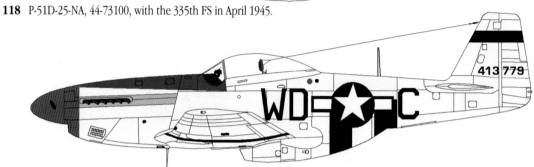

119 Col. Donald Blakeslee, July 1944.

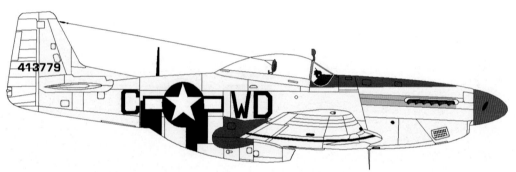

120 Col. Donald Blakeslee, October 1944.

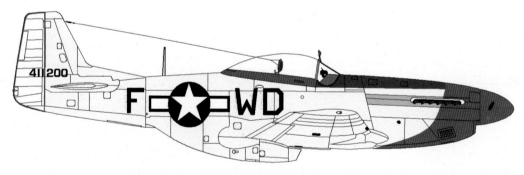

121 1st Lt. Paul J. Lucas Jr, Shamoki, Pennsylvania. To 335th FS 24/1/45 until 18/9/45.

1/72 Scale

118: *This P-51D-25NA 44-73100 was with 335th FS in April 1945. No bands or stripes, red outline to white rudder, red outline on codes.*

119: *P-51D-5 44-13779 was Blakeslee's assigned aircraft from July 1944. NMF overall, black ETO bands on wings and horizontal tail. D-Day stripes lower fuselage only. See 88, 103-104, 120.*

120: *Same aircraft as above in October 1944. Black ETO bands, wings and horizontal tail, only black stripes remaining of D-Day markings. White rudder. Aircraft has had fin fillet and mirror added, this and the canopy frame being red.. OD wing fillet borrowed from another aircraft. See 88, 103-104, 119.*

121: *Lucas flew this P-51D-5-NT in spring of 1945. It has no ETO bands or D-Day stripes, 1945-style red nose colouring, canopy frame and mirror also red, as is outline to white 335th Squadron rudder colour.*

335th Fighter Squadron

122 1st Lt. Donald Peterson, hometown unknown. To 335th FS 27/7/44 until 24/4/45 when he returned to USA.'D' Flight CO from 24/2/45

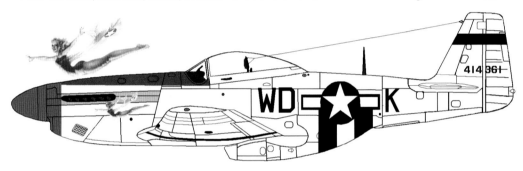

123 Capt. Robert J. Mabie, Marshalltown, Indiana. To 335th FS until 4/5/45 then to USA.
Capt. Donald D. Perkins, Palos Park, Illinois, To 335th FS 4/4/44 until 4/11/44 then to USA. 'D' Flight CO from 26/5/44.

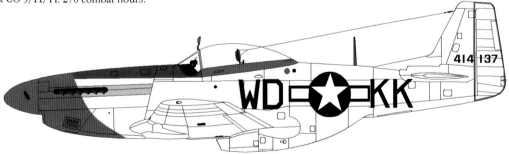

124 1st Lt. Darwin L. Berry, hometown unknown. To 335th FS 5/6/44 until tour finished 17/12/44. 'C' Flight CO 16/9/44, 'A' Flight CO 9/11/44. 270 combat hours.

125 Capt. George D. Green, Whittier, California. With 335th FS from 13/7/44 until 9/7/45.. 'B' Flt CO from 23/3/45.

1/72 Scale

122: *Peterson's P-51D -5-NA in March 1945. Bar after the code 'H' indicates it is the second H-coded aircraft in the squadron. No ETO bands, no D-Day stripes. Red outlined white rudder. Crew Chief J. Gibson.*
123: *The P-51D-5-NA shared by Mabie and Perkins in Autumn 1944. It has black ETO bands on tail surfaces, but not on the wings, and D-Day stripes under rear fuselage only.*
124: *The P-51D-10-NA flown by Berry in November 1944. It has black ETO bands on wing and tail surfaces and D-Day stripes under rear fuselage only.*

Name 'Fiesty Sue' is in white and not very legible, above the exhausts. It was later assigned to Lt. Elmer N. McCall. Lost 21/3/45 when 1st Lt. Robert A. Cammer was shot down by flak over Achmer airfield, and became a POW.
125: *This P-51D-10-NA was flown by George Green at war's end. Note use of second letter K, instead of a bar. Crew Chief B. Schultz, Asst. C/Chief 'Cess' Poole. WD has red outline, KK does not. See 126.*

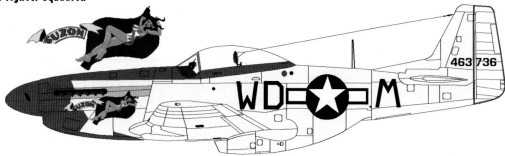

126 Capt. George D. Green, Whittier, California.

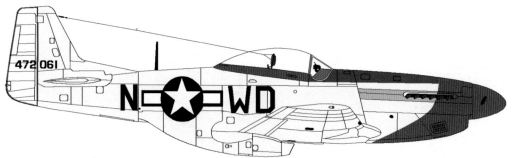

127 This P-51D-20-NA, 44-72061, was with the 335th FS in April 1945.

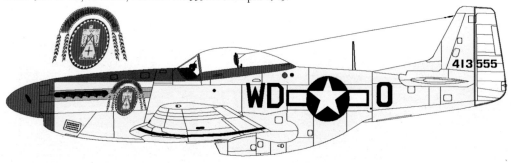

128 Capt. Ted E. Lines, Mesa, Arizona.

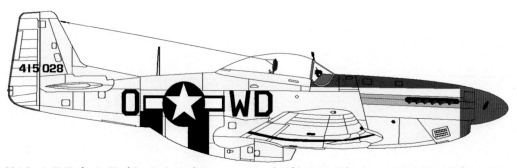

129 Maj. Louis H. Norley Jr ('Red Dog'), Conrad, Montana. Joined 336th FS 10/7/43, then to 335th FS 30/8/43, until he went to 334th FS 25/1/45 as CO, serving until 9/1945. Thus he served with all three 4th FG Squadrons in a long and eventful career. He was credited with 10.33 air and 5 ground victories.

1/72 Scale

126: *This P-51D-20-NA, 44-63736, was the aircraft Green landed in a German field to pick up his CO, Pierce McKennon, on 18/3/45. NMF overall, white rudder with red outline, red nose and canopy frame. No mirror, no black bands. Nose panels probably not original to this aircraft.*

127: *This P-51D-20-NA, 44-72061, was with 335th FS April 1945. Red outline to codes, also around white rudder.*

128: *Line's assigned aircraft in November 1944 was this P-51D-5-NA 44-13555, also named 'Thunder Bird'. It carries black ETO bands on wings and hori-*

zontal tail, red canopy frame and white rudder with red outline. Later recoded WD-D and passed to 1st Lt. Charles E. Konsler until end of the war. Crew Chief S. Koenig. See 105.

129: *Norley's P-51D-15-NA with the 335th FS in late October 1944. NMF overall, D-Day stripes under fuselage only, ETO bands on wings and horizontal tail surfaces. White rudder outlined red. Aircraft passed to Calvin Willruth as WD-Y in spring 1945. See 69-71, 137, 178.*

335th Fighter Squadron

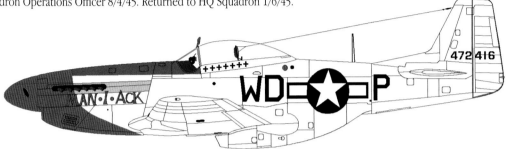

130 Maj. Robert A. Ackerley, Middletown, New York. To HQ Squadron, then to 335th FS on 28/1/45. 'C' Flight CO 23/3/45. Squadron Operations Officer 8/4/45. Returned to HQ Squadron 1/6/45.

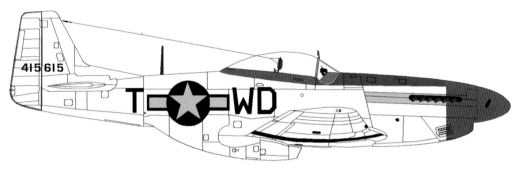

131 Maj. Robert A. Ackerley, Middletown, New York.

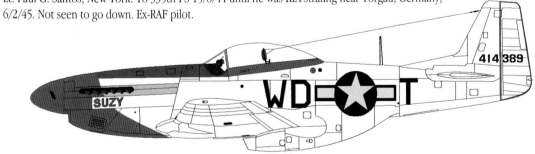

132 Capt. Brack Diamond, hometown unknown. With 335th FS 5/6/44 until 13/1/45, then to USA. 'D' Flight CO 16/9/44. Lt. Paul G. Santos, New York. To 335th FS 15/8/44 until he was KIA strafing near Torgau, Germany, 6/2/45. Not seen to go down. Ex-RAF pilot.

133 Lt. Robert C. Bucholz, Oklahoma City. To 334th FS 16/11/44. KIA 9/4/45, hit by flak, Munich/ Brunnthal airfield, crashed with aircraft. 3 ground kills before being hit.   **1/72 Scale**

130: *The P-51D-20-NA assigned to Ackerley in early 1945. Note white rudder lacks red outline. No bands or stripes. Name 'Rita Marie' is black. Aircraft later re-named 'Man-I-Ack'. Crew Chief E. Cool.*

131: *'Rita Marie' as 'Man-I-Ack' at the end of the war. Rudder now has a red outline, 7 Kills on canopy frame. Assigned pilot unknown. Aircraft later sold to Swedish Air Force as 26101 and then to Nicaraguan Air Force.*

132: *This P-51D-15-NA, 44-15615, was shared by Diamond and Santos in winter 1944-45. It is NMF overall, with black ETO bands on wings and hori-*

zontal tail. White rudder has red outline. Note greyed-out insignia. Lt. Santos was KIA in this aircraft on 6/2/45.

133: *P-51D-10-NA 44-14389 was with 335th FS from 31/8/44 until it went missing on 9/4/45 with Lt. Bucholz. NMF overall, black ETO bands on wings and horizontal tail. Fuselage stars light grey.*

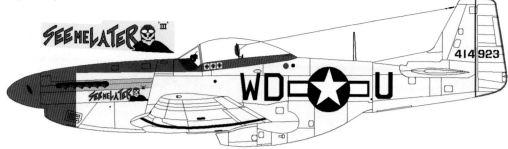

134 1st Lt. Wilbur B. Eaton, Portland, Oregon. To 335th FS 29/6/44 until tour expired 15/2/45. 'C' Flight CO 16/1/45. Reconnaissance pilot in Spitfires and P-38s before joining 4th FG.

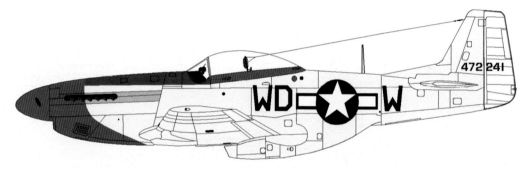

135 P-51D-10-NA 44-14438 in March 1945 colours. Pilot assignment not known.

136 This P-51D-20-NA served with the 335th FS in spring 1945. Assigned pilot not known.

137 Capt. Calvin W. Willruth, Lancaster, Massachusetts. To 335th FS 4/9/44 until unknown date.

1/72 Scale

134: This was Lt. Eaton's P-51D-15-NA at the end of December 1944. NMF overall, has black ETO bands on wings and horizontal tail. Extended 24 inch red nose, white rudder with red outline, 3 kills on canopy frame. Aircraft was lost 3/3/45 when Lt. Ken Green became POW, hit by flak south of Rotterdam.

135: P-51D-10-NA 44-14438 in March 1945 colours. 'Little Nan' has white rudder outlined in red, as is the canopy frame. No stripes or bands. Pilot assignment not known. Crew Chief George Lee.

136: This P-51D-20-NA served with the 335th FS in Spring 1945. Assigned pilot not known. Red-outlined white rudder, no bands or D-Day stripes.

137: Willruth's assigned A/C in April 1945 was Louis Norley's WD-O re-coded WD-Y and named 'DOTTY'. It now has the 1945 swept-under nose colouring, red canopy frame and mirror. D-Day stripes removed, but black ETO bands still on wings and horizontal tail surfaces. See 129.

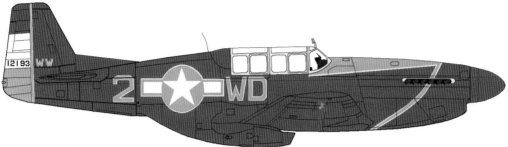

138 This is the first two-seater in the 4th FG, summer 1944.

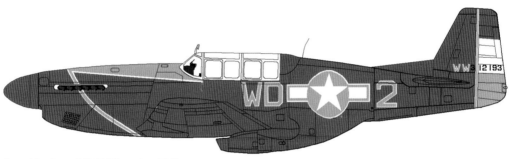

139 The same aircraft in spring 1945.

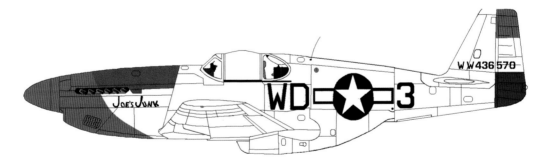

140 Port side view of 43-12193, spring 1945.

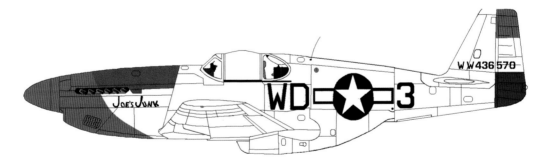

141 This P-51B-7-NA,44-36750, was with the 335th FS from 15/11/44 until the end of the war.

1/72 Scale

The 4th FG used several two-seat converstons and 'War-Weary' aircraft for ETO introduction for new pilots and to give ground crews and others a taste of what their hard work achieved.

138: The 335th FS had the first two-seater in the group, P-51B-1-NA 43-12193, converted by T/Sgt. Woody Jensen, Squadron Technical Inspector, in summer 1944. Note the tiny pin-up girl!

139: The same aircraft in spring 1945. Note the starboard side serial number presentation lacks the first digit — 3. The pin-up did not survive the re-paint, but the aircraft survived with the 4th FG until the summer of 1945.

140: The codes, national insignia, and anti-glare panelling are outlined with natural metal (silver). The canopy frames are also natural metal.

141: This P-51B-7-NA, 44-36750, was with the 335th FS from 15/11/44 until the end of the war. NMF, 1945-style nose colouring, 'Clobber College' rudder. Name on port side only. Note OD of anti-glare panel does not reach all the way back to the windshield. Crew Chief Joe Sills.

336th Fighter Squadron

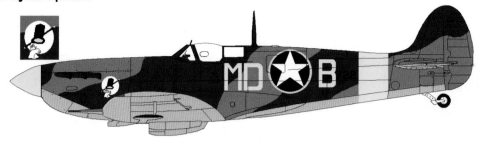

142 Maj. Leroy Gover, San Carlos, California. Joined 335 Squadron 23/9/42, until 4/1/44, when transferred to 4th FG HQ Squadron. Earned first Silver Star awarded to Group. Squadron Operations Officer from 26/9/43. CO from 10/10/43 to 10/11/43. Returned to USA after 257 combat sorties.

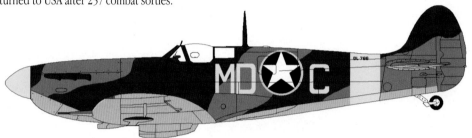

143 Spitfire Vb BL766. Assigned pilot uncertain, possibly Donald Blakeslee, CO of 335th FS, during October/November 1942, despite 336th FS markings.

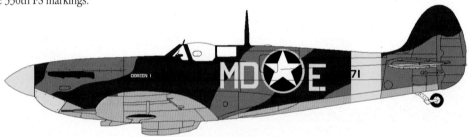

144 Maj. John G. Dufour. Alameda, California. Joined 335th FS 9/10/42. Went to Eighth Fighter Command HQ 2/9/43. Squadron CO from 4/3/43.

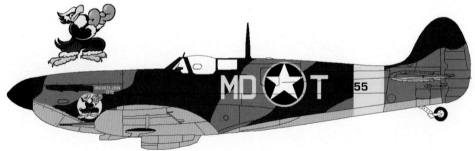

145 Capt. Dominic Salvatore Gentile ('Don'), Piqua, Ohio. Joined 336th FS 28/9/42, left end April 1944. 'B' Flight CO 26/9/43.

1/72 Scale

142: Spitfire Vb BL722, MD-B was Gover's first aircraft after the Eagle Squadrons became the 4th FG USAAF in August 1942. It wears the RAF colours of Dark Green and Ocean Grey over Medium Sea Grey undersides, with Sky spinner and tail band. Yellow stripe on wing leading edge outboard of guns. The US star insignia was painted over the RAF roundels on fuselage and port upper, starboard lower wings. The wing insignia did not have the yellow surround. See 151, 155.

143: Spitfire Vb BL766. Assigned pilot unknown for certain, possibly Blakeslee

during October/November 1942. Standard RAF colour scheme but note serial repainted on sky band in very small (2 inch?) figures.

144: Spitfire VB 'Doreen I' as assigned to John Dufour, 336th FS during Oct 1942. Standard period RAF scheme with US insignia in 4 positions. Only the fuselage stars had yellow surround. Note Sky panel under nose. See 148.

145: Gentile's Spitfire V, 'Buckeye Don', with the 336th FS, shortly after 133 Eagle Squadron was transferred to the USAAF. The two swastika kills represent the victories he scored at Dieppe, but not in this aircraft. See 161, 183.

336th Fighter Squadron

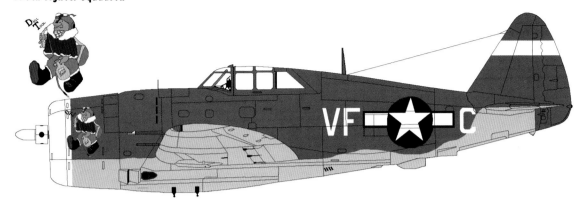

146 1st Lt. George K. Villinger, Palmyra, New Jersey. Joined 336th FS 27/8/43 until KIA 2/3/44 near Frankfurt, Germany. Circumstances unknown.

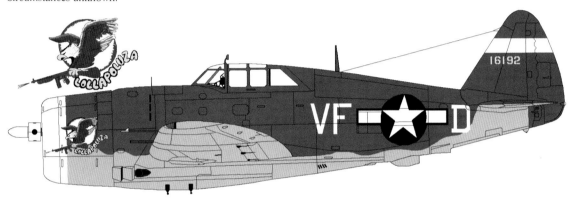

147 1st Lt. Woodrow F. Sooman ('Woody'), Republic, Washington. To 336th FS autumn 1943 until 18/3/44 when his P-51 aircraft developed a glycol leak near Frankfurt, Germany and he failed to reach home. Became POW.

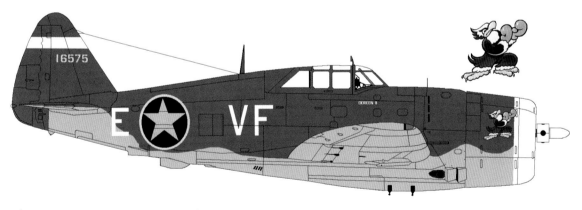

148 Maj. John G. Dufour, Alameda, California.

1/72 Scale

146: P-47C 'Dull Tool' assigned to Villinger in September 1943. Serial not known. OD and NG with white nose and tail bands. See 167.

147: P-47C-2-RE. Flown by Sooman in late 1943 and early 1944. Originally a 334th FS aircraft. OD and NG, white nose and tail bands. See 170.

148: This P-47C-5-RE 41-6575, VF-E, was Dufour's aircraft in April 1943. OD and NG with white bands on the tail surfaces. Name 'Doreen II' under windscreen. See 144, 149.

336th Fighter Squadron

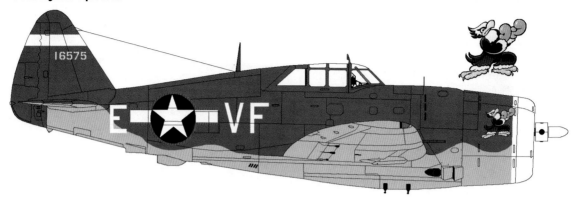

149 Capt. Kendal E. Carlson ('Swede'), Red Bluff, California. To 336th FS 25/7/43 until 25/2/45 when he became POW.

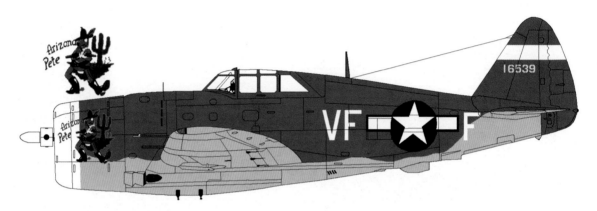

150 Capt. Kenneth D. Peterson ('Blacksnake'). Joined 336th FS 9/10/42 until shot down 29/3/44. Single-handedly attacked 12 enemy aircraft to protect a B-17. Shot down 2 FW 190s before being forced to bale out to become POW. He was awarded a DFC for this action.

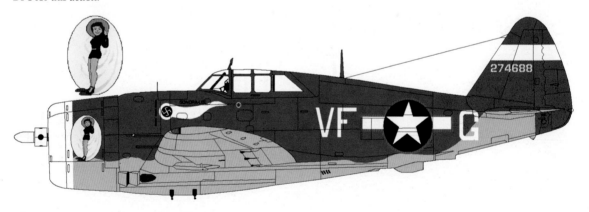

151 Maj. Leroy Gover, San Carlos, California.

1/72 Scale

149: This was previously John Dufour's machine, taken over by Carlson and shown how it appeared in August 1943. Name 'Doreen' has been removed but nose art retained. Markings updated with bars added to stars and the July/August red surround to the insignia. Don Allen nose art. See 148.

150: P-47C-5-RE 41-6539 'Arizona Pete' was Peterson's assigned aircraft for much of 1943. He shot down a FW 200 Condor off Bordeaux, France 5/3/44 flying a P-47. Standard OD and NG scheme, with ETO bands, nose and tail

surfaces. Crew Chief was S/Sgt. L. Engber. See 172.

151: Gover's P-47D-6-RE in late 1943, when he flew his final missions. After completing his tour he returned to the USA as an instructor. Standard OD and NG scheme. Note Insignia Red surround to stars and bars, which was used between July-August 1943. He flew his 100th mission in this aircraft. See 142, 155.

336th Fighter Squadron

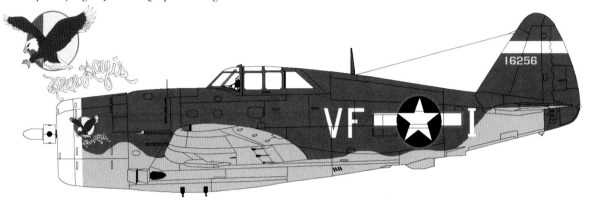

152 1st Lt. Conrad Ingold ('Connie'), New York City. Joined 336th FS 25/5/43 until 5/2/44 when he was taken off flying due to poor eyesight. Joined HQ Squadron as ground officer.

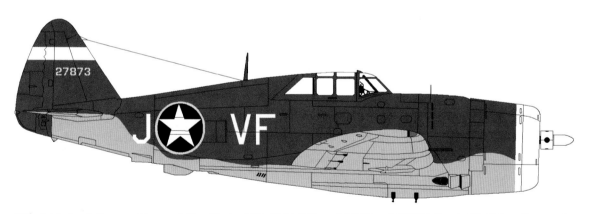

153 Capt. Robert D. Hobert, Woodland, Washington. Joined 336th FS 28/5/43. Was KIA 5/4/44.

154 1st Lt. Joe L. Bennett, Tucumari, New Mexico. With 336th FS from 9/10/42 until 29/2/44, then to 8th Fighter Command. Ex-Eagle Squadron member.

1/72 Scale

152: *This P-47D-6-RE was assigned to Ingold in September 1943. Completely standard colours and markings for period.*

153: *'Blue Roofis', Hobert's P-47C-2-RE in September 1943. Aircraft previously VF-G, assigned to Leroy Gover and was again re-coded to VF-C, in January 1944, after Hobert's use of it. It wears the standard OD and NG finish, with the white nose and tail ETO bands.*

154: *P-47D-1-RE 42-7873 was crashlanded and burnt out on 17/6/43 in the grounds of the 'Carpenters Arms' pub, North Weald, after an engine fire in the air. OD and NG, white nose and tail bands, yellow circle around fuselage insignia only.*

336th Fighter Squadron

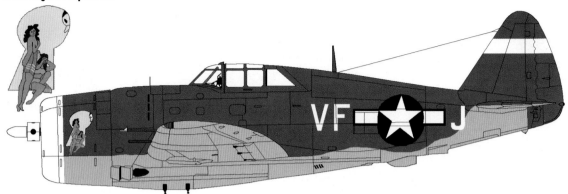

155 Maj. Leroy Gover, San Carlos, California.

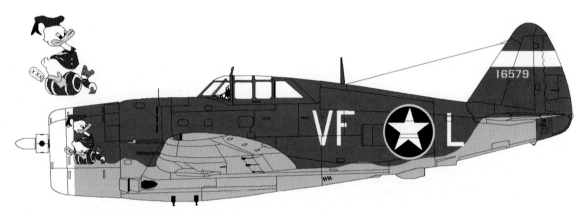

156 Maj. Carl H. Miley, Toledo, Ohio. To 336th FS 9/10/42 until 10/11/43 when he returned to USA. Squadron CO 1/9/43.

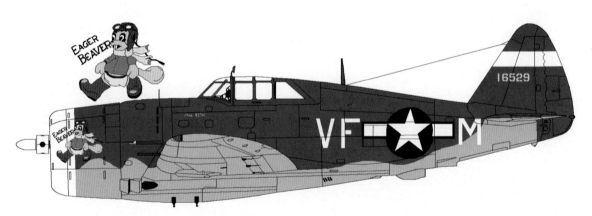

157 1st Lt. Jack L. Raphael, Tacoma, Washington. Joined 336th FS 18/8/43. Transferred 28/6/44.

1/72 Scale

155: This P-47C is also believed flown to have been flown by Gover in September 1943. (See 151). Serial is not known. Standard colours and white markings.

156: Miley's P-47C-5-RE in June 1943 was 41-6579. In OD and NG, with the white tail bands. Yellow circle around stars on fuselage only. Later coded VF-H and assigned to Lt. Conrad Ingold. See 152.

157: P-47C-5-RE 416529 was Raphael's Thunderbolt from August 1943 until February 1944 when the 4th received Mustangs. OD and NG with standard white bands on nose and all tail surfaces. Beaver on port side only. 'Miss Beth' below windshield.

336th Fighter Squadron

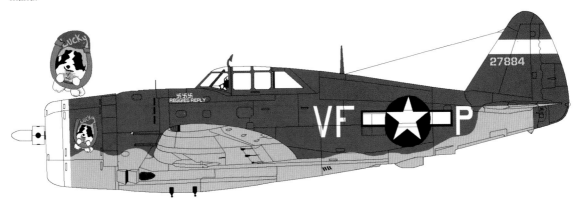

158 1st Lt. Donald D. Nee, Long Beach, California. To 336th FS 9/10/42, until 26/11/43 when he went to 9th Fighter Command.

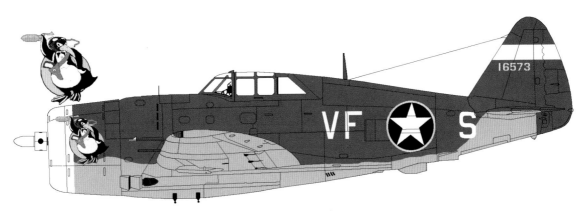

159 Maj. John Trevor Godfrey ('Johnny'), Woonsocket, Rhode Island. Joined 336th FS 22/9/43. POW 24/8/44.

160 1st Lt. Andrew J. Stephenson, Los Angeles, California. To 336th FS 9/10/42 until 26/12/43. Ex-133 Eagle Squadron.
1st Lt. Peter G. Lehman, New York City, New York. To 336th FS 25/8/43 until killed in flying accident 31/3/44.

1/72 Scale

158: *P-47C-2-RE 'Sandman' flown by Lt. Nee in late 1943, in the standard colours and markings of the period, ODand NG with white identity bands on nose and tail surfaces. Serial not known.*
159: *P-47D-1-RE assigned to Godfrey named after his dog 'Lucky'. The inscription 'Reggie's Reply' is for his brother killed in the Battle of the Atlantic. Standard OD and NG with white ETO bands, nose and all tail surfaces. He scored 3.5 kills in Thunderbolts, 1.5 in this aircraft. See 180-181, 204.*
160: *P-47C-5-RE 41-6573 was assigned to Stephenson from April to December 1943 then passed to Lehman. Standard colours and markings for mid-1943, with OD and NG, white nose and tail bands, yellow surround to fuselage insignia only.*

336th Fighter Squadron

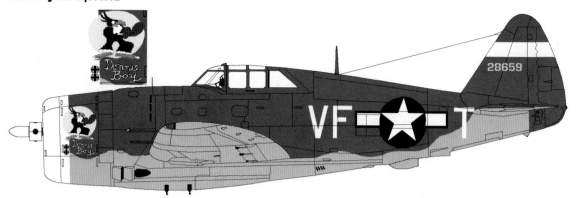

161 Capt. Dominic Salvatore Gentile ('Don'), Piqua, Ohio. Joined 336th FS 28/9/42, left end April 1944. 'B' Flight CO 26/9/43.

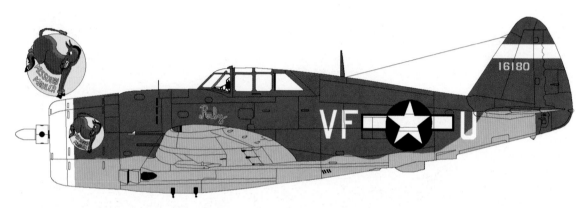

162 Maj. Willard W. Millikan, Rockport, Missouri. Joined 336th FS autumn 1943. Stayed until lost (POW) 30/5/44. Acting Squadron CO 13/4/44 until 10/5/44 while Goodson was in the Mediterranean area.

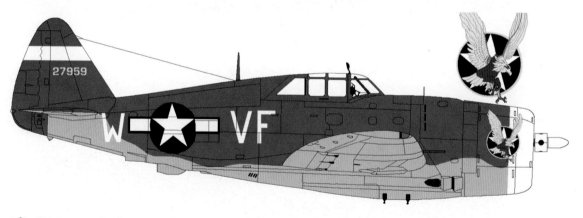

163 Maj. James A. Goodson ('Goody'), New York. Joined 336th FS 9/10/42. Served until became POW 20/6/44. Detached service with Mediterranean FG 12/4/44 TO 10/5/44. 'A' Flight CO from 26/9/43. Squadron CO 8/3/44 until lost 20/6/44.

1/72 Scale

161: Gentile's P-47D-5-RE 'Donnie Boy'. OD and NG, white ETO bands, nose and all tail surfaces. Two kill crosses represent victories during Dieppe Operation. He scored 4.3 kills in Thunderbolts, 3 of them in this aircraft. See 145, 183.

162: Millikan's P-47C-2-RE 41-6180 in which he scored 2 of his 3 Thunderbolt victories. Standard OD and NG with white bands on all tail surfaces. As well as his 'Missouri Mauler' artwork, his English wife's name, 'Ruby' is painted below the windshield. See 188.

163: This P-47D-2-RE was Goodson's assigned aircraft from June 1943 until February 1944, when the group received Mustangs. Standard colours and markings. He scored 5 victories in Thunderbolts, 2 of them in this aircraft. See 165-166, 196.

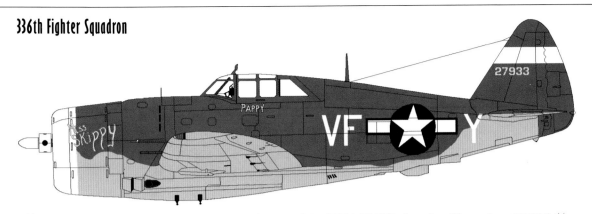

164 Capt. Phillip H. Dunn ('Pappy'), Vancouver, Washington. Joined 336th FS 1942. Served until becoming a POW 3/3/44.

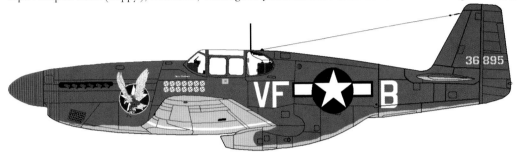

165 Maj. James A. Goodson ('Goody'), New York.

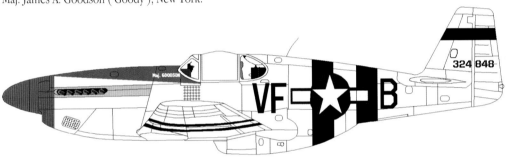

166 Maj. James A. Goodson ('Goody'), New York.

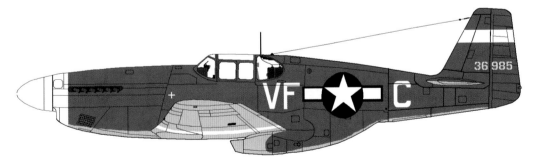

167 1st Lt. George K. Villinger, Palmyra, New Jersey.

1/72 Scale

164: P-47D-1-RE 42-7933, was 'Pappy' Dunn's assigned aircraft from September 1943 until the 4th converted to Mustangs, February 1944. Standard OD and NG with white bands, nose and tail. 'Miss Skippy' on nose, yellow with red outline, 'Pappy' below cockpit, yellow with black outline. Crew Chief E. Rowe, Asst. C/Chief D. Ratcliffe. Ying-Yang marking on wheel covers.
165: P-51B-7-NA 43-6895 was Goodson's first assigned Mustang. He did not score in this aircraft. 14 kill marks represent both air and ground victories. OD and NG. ETO bands on wings only. See 163, 166, 196.

166: P-51B-15 43-24848. NMF overall, black ETO bands on all tail surfaces. Full D-Day stripes on wings and fuselage. 30 black swastika kill marks under windscreen in 5 rows of 6. 'Maj. Goodson' on anti-glare panel ahead of windshield. Flown on Russia shuttle mission by Capt. Neal 'Dutch' Van-Wyk. See 163, 165, 196.
167: This P-51B-5-NA, 43-6985, was the aircraft in which Villinger was lost on 2/3/44. OD and NG, white nose, spinner, wing and tail ETO bands. See 146.

336th Fighter Squadron

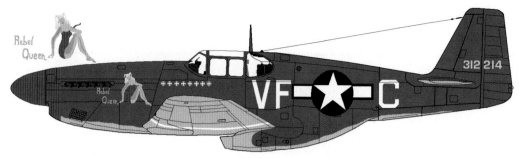

168 Maj. Frederick W. Glover ('Freddie'), Asheville, North Carolina. To 336th FS 20/2/44 until 1/6/45. Squadron Operations Officer 17/8/44, Squadron CO 24/8/44. Evader during May 1944.

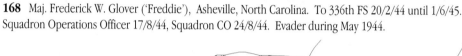
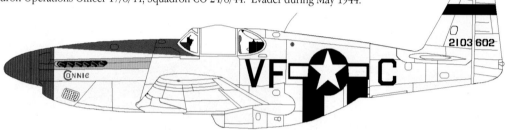

169 1st Lt. George C. Smith, Los Angeles, California. To 336th FS 25/2/44 until 18/12/44 when tour completed.

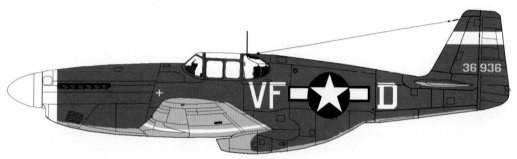

170 1st Lt. Woodrow F. Sooman ('Woody'), Republic, Washington.

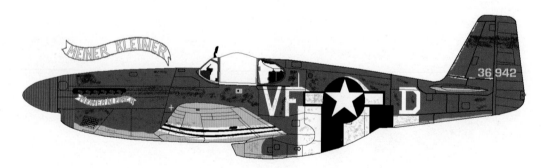

171 Capt. Joseph W. Higgins, Philadelphia, Philadelphia. Joined 336th FS 17/4/44, completed his tour and left for home on 30/9/44. Flew this P-51B-5-NA on Russia shuttle mission.

1/72 Scale

168: *P-51B-1-NA 43-12214 flown by Glover during March/April 1944. OD and NG, with group red nose colour, from 15/3/44. White tail bands were removed from 23/3/44, but remained on wings. 8 white kill crosses below windscreen. Crew Chief J. Wilson, Asst. C./Chief N. Meyers. See 198-199.*

169: *P-51C-5-NT 42-103602 'Connie' was Smith's assigned aircraft. Black ETO bands on all tail surfaces, but none on wings. D-Day stripes under fuselage only, fitted with Malcolm hood. Smith flew it on the Russian shuttle mission July 1944. It ended the war as a training aircraft coded VF-5. See 192.*

170: *Sooman was lost in this P-51B-5-NA, 43-6936. OD and NG with white bands on wings and all tail surfaces. White nose band and spinner may have been red by the time it was lost, most 4th FG aircraft being painted over the period 15-18 March 1944. See 147.*

171: *Higgins' only assigned aircraft. Lost 21/11/44 while being flown by 2nd Lt. George Klaus (POW). Extremely scruffy worn OD and NG scheme, D-Day stripes on lower surfaces, no ETO bands. 'Meiner Kleiner' yellow, outlined red on a white scroll, outlined in red. Crew Chief S/Sgt. Glesner Weckbacher.*

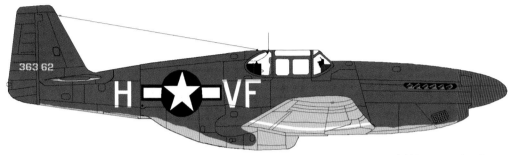

172 Capt. Kenneth D. Peterson ('Blacksnake'). Joined 336th FS 9/10/42 until shot down 29/3/44.

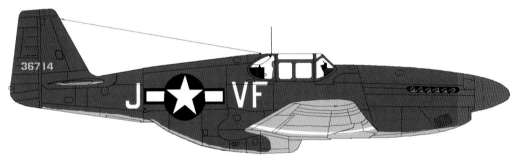

173 This P-51B-5-NA 43-6362 crash-landed at Manston on return from an operation on 30/4/44 by Lt. Fredericks. Assigned pilot unknown.

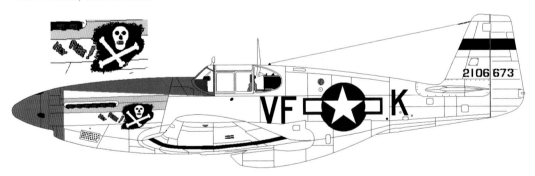

174 This P-51B-5-NA 43-6714 was lost in a mid-air collision on 7/6/44. Capt. Donald Pierini baled out safely after colliding with Lt. Kenneth D. Smith, who was killed.

175 Capt. Reuben Simon ('Rube'), Los Angeles, California. With 336th FS from 30/7/43 until 25/5/44, then to 496th Fighter Training Group, Atcham.

1/72 Scale

172: This P-51B-5, 43-6696 was Peterson's only assigned Mustang and in which he was shot down 29/3/44. Red nose may have been added by then, having been ordered from 13/3/44. ETO bands on wings and all tail surfaces. See 150.

173: P-51B-5-NA 43-6362 is in the early 1944 scheme of OD and NG. Red nose from March 1944, white ETO bands on wings only.

174: This P-51B-5NA 43-6714 was lost in a mid-air collision on 7/6/44. Capt. Donald Pierini baled out safely, after colliding with Lt. Kenneth D. Smith,

who was killed. OD and NG aircraft, white bands on wings only.

175: P-51B-10-NA 42-106673 was Simon's aircraft in May 1944. Aircraft is NMF overall with black codes and ETO bands. Nose art is white skull and crossbones on black background, name 'Hey Rube!' is red with black outline. See 207.

336th Fighter Squadron

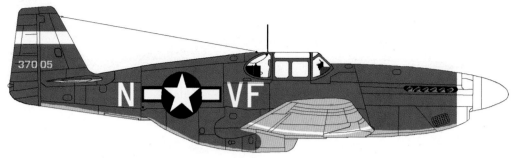

176 Lt. Glenn A. Herter, East Windsor, Ontario, Canada. To 337th FS 25/5/43, until KIA 3/3/44. Shot down in fight with 60+ enemy fighters near Wittenburg, Germany.
Capt. Robert H. Wehrman, Old Greenwich, Connecticut. With 336th FS 1/9/43 until 30/10/44.

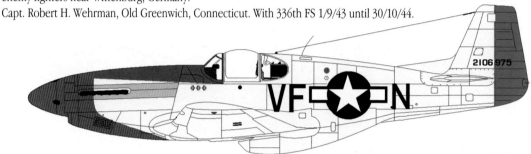

177 P-51B-15-NA 42-106975 served in 335th FS in early 1945. Pilot assignment not known, although the aircraft has three kill crosses ahead of the canopy.

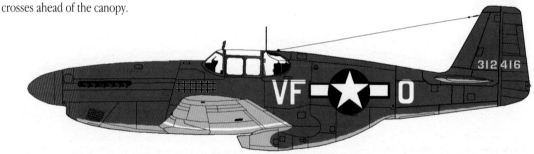

178 Maj. Louis H. Norley Jr. ('Red Dog'), Conrad, Montana. Joined 336th FS 10/7/43, then to 335th FS 30/8/43.

179 P-51B-10 assigned to Nicholas F. Hurley.

1/72 Scale

176: *This P-51B-7-NA was assigned to Glenn Herter when it arrived in the 336th FS on 28/2/44. It was written off on 5/3/44 when Lt. Bob Wehrman glided a long way to crashland at Heathfield, UK, after the plugs fused. OD and NG with full white ETO bands on nose and tail surfaces. Aircraft had a service life of 5 days!*

177: *P-51B-15-NA 42-106975, served with 335th FS in early 1945. Pilot assignment not known, although the aircraft has three kill crosses ahead of the canopy. NMF overall with late war nose colour demarcation and 336th FS*

blue rudder, no bands or stripes carried.

178: *Norley's P-51B-1-NA 43-12416, with 336th FS mid-1944. He did not score in this aircraft although it carries 14 kill marks, for his air and ground claims to date. It is in the standard OD and NG scheme, with white ETO bands on wings only. Crew Chief V. Giovenco. See 69-71, 129.*

179: *This aircraft was left in Italy with the 325th FG after the Russian shuttle mission, July 1944. Although this was not his assigned machine, John Godfrey shot down a Bf 109 on 1 May 1944 with it.*

336th Fighter Squadron

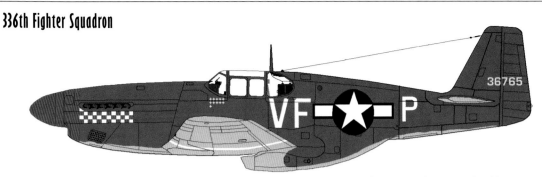

180 Maj. John Trevor Godfrey ('Johnny'), Woonsocket, Rhode Island. Joined 336th FS 22/9/43. POW 24/8/44.

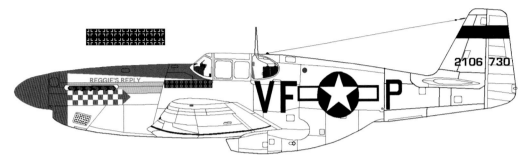

181 Maj. John Trevor Godfrey ('Johnny'), Woonsocket, Rhode Island.

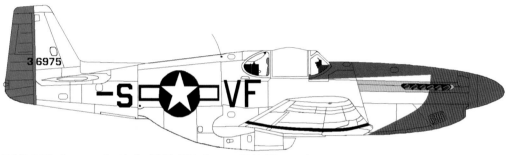

182 P-51B-7-NA that served with the 336th FS in January 1945. Pilot not known.

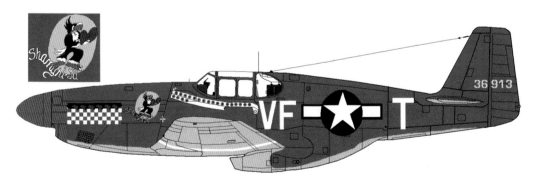

183 Capt. Dominic Salvatore Gentile ('Don'), Piqua, Ohio.

1/72 Scale

180: *P-51B-5-NA 43-6765, Godfrey's first P-51. White ETO bands on wings only. Note only 3 rows of red/white checks, both sides. 11 white cross kill marks below windshield. Crew Chief S/Sgt. Larry Krantz. See 159, 181, 204.*
181: *P-51B-1-NA 42-106730. Godfrey's second P-51. Flown until April 1944. He scored 4 kills in this aircraft. On 27/4/44 his room-mate, Lt. Robert Tussey, crash-landed it at Martlesham Heath. NMF with black ETO bands, wings and all tail surfaces. Red/white checks and name 'Reggie's Reply' both sides, kill marks port side only. see 159, 180, 204.*

182: *P-51B-7-NA that served wuth the 336th FS in January 1945. Pilot unknown. 1945-style nose colouring, blue rudder and retro-fitted fin fillet and Malcolm hood. Black bands on wings and horizontal tail surfaces. 43-6975 was the second S in the squadron, indicated by the bar aft of the code.*
183: *Gentile's only P-51 (a B-5-NA). He flew this aircraft until the end of his tour and crashed it at Debden during a low pass for the press. OD and NG, white bands on wings only. 4 rows of red/white checks appeared port and starboard, emblem and scroll on port side only. See 145, 161.*

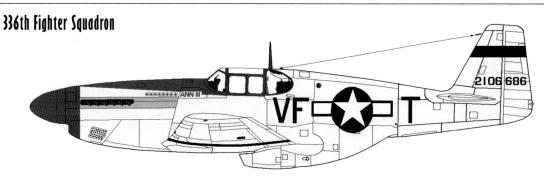

184 Capt. Joseph H. Bennet (Joe), Moreton, Texas. To 336th FS until 4/4/44 when he became POW after being shot down by fighters near Strasbourg.

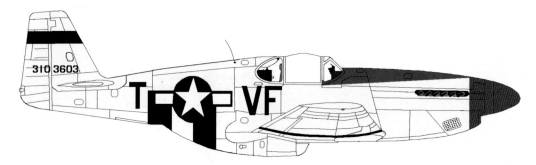

185 Capt. Francis M. Grove ('Lefty', 'Pappy'), Glen Cove, New York. To 336th FS 1/5/44 until Group de-activated in USA in late 1945. Last Squadron CO of the era, from 22/9/45.

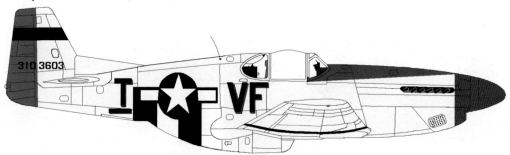

186 Capt. Francis M. Grove ('Lefty', 'Pappy'), Glen Cove, New York.

187 Maj. Willard W. Millikan, Rockport, Missouri. Joined 336th FS autumn 1943. Stayed until lost (POW) 30/5/44.

1/72 Scale

184: This P-51B-10-NA was Bennett's aircraft in spring 1944. NMF with full black ETO bands wings and tail. Note OD canopy framing. Name 'Ann III' and 8 kill crosses ahead of windscreen. This aircraft shared with Lt. Grove. Crew Chief S/Sgt. John Ferra.

185: Grove's P-51C-5-NT 42-103603 in July/August 1944. Full black ETO bands on wings and all tail surfaces, D-Day stripes under fuselage only. Malcolm hood fitted. See 186, 217-218.

186: This is the same aircraft as above in December 1944. Retro-fitted with

fin fillet. NMF overall, ETO bands and D-Day stripes as before. Aircraft now coded T-bar, indicating it is the second aircraft in the squadron with this code. Blue Squadron rudder colouring, and the codes are shadow-shaded red, but the red nose colour has not been extended. See 185, 217-218.

187: P-51B-5-NR 43-6997, in which Millikan scored 8 kills in 14 days during April 1944. White ETO bands on wings only. Not thought to have had art-work on this aircraft, which was crash-landed at Debden, out of fuel, 18/6/44, by Lt. Henry A. Ingalls. See 162, 188.

336th Fighter Squadron

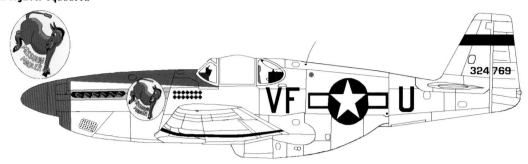

188 Maj. Willard W. Millikan, Rockport, Missouri. Joined 336th FS autumn 1943. Stayed until lost (POW) 30/5/44.

189 Capt. Neil Van Wyk ('Dutch'), Paterson, New Jersey. Joined 336th FS 10/10/43 until 8/11/44, then to 335th FS until 27/2/45. 335th FS 'C' Flight CO from 29/11/44.

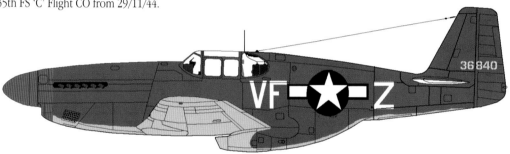

190 Capt. Joseph H. Patteuw ('Patt') Detroit, Michigan. Joined 336th FS 4/4/44, left 10/11/44 on completion of tour.

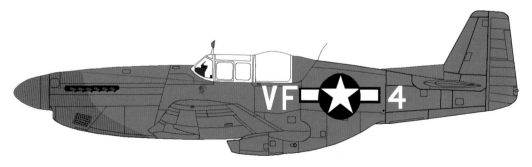

191 This two-seater served in the 336th FS in early 1945. The serial number is not known.   **1/72 Scale**

188: *Millikan's last assigned aircraft was this P-51B-15-NA, 43-24769. He scored one kill in it on 22/5/44. On 30/5/44 he was flying this aircraft when he collided with his wingman over Germany and went down to become a POW. NMF overall, full black ETO bands on wing and all tail surfaces. 14 red-outlined black crosses ahead of cockpit. See 162, 187.*

189: *P-51B-5-NA 43-6772 was Van Wyk's aircraft in April 1944. NMF with full black ETO bands on wings and all tail surfaces.*

190: *P-51B-5-NA 43-6840 was assigned to Patteuw when he joined the squad-*

ron. It was written off by a new pilot on 10/5/44 who broke the landing gear on landing, almost ran down the duty flagman(Patteeuw), and slid neatly into a revetment. Aircraft nickname was 'Zed' but was not painted on. Crew Chief O. Garrison, Asst. C/Chief N. Meyer. See 221.

191: *This two-seater served in the 336th FS in early 1945. Overall blue, red trim, natural metal canopy framing. White codes with red shadow-shading. Malcolm hood over second cockpit. Serial number is not known.*

336th Fighter Squadron

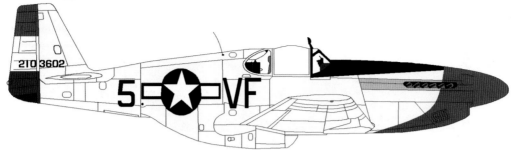

192 This is how Lt. George Smith's 'Connie' ended the war.

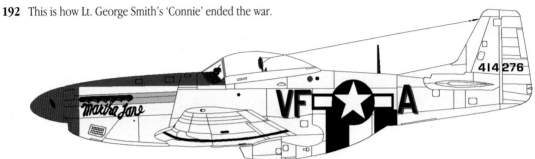

193 Capt. Franklin W. Young, Marmora, New Jersey. To 336th FS 15/6/44 until 10/5/45, then to USA.

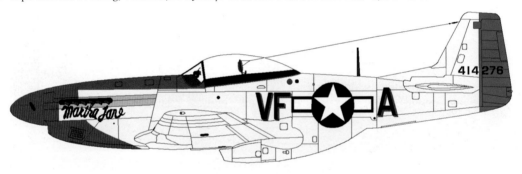

194 Capt. Franklin W. Young, Marmora, New Jersey.

195 1st Lt. James R. McMahon, Camden, New Jersey. To 336th FS 15/2/45 until end of war. Later flew 100 missions in the Korean War.

1/72 Scale

192: This is how Lt. George Smith's 'Connie' ended the war. After service with the squadron 'Clobber College', she appeared in this livery at Bassingbourn at the end of the war, where she was broken up. See 169.

193: Young's P-51D-10-NA in September 1944. D-Day bands under rear fuselage. Black ETO bands on wings and horizontal tail surfaces. Codes with red shadow-shading. See 194-195.

194: 'Martha Jane' in March 1945, just before it passed to Jim McMahon and became 'Marcy'. ETO bands and D-Day stripes removed. Canopy rail and

rudder painted. Nose colour swept back in January 1945. See 193, 195.

195: 'Martha Jane' became 'Marcy' as seen here when it passed to Jim McMahon in April 1945. Aircraft now has no ETO or D-Day bands and 1945-style nose colour. Canopy frame black. Crew Chief G. Anderson. Asst. Crew Chief M. Weddle. Amr. J. Terrill. See 193-194.

336th Fighter Squadron

196 Maj. James A. Goodson ('Goody'), New York.

197 Capt. Donald R. Emerson, Pembina, North Dakota. Joined 336th FS 9/3/44. Squadron Operations Officer 8/7/44. 'A' Flight CO August 1944. KIA on Christmas Day 1944, shot by ground fire crossing front line, died before crashing in Belgium.

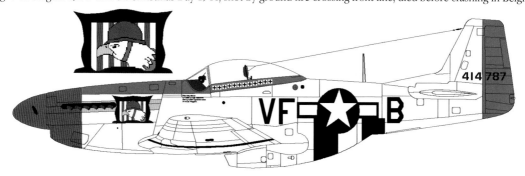

198 Maj. Frederick W. Glover ('Freddie'), Asheville, North Carolina.

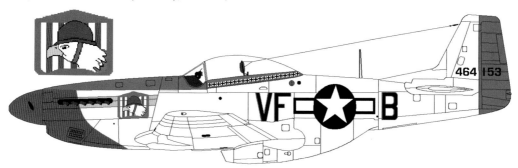

199 Maj. Frederick W. Glover ('Freddie'), Asheville, North Carolina. Glover's last wartime aircraft with the 4th FG was this P-51D-20-NA, 44-64153.

1/72 Scale

196: Goodson's D-5 model, in which he was shot down by flak to become a POW on June 20th 1944, Neubrandenburg airfield. He did not score in the P-51D. NMF overall with full D-Day bands. Black ETO bands on tail surfaces. 30 swastikas represent his total air and ground kills. See 163, 165-166.
197: This P-51D-5-NA was Emerson's assigned aircraft in summer 1944. He flew it on the Russia Shuttle in July. D-Day bands on lower surfaces, black ETO bands on tail surfaces, 7 black white outlined kill crosses under windscreen. Aircraft lost 26/3/45, Lt. Harry L. Davis diving into the ground at

Woodbridge, Suffolk, with his wing on fire, KIA. C/Chief Larry Jones. See 201.
198: Glover's P-51D-10-NA in late 1944. NMF overall, black ETO bands on wings and horizontal tail. Blue rudder, anti-glare panel and canopy frame, red outline to anti-glare panel and canopy. 12 kill crosses on canopy frame. Half D-Day stripes on lower fuselage. See 168, 199.
199: NMF overall, no ETO or D-Day bands. Blue anti-glare panel and rudder, red outlined codes. Red outline to anti-glare panel and cockpit frame. 23 kills marks on canopy frame. See 168, 198.

336th Fighter Squadron

200 Lt. James E. Hileman, New Kensington, Pennsylvania. To 336th FS 28/10/44 until 23/4/45, then to USA.

201 2nd Lt. Earl A. Quist. Joined 336th FS 12/7/44. Became POW 8/11/44.

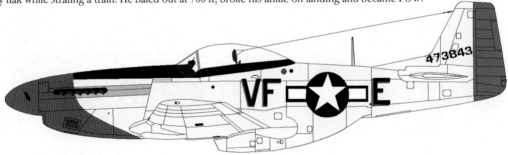

202 Capt. George H. Davis ('Ink'), Berlin, Maryland. Joined 336th FS 30/9/44, left 26/1/45 to go to 335th FS until 3/3/45, when hit by flak while strafing a train. He baled out at 700 ft, broke his ankle on landing and became POW.

203 2nd Lt. William H. Hastings, Washington Courthouse, Ohio. Joined 336th FS 5/2/45 until 15/9/45.

1/72 Scale

200: *44-15191, P-51D-15-NA 'Mary Belle' was Hileman's assigned aircraft in December 1944. It is in NMF, black ETO bands on wings and horizontal tail. 1945 style nose colouring, blue rudder, black canopy frame. Name red with black outline. Single black mirror.*

201: *This P-51D-15-NA was flown by Quist until he went down in November 1944. It was then taken over by Don Emerson, who was killed in it on Christmas Day 1944. NMF overall, D-Day bands remaining on lower fuselage only. Black ETO bands on wings and tail, but none on fin and rudder. Black anti-*

glare panel and canopy frame. Crew Chief Glesner Weckbacher, Asst. Crew Chief L. Brown. See 210.

202: *This P-51D-20-NA was Davis's assigned aircraft with the 336th FS in January 1945. NMF overall, blue Squadron rudder colour. No black bands.*

203: *Hastings' assigned aircraft in April 1945 was this P-51D-25-NA, 44-73843. It is NMF overall, no stripes or bands, black anti-glare panel and canopy frame. Red shadow blocking on black codes.*

336th Fighter Squadron

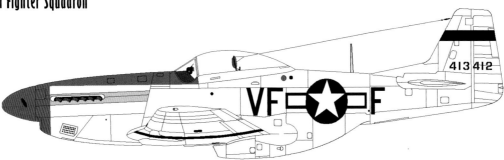

204 Maj. John Trevor Godfrey ('Johnny'), Woonsocket, Rhode Island.

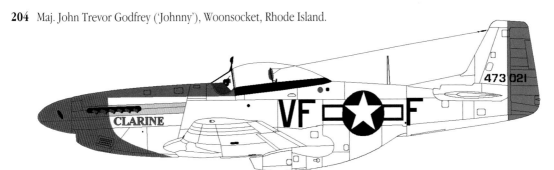

205 This P-51D-25-NA was with the 336th FS in spring 1945. Pilot assignment not known.

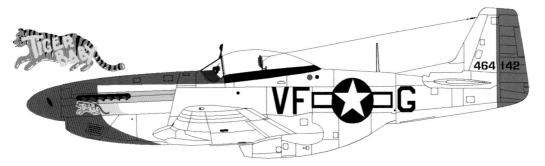

206 1st Lt. John P. Murchake Jr ('Tiger'), Annapolis, Maryland. With 336th FS 24/1/45 until 21/9/45 and then to 64th Fighter Wing.

207 Capt. Donald J. Pierini, Trenton, New Jersey. Flew a tour with 336th FS from 25/5/44 until 8/3/45, then returned to USA.
1st Lt. Harold H. Fredericks, Oakland City, Indiana. With 336th FS from 20/2/44 – 29/5/45. Evader 6/6/44 – 5/9/44. **1/72 Scale**

204: P-51D-5-NA. This is the aircraft Godfrey was flying when shot down by his wingman over a Luftwaffe airfield near Nordhausen on 24 August 1944. Became a POW. Not known if this was his assigned aircraft though he flew it on the second, fourth and last of the 12 missions of his second tour. Black bands on wings and all tail surfaces. See 159, 180-181.

205: This P-51D-25-NA was with the 336th FS in spring 1945. It shows typical period markings, with no bands or stripes, swept nose colouring and blue 336 rudder. Pilot assignment not known.

206: P-51D-20-NA 44-64142 'Tiger Baby' was Murchake's aircraft at war's end. It is in NMF overall with the late-war style nose markings and blue rudder. No bands or stripes, canopy frame is black.

207: This P-51D-10-NA 44-14277 was assigned to Pierini until his tour finished, then passed to Lt. Fredericks. It went missing 16/4/45, with 2nd Lt. Benjamin L. Griffin, of Jacksonville, Florida, who became POW when shot down by flak over Praha airfield, Czechoslovakia. It is NMF with no black bands, codes outlined in red. Crew Chief S/Sgt. Frank Mason. See 175.

336th Fighter Squadron

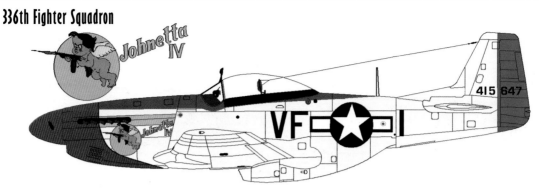

208 1st Lt. Douglas N. Groshong, Selma, California. Joined 336th FS 22/9/44. Returned to USA 21/7/45.

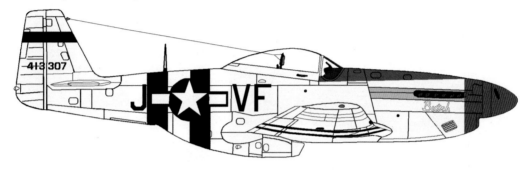

209 1st Lt. James C. Lane, Medford, Massachusetts. To 336th FS 4/4/44, stayed until 12/9/44 when he baled out north of Trier, Germany, owing to loss of engine coolant and became a POW.

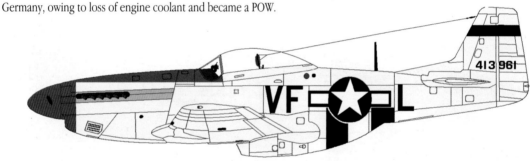

210 2nd Lt. Earl A. Quist. Joined 336th FS 12/7/44. Became POW 8/11/44.

211 Flight Officer Clarence H. Bousefield, Centreville, South Dakota. Joined 336th FS 18/4/45 until 18/9/45.

1/72 Scale

208: This P-51D-15-NA 44-15647, 'Johnetta IV', was Groshong's aircraft in spring 1945. NMF with Squadron blue rudder. No black bands. Anti-glare panel extends back to antenna and is outlined red. Note red formation lights in bar of insignia and aft of exhaust. Red nose marking is outlined in black.

209: In June/July 1945, 44-13307 was Lane's assigned P-51D-5-NA. 'Butch' was NMF overall, full D-Day stripes on wings and fuselage. Name is white with red outline.

210: This P-51D-5-NA was being flown by Earl Quist when he was shot down to become POW. NMF overall with D-Day stripes on lower fuselage only. No ETO bands on wings, but on horizontal tail.

211: Bousefield's P-51D-15-NA 44-15613, 'Peaches', in March 1945 with no bands or stripes, 1945-style nose and rudder colours. Anti-glare panel and canopy frame black. Note position of serial on fin.

336th Fighter Squadron

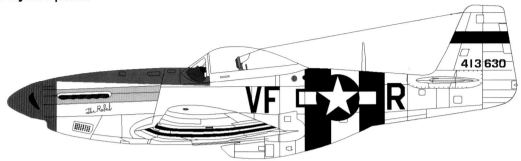

212 Capt. Joseph H. Joiner, Corpus Christi, Texas. 336th FS from 25/5/44 to 1/6/45, then to 128th FG HQ.

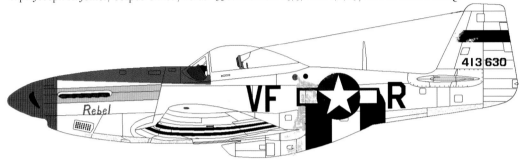

213 Capt. Joseph H. Joiner, Corpus Christi, Texas.

214 Capt. Melvyn N. Dickey, Tampa, Florida. To 336th FS 12/7/44 until 6/6/45 then to USA.

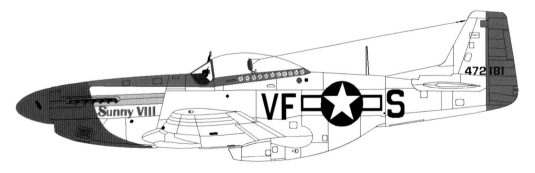

215 Col. Everett W. Stewart, Abilene, Kansas. Became Group CO 21/2/45 until end of war. Previously 355th FG CO and served in Pacific.

1/72 Scale

212: P-51D-5-NA 44-13630 was Joiner's aircraft in June 1944. It is in overall NMF finish with full D-Day stripes wings and fuselage, also ETO bands on all tail surfaces. Name 'The Rebel' is red. Later passed to Melvyn Dickey and became 'Betty Jane II'. See 213.

213: Same aircraft in July/August 1944, after much hard usage. 'The' has been removed and name 'Rebel' repainted. D-Day stripes removed from top surfaces. Aircraft has very dirty, well-worn look. See 212.

214: Dickey's machine in February 1945 was this P-51D-5-NA. NMF overall,

1945-style nose colouring, blue rudder, black canopy frame and mirror.

215: Col. Stewart's P-51D-20-NA in April 1945. NMF with blue anti-glare panel and canopy frame, both with red outline. 11 kill swastikas on canopy. No bands or D-Day stripes. Crew Chief Glesner Weckbacher, Asst. Crew Chief Louis Brown, Armourer Vervene Young.

216 2nd Lt. Maurice W. Miller Jr, Jackson Heights, New York. To 336th FS 24/1/45 until POW 16/4/45. Downed by flak at Praha airfield, Czechoslovakia.

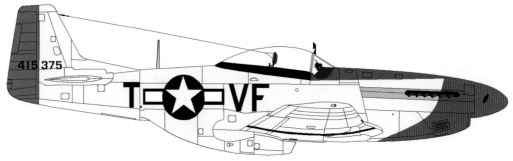

217 Capt. Francis M. Grove ('Lefty', 'Pappy'), Glen Cove, New York.

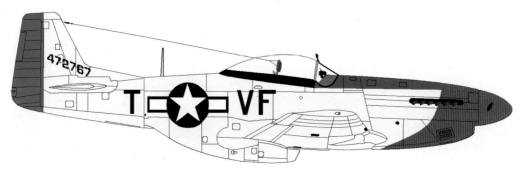

218 Capt. Francis M. Grove ('Lefty', 'Pappy'), Glen Cove, New York.

219 Capt. Harry N. Hagan, Yorkville, Ohio. Joined 336th FS 1/6/44. Injured after baling out 17/1/45, landing in a tree near Folkestone, UK. Awarded Purple Heart. Left for USA 10/5/45.

1/72 Scale

216: *This P-51D-10-NA was Miller's assigned aircraft and the one he was flying when he was shot down. NMF overall, 1945-style nose colouring, blue rudder, black mirror and canopy frame. Codes outlined red.*

217: *Lefty Grove's P-51D-15-NA in January 1945. Swept-back nose colour, blue rudder, black canopy frame and mirror. See 185-186, 218.*

218: *Grove's last wartime aircraft was this P-51D-25-NA, 44-72767. It has no bands or D-Day stripes and is quite a plain example of the Squadron's late-war scheme — except for the positioning of the serial number angled across*

the fin. Crew Chief John Ferra. See 185-186, 217.

219: *This P-51D-10-NA was Hagan's aircraft in summer 1944 and early 1945. It is NMF overall, with black ETO bands on wings and horizontal tail, code shadow-shaded red. Black canopy rail and mirror, blue rudder of the 336th FS from October 1944. This was the aircraft he baled out of. Crew Chief E. Rowe. See 220.*

336th Fighter Squadron

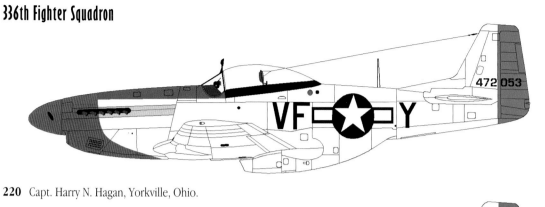

220 Capt. Harry N. Hagan, Yorkville, Ohio.

221 Capt. Joseph H. Patteuw ('Patt') Detroit, Michigan.

1/72 Scale

220: Harry Hagan's aircraft in February 1945 was this P-51D-20-NA, 44-72053. It was NMF overall, no black bands, 336th FS blue rudder colour. Anti-glare panel OD, canopy frame black. Crew Chief E. Rowe. See 219.

221: P-51D-5-NA 44-13325 'Rosie's Beau' was Patteauw's assigned D model. When he left it went into storage for a time. It has the spring-1945 scheme with the swept-under red nose, blue 336th FS rudder colour, and anti-glare panel, mirror and canopy frame in black. Codes are thinly out-lined in red. Note the sloping serial number on the fin and the use of a

double aircraft letter Z, instead of a bar. No known assigned pilot in 1945.

Right: Shown in post-January 1945 after the revised swept red nose markings were introduced, this P-51B-15-NA, 42-106975, of the 336th Fighter Squadron, taxies past a hangar towards the tower and the 336th FS's flight line. Despite the three kills marked under the windscreen, the as-signed pilot of VF-N remains unidentified. See colour pro-file 177.

Left: This is Capt. Franklin K. Young's P-51D-10-NA in mid-summer 1944. 44-14276 still retains D-Day bands under the fuselage, type identity bands on the wings and tail and shadow-shaded codes. In September the fin band had been removed. By March 1945 the red nose marking had been extended and the Squadron blue colour applied to the rudder. By April Young had completed his tour, and Martha Jane had become Marcy in the hands of 1st Lt. James R. McMahon. See colour profiles 193-195.

Centre left: This P-51B was converted to a two-seater with the 336th Fighter Squadron and served as a hack in 1945. Its original identity is unknown. See colour profile 191.

Left: Major James Goodson of the 336th Fighter Squadron in the cockpit of his P-51B, 43-24848, VF-B, posing for the benefit of the cameraman. Goodson was a strafing expert, fifteen of his victories being scored on the ground. Looking on is Lt. Ralph 'Kid' Hofer from the 334th Fighter Squadron. The photo dates from about June 1944, shortly before Hofer was killed in action and Goodson was shot down (on 20 June) in a P-51D to become a POW. See colour profiles 43, 166 and 196.

THE 20TH FIGHTER GROUP
Victory by Valour

The 20th Fighter Group arrived at Kingscliffe in Northants on 26 August 1943, without aircraft. Kingscliffe was built as a satellite of RAF Wittering, to accommodate two squadrons, so the 55th Fighter Squadron was based at Wittering until additional barracks could be built.

By November the group had received 16 P-38H aircraft, and on the 3rd of the month, ten pilots of the 79th Fighter Squadron took ten of these to Nuthampstead, to fly with the 55th Fighter Group to gain operational experience, flying their first operation on 5th November 1943. These pilots were replaced by members of the 77th on 11th November 1943 and then the 55th sent pilots on 21 December 1943.

The group finally flew its first full mission as a unit on 28th December 1943. During operations with the 55th, six pilots were lost.

The 20th first received P-38H type aircraft; these were progressively replaced by the J-model from the beginning of 1944. Initially, all these aircraft were received in the standard colour scheme for the type, of Olive Drab top surfaces, with Neutral Gray undersides. From February 1944, the J-models were received in natural metal finish.

Codes were assigned to the squadrons prior to starting operations: KI for the 55th, LC for the 77th and MC for the 79th. These were applied in white to the port and starboard booms, with the individual code letter on the coolant radiator housing, and the squadron code on the rear section of the boom. These were 18 inches high by 9 inches wide.

It was soon evident that the codes were not very visible beyond about 400 yards, and so, in January 1944, geometric symbols were applied to the outer surfaces of the vertical tail, these being a triangle for the 55th, a disc for the 77th, and a square for the 79th. These had a maximum width of 30 inches.

When the J-models began arriving in natural metal finish in February, these markings were applied in black. In March 1944 it became standard practice to carry the aircraft's individual code letter on the inner face of the vertical tail surfaces, again 30 inches high.

In March 1944, the Eighth Air Force introduced a system of colour identification for fighter groups, the 20th being assigned yellow. This was applied to spinners and the first 12 inches of both engine cowlings.

From spring 1944 most P-38s were marked with a 'Droopsnoot' simulation, consisting of an 8 inch white band around the aft part of the nose cone, the remainder of the nose cone being highly polished to simulate a transparency. This marking was carried until July 1944, which coincided with the 20th switching to Mustangs.

Above: The distinctive shape of the P-38 Lightning was unmistakeable. As a consequence it needed no type identification bands as did the P-47 and P-51. This particular P-38J-15-LO, 42-104087, which may have served with the 20th Fighter Group, is shown as it was received in the UK, in overall natural metal finish with the basic national insignia.

On P-38s, anti-glare panels were painted on the upper nose area ahead of the cockpit and on the upper inner half of each engine nacelle, in Olive Drab, on all natural metal finish aircraft.

In May 1944, in anticipation of Allied landings in Europe and fearing that bright metal aircraft finishes would reveal advanced landing grounds to the enemy, fighter Groups were instructed to camouflage the uppersurfaces of their aircraft. This was carried out in the field using available paints, more or less haphazardly.

On 21 July 1944 the 79th FS flew the last operation with Lightnings, the other two squadrons having already begun to operate P-51 Mustangs. During its time operating the P-38, the 20th lost 87 pilots to all causes, for 89 confirmed victories. In the first month of flying the Mustang, they scored 70 victories for a loss of 14. This ratio improved as experience was gained in P-51s — the Lightning was not ideally suited to the ETO.

Mustangs were in natural metal finish from the start, and many received Olive Drab or Dark Green on upper surfaces at unit level, in anticipation of soon moving to the Continent. In the 20th this painting was confined to the upper wing and tail surfaces, and the extreme top of fuselage and vertical tail areas, in a random pattern. Squadron codes were applied in black in the usual position either side of the fuselage insignia. The geometric symbols as carried on Lightnings were now applied to both sides of the vertical tail surfaces, 30 inches at the widest part, in black, with the aircraft letter superimposed on it, usually in white, though sometimes it was masked out and left in natural metal when the symbol was sprayed on.

Group colours changed on the P-51 to black and

white, applied to the nose. The front third of the spinner was white, the remaining two-thirds plus the leading 12 inches of the cowling were black, backed by an 8 inch wide white band, which ended roughly in line with the front of the exhaust outlet.

Two or three aircraft initially carried yellow in place of the white of the nose markings, a carry-over from the yellow allocated on the Lightnings, but this was very short lived.

In November 1944, seven black stripes were added aft of the white band on the cowling, from the lower edge of the anti-glare panel down to below the exhaust panel, curving down towards the nose. The spaces between these black bands were usually painted white, though some aircraft had these left in natural metal. These markings quickly became famous as 'Piano Keys', and were kept for the remainder of the war.

The application of the geometric symbols to the tails of both types usually obliterated the serial number, and these were not always reinstated. ETO bands and D-Day stripes were carried and removed in accordance with promulgated orders, though as always, variations were common.

As ever, photographs of the particular subject are essential for the modeller.

Left: Lt. Arthur W. Heiden shaking hands with his crew chief, T/Sgt. Max Pyle, in front of P-38J-10-LO 42-67427, MC-H. Heiden completed his tour in August 1944, but the 'lady' was not so lucky, being written off in a crash on 23 April while being flown by another pilot. The various shades of metal on the dummy 'droopsnoot' are noteworthy. Just visible forward of the scoreboard is a pin-up photo of an actress named Lorraine Day who corresponded with the crew. See colour profiles 310-311.

Left: A famous lineup showing the various Fighter Group commanders' aircraft at Bottisham on 31 August 1944, shortly before Allied forces entered Germany. Nearest aircraft is the P-51D-5-NA, 44-13337, MC-R, of Col. Harold Rau, commander of the 20th Fighter Group (for the second time) from 27 August. At this time the 20th's 'piano keys' nose marking had not yet been introduced. See colour profile 365. The third Mustang from the front is Da Quake, P-51D-10-NA 44-14291 of Lt. Col. John L. McGinn, wearing 338th Fighter Squadron codes and 55th Fighter Group nose colours. The aircraft was lost some 40 miles south-west of Leipzig on 7 October 1944 with Capt. Peter Dempsey at the controls who became a POW. See colour profile 448.

Right: Major Jack M. Ilfrey, CO of the 79th Fighter Squadron and his ground crew in front of their charge, P-51D-5-NA 44-13761, in June 1944. From the left: Sgt. S. Brusko, Sgt. R.E. Burgess (the Crew Chief), Sgt. O.N. Heim, Ilfrey and Sgt. R.R. Miller. The aircraft has the early style Group nose markings and a scoreboard showing mission markings and victories. See colour profiles 351-352.

Centre right: Capt. William W. Smith perched on the wing of his P-51D-5-NA, 44-13791, MC-S, his last aircraft with the 79th FS. It wears early Group P-51 markings, Olive Drab top surfaces and natural metal finish below. The name is black and yellow, later changed to Guardian Angel when it was assigned to Lt. John L. Armstrong, who was lost in it on 28 August 1944 to become a POW. See colour profile 369.

Below right: Seen in April 1944, this is Col. Harold J. Rau, newly assigned CO of the 20th Fighter Group, and his ground crew. The aircraft is P-38J-15-LO 43-104308, MC-R, which displays a very good example of the 'droop-snoot' simulation marking. Only one of the victories shown was claimed in air combat, all the others were achieved by ground strafing. See colour profiles 328-329.

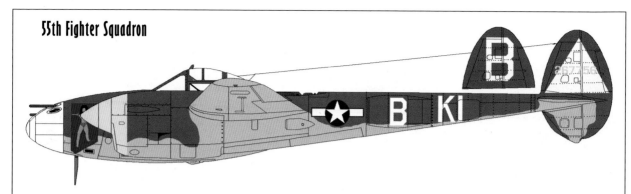

222 Capt. Jerome C. Serros ('Jerry'), Orlando, Florida. Joined 55th FS 2/8/43. Flew 2 tours. KIA 2/11/44, mechanical failure, crashed near Quackenbruck in P-51D-5-NA 44-13838 'Okie Bloke'. Claimed .5 Bf 110 in the air.

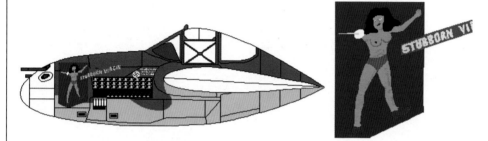

223 Capt. Jerome C. Serros ('Jerry'), Orlando, Florida.

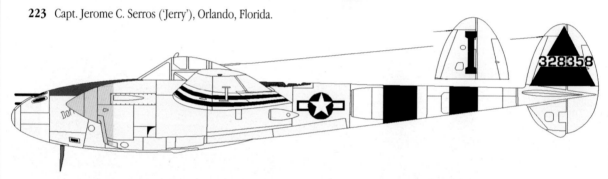

224 1st Lt. Rodney F. Watson ('Rod'), Modesto, California. To 55th FS 27/2/44. Flt. CO 13/8/44 to 7/9/44, then to USA, tour completed. Destroyed 1 Bf 109 in the air.

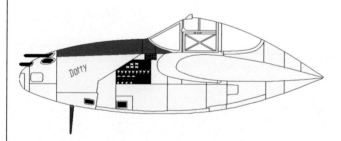

225 1st Lt. Rodney F. Watson ('Rod'), Modesto, California.

1/72 Scale

222/223: P-38J-10-LO 42-67756 was assigned to Serros in May 1944. It is in OD and NG with droopsnoot simulation on nose, and yellow group colouring on spinners and forward cowlings. White codes and 55th FS triangle on tail, serial in yellow. Mission tally on black panel, and one swastika kill mark.

224/225: P-38J-15-LO 43-28358 as flown by Watson in June 1944, just after D-Day. NMF overall with yellow Group colours on forward cowlings, full D-Day stripes cover code KI-I on booms. Black 55th FS triangle, serial, and

individual code 'I' on tail. Mission marks are white on black panel, name 'Dotty' is red.

55th Fighter Squadron

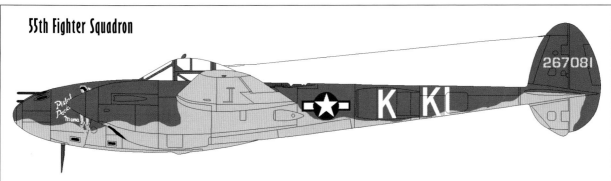

226 Maj. Donald H. McAuley ('Mac'), Los Gatos, California. To 55th FS 25/1/43. Squadron CO 18/3/44 to 23/4/44. Claimed 1 FW 190 and 1 Bf 109 in the air. Shot down and KIA on 23/4/44.

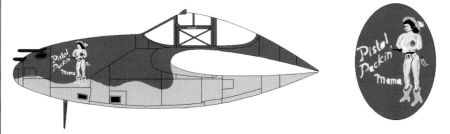

227 Maj. Donald H. McAuley ('Mac'), Los Gatos, California.

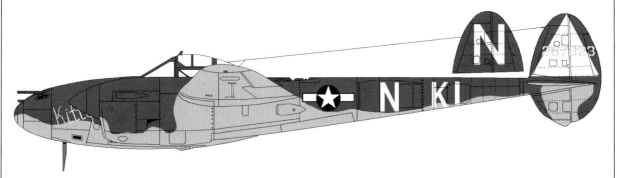

228 1st Lt. Harry E. Bisher ('Angel'), Gladstone, Illinois. To 55th FS 30/9/42, Flt. CO 31/12/42 to 3/2/43. Assistant Squadron Operations Officer 3/2/43 to 4/3/44. Shot down 4/3/44, evaded, returned 17/6/44 and sent back to USA on 30/7/44.

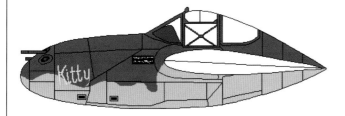

229 1st Lt. Harry E. Bisher ('Angel'), Gladstone, Illinois.

1/72 Scale

226/227: *P-38H-5-LO 42-67081 'Pistol Packin' Mama' was McAuley's aircraft in December 1944. It wears the factory applied OD and NG finish with serial in yellow, codes white. This aircraft was passed to the 55th Fighter Group in December 1944 when the 20th FG received the J model. It then went to Italy for use by the fighter groups based there.*

228/229: *Bisher flew this P-38J-10-LO 42-67823 in February 1944. It was lost 5/5/44 when Lt. Roy Scrutchfield took his crewchief up for a flight, demonstrated engine failure, and failed to re-start the engines. The aircraft was written off in the resultant crash landing, though neither man was injured. This aircraft was used by Lt. Willis Taylor to score a Bf 109 kill on 24/4/44. It wears the standard OD and NG scheme, with codes and 55th FS triangle in white, and the serial and name 'Kitty' in yellow.*

55th Fighter Squadron

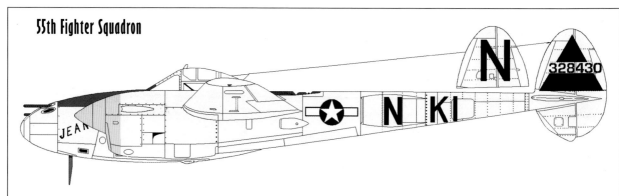

230 Capt. Roy M. Scrutchfield ('Scrutch'), Richards, Missouri. Joined 55th FS 30/9/42. Flt. CO 21/10/44 to 2/11/44. Squadron Operations Officer 2/11/44 to 30/11/44. To USA 2/12/44, tour complete.

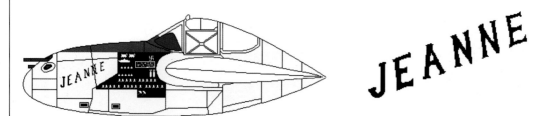

231 Capt. Roy M. Scrutchfield ('Scrutch'), Richards, Missouri.

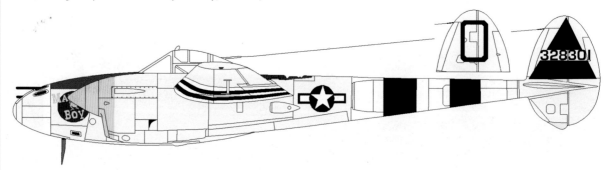

232 1st Lt. Edwin E. Wasil ('Ed'), Chicago, Illinois. To 55th FS 22/4/44 until completion of tour 30/9/44 then to USA. Destroyed 2 Do 18s on the water.

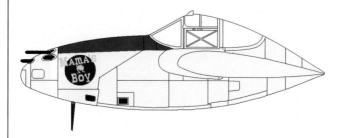

233 1st Lt. Edwin E. Wasil ('Ed'), Chicago, Illinois.

1/72 Scale

230/231: P-38J-15-LO flown by Scrutchfield May/June 1944 just before D-Day. NMF overall, with black codes, serial and squadron triangle, and his wife's name on the nose. White mission marks on black panel. Yellow group colours on spinners and cowl fronts, standard droopsnoot simulation.
232/233: P-38J-10-LO 43-28301 was Wasil's aircraft during the D-Day period. NMF overall, full D-Day stripes, code, serial and Squadron symbol in black. Yellow Group markings on spinners and forward cowlings. Name is yellow on blue backing disc.

55th Fighter Squadron

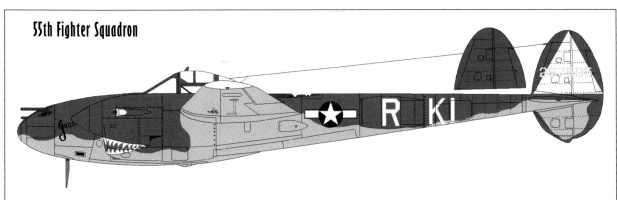

234 Capt. Roy M. Scrutchfield ('Scrutch'), Richards, Missouri.

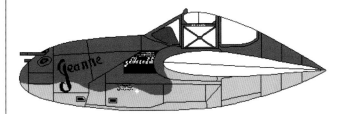

Jeanne

235 Capt. Roy M. Scrutchfield ('Scrutch'), Richards, Missouri.

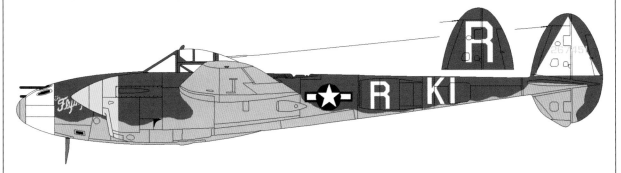

236 2nd Lt. William G. Schultz ('Dutch'), Holdenville, Oklahoma. Joined 55th FS 27/2/44 until he was killed in action 1/5/43, brought down by flak near Le Culot. Claimed 1.5 Bf 109s in the air.

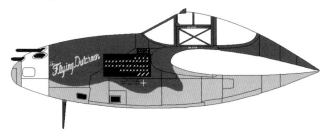

237 2nd Lt. William G. Schultz ('Dutch'), Holdenville, Oklahoma.

1/72 Scale

234/235: *P-38J-10-LO 42-67505 was flown by Scrutchfield in February/March 1944. OD and NG with white codes and 55th triangle symbol, yellow serial. Wife's name in black, mission marks in white on black panel. Sharkmouths in red and white, eyes in blue and white. Note white wingtips.*

236/237: *This P-38J-10-LO 42-67451 'The Flying Dutchman' was Schultz's assigned aircraft. It completed 82 sorties without an abort, a record for the P-38 at that time. The aircraft is in the standard OD and NG scheme, with codes and Squadron symbol in white, serial and group markings in yellow.*

Droopsnoot simulation on nose, the tip is a darker area of NMF not a painted colour. Name and mission marks are also in yellow, the latter on a black background panel. Crewchief S/Sgt. Coleman Kilpatrick.

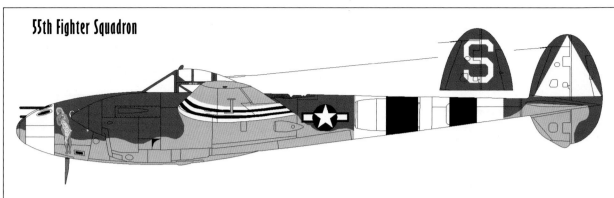

238 Lt. Richard O. Loehnert ('Dick'), Long Beach, California. Assigned 55th FS 17/11/43, completed his tour 12/11/44. Destroyed 2 Bf 109s in the air on 7/7/44.

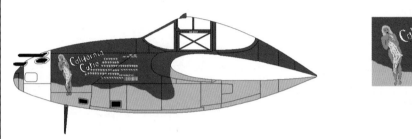

239 Lt. Richard O. Loehnert ('Dick'), Long Beach, California.

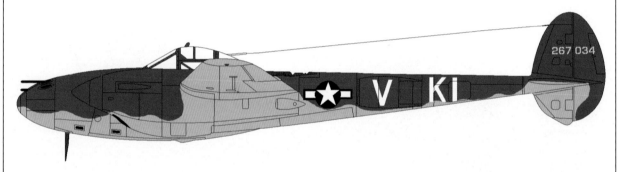

240 1st Lt. Everett E. Geiger, New Richmond, Indiana. To 55th FS 2/8/43 until MIA 24/2/44. POW. Claimed one Cant Z.506b in the air on 22/2/44.

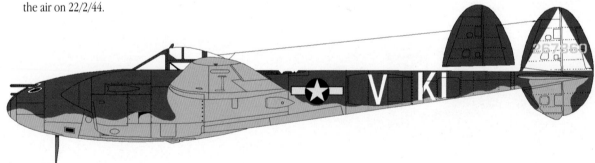

241 1st Lt. Everett E. Geiger, New Richmond, Indiana.

1/72 Scale

238/239: P-38J-10-LO 42-67916 KI-S 'California Cutie' was Loehnert's assigned aircraft in July 1944 and he flew it to score his two victories on 7/7/44. OD and NG with full D-Day stripes, 55th FS triangle on tail and individual code 'S' on inner tail surfaces in white.
240: Geiger's first aircraft was this P-38H-5-LO 42-67034, in the factory applied OD and NG scheme. Yellow serial and white codes.
241: Geiger's P-38J-10-LO 42-67860 in February 1944. Standard OD and NG with white codes and 55th FS triangle, yellow serial.

55th Fighter Squadron

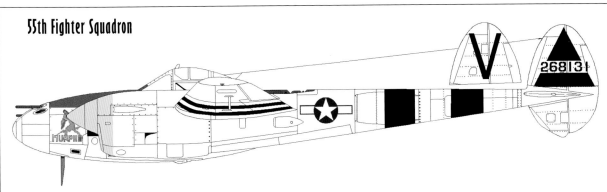

242 Maj. Maurice R. McLary ('Mac'), Pendleton, Indiana. Joined 55th FS 6/8/43. Flt. CO from 23/9/43 to 23/4/44, Sqdn. CO 23/4/44 TO 24/4/44, Group Tactical Inspector, 23/6/44 until 4/8/44, then to 77th FS as CO from 4/8/44 until 11/9/44, when he returned to USA, tour complete. Destroyed 1 FW 190, 1 Bf 110 and 1 Me 410 in the air.

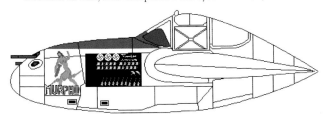

243 Maj. Maurice R. McLary ('Mac'), Pendleton, Indiana.

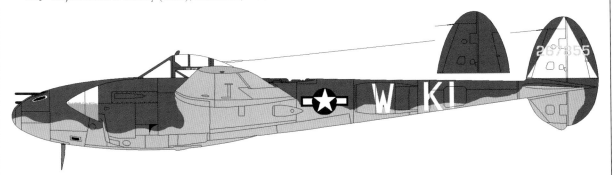

244 2nd Lt. Royal D. Frey (' Junior '), Columbus, Ohio. Joined 55th FS 2/8/43 until he was shot down 10/2/44 and became POW. Claimed 2 Bf 110s in the air.

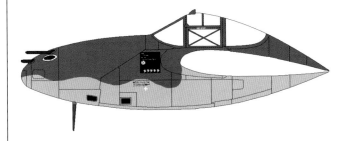

245 2nd Lt. Royal D. Frey (' Junior '), Columbus, Ohio.

1/72 Scale

242/243: *'Murph III' was McLary's P-38J-10-LO 42-68131 in June 1944. It was lost on 22/6/44, Lt. John A. Pierson being KIA. NMF overall, full invasion stripes on wings and fuselage, 55th FS triangle and code V on tail in black. White wingtips as seen on several 55th FS aircraft at this time. Three kill marks and numerous mission symbols on black panel on fuselage pod.*

244/245: *P-38J-10-LO 42-67855 was Frey's assigned aircraft which he was lost in on 10 February 1944. He had the spinners and wingtips painted blue for a short time, but was ordered to remove it. Aircraft is in the factory scheme*

of OD and NG, with white codes and squadron symbol. The individual letter 'W' has not yet been applied to the inner face of the vertical tail. Scoreboard on black panel shows one swastika kill mark and five top hat escort mission symbols. Crew Chief S/Sgt. L.G. Brenton.

55th Fighter Squadron

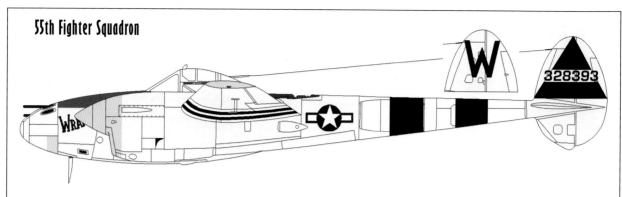

246 Lt. Col. Cy Wilson, West Point, Texas. Joined 20th FG 12/4.44, 55th FS CO 24/4/44 until 25/6/44. Group CO 25/6/44 to 27/8/44, when he was hit by flak and became POW. He claimed 2 Bf 109s and 1 FW 190 in the air.

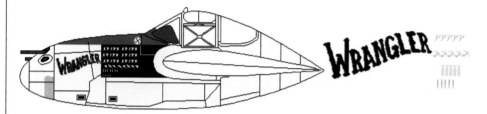

247 Lt. Col. Cy Wilson, West Point, Texas.

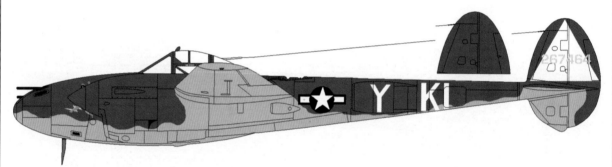

248 Maj. Maurice R. McLary, 'Mac', Pendleton, Indiana.

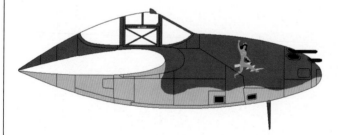

249 Maj. Maurice R. McLary ('Mac'), Pendleton, Indiana.

1/72 Scale

246/247: *The P-38J-15-LO 43-28393 assigned to Cy Wilson while CO of the 20th FG just prior to the change over to Mustangs. It is NMF overall, with codes and Squadron symbol in black, and the yellow Group colours on the spinners and first 12 inches of the cowlings. Full D-Day stripes are carried. Name is dark blue with red shading. Various mission marks are in yellow on a black panel.*

248/249: *This P-38J-10-LO 42-67464 was McLary's aircraft in January 1944. It was bellied in at Rougham, home of the 94th Bomb Group, after battle damage on 29/1/44. OD and NG, white codes and 55th FS symbol, yellow serial. Artwork appeared on both sides of the nose. See 242, 250-251, 279.*

55th Fighter Squadron

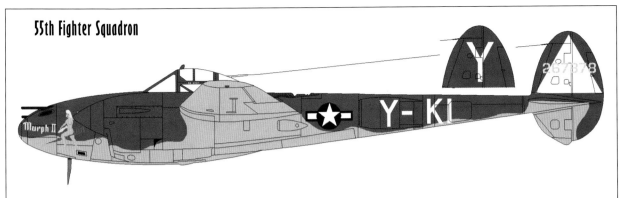

250 Maj. Maurice R. McLary ('Mac'), Pendleton, Indiana.

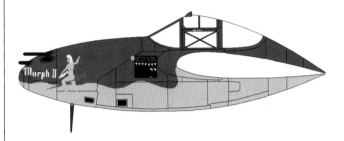

251 Maj. Maurice R. McLary ('Mac'), Pendleton, Indiana.

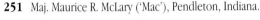

252 Maj. Robert H. Reimensnider ('Bobby'), Somonauk, Illinois. Joined 55th FS 9/1/44. Assistant Operations Officer 5/7/44 to 8/10/44. Flt. CO 9/10/44 to 15/11/44. Assistant Group Operations Officer 16/11/44 to 26/2/45. Squadron Operations Officer 27/2/45 to 21/7/45. 55th FS CO from 22/7/45. Destroyed 1.5 Do18s on the water and a twin-engined trainer on the ground.

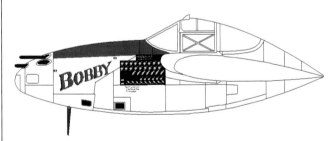

253 Maj. Robert H. Reimensnider ('Bobby'),Somonauk, Illinois.

1/72 Scale

250/251: 'Murph II' was P-38J-10-LO 42-67878, assigned to McLary in February 1944. It was lost on 24/2/44 when it crashed, out of fuel, near Schluctern, 2nd Lt. Otto A. Quiring being killed in the crash. It is in standard OD and NG scheme, with codes and Squadron symbol in white. See 242, 248-249, 279.
252/253: P-38J-10-LO 42-68108, 'Bobby', as flown by then Capt. Reimensnider around D-Day. NMF overall, full D-Day stripes on wings and tailbooms, covering up codes KI-Y. Black serial and 55th FS triangle, and individual code Y on tail. Yellow Group colours on spinners and forward cowlings.

Name is red with black shading, mission symbols are yellow on black panel. Crew Chief S/Sgt. Herbert C. Macrow, Asst. Sgt. Carl T. Penkalski.

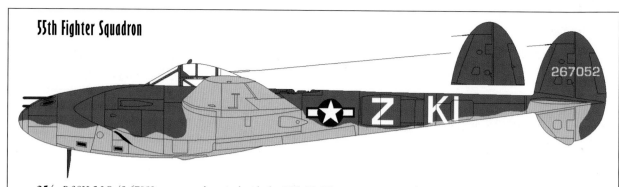

254 P-38H-5-LO 42-67052 was an early arrival with the 55th FS. Pilot assignment not known.

255 Capt. Harley L. Brown ('Lefty'), Wichita, Kansas. Joined 55th FS 11/8/44 until 11/3/45, then to USA tour complete. Flt. CO 6/12/44 to 10/3/44. Claimed 3 FW 190s and 3 Bf 109s in the air.

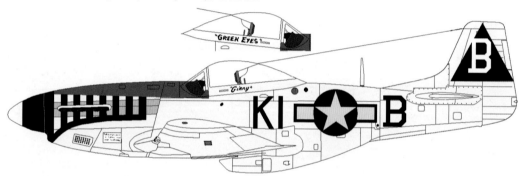

256 1st Lt. Richard P. Iehle ('Wiley'), Sandusky, Oregon. To 55th FS 13/2/45 until end of war.

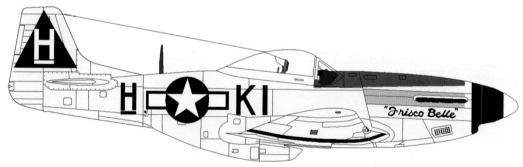

257 Capt. Edward H. Cosgriff Jr ('Grief'), Burlingame, California. To 55th FS 19/9/44 until end of war. Assistant Squadron Operations Officer from 7/12/44.

1/72 Scale

254: P-38H-5-LO 42-67052 was an early arrival with the 55th FS. It wore the standard P-38 scheme of OD and NG, with white codes and yellow serial. Pilot assignment not known.

255: This P-51D-5-NT, 44-11205, KI-A bar, was Brown's aircraft in late 1944. Name 'Be Good' on nose is red and yellow, 'Brownie's Ballroom' on canopy frame is yellow on a red background. Aircraft is NMF overall with black codes and 55th triangle. No stripes or bands.

256: P-51, serial not known, KI-B, was Iehle's assigned aircraft. NMF over-

all, Group markings are black only. 55th FS triangle and codes in black, as are names 'Ginny' and 'Green Eyes' on canopy rail. No stripes or bands carried.

257: P-51D-15-NA 44-14880 KI-H bar was Cosgriff's mount early in his tour. It has the early Group nose marking in black and white, black codes and 55th triangle, as is name 'Frisco Belle', but it has not had OD applied to upper surfaces. Black ETO bands on wings and horizontal tail.

55th Fighter Squadron

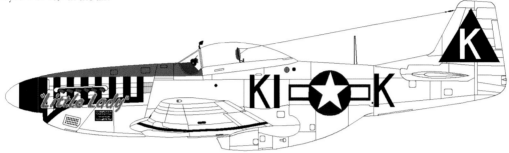

258 1st Lt. Dale L. Larabee ('Larry'), Redding, California. Joined 55th FS 22/4/44 until 27/9/44. To USA when tour complete. Destroyed 1 Bf 109 in the air.

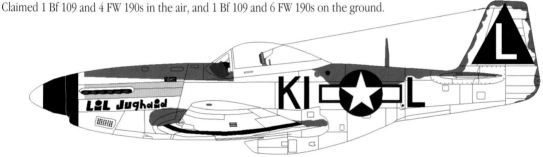

259 Capt. Charles H. Cole ('Tink'), St. Joseph, Missouri. Joined 77th FS 29/9/44. Flight CO 5/12/44 to 6/1/45. Assistant Squadron Operations Officer 6/1/45 to 25/2/45. Transferred to 55th FS 21/2/45. MIA 25/2/45, POW. Claimed 1 Bf 109 and 4 FW 190s in the air, and 1 Bf 109 and 6 FW 190s on the ground.

260 1st Lt. James E.Burford ('Jim'), Webster, Wisconsin. To 55th FS 28/3/44. Claimed 1 Bv 140 and 1 Hs126 , both on ground. To USA 7/9/44, tour complete.

261 Capt. Joseph T. McKeon ('Mac'), Maspeth, Long Island, New York. To 55th FS 7/7/44. Flt. CO 15/7/44 to 7/10/44. Crashed Zartzig after collision, became POW. Previously completed tour in South Pacific, destroying 4 Zeros and 1 Val in the air. With the 20th FG he destroyed 1 Bf 109 in the air and 2 Do 24s on water.

1/72 Scale

258: *P-51D-5-NA 44-13778, KI-J, flown by Larabee in July and August 1944. Early Group nose colours, D-Day stripes on lower surfaces, black codes and 55th FS triangle. Aircraft later passed to Lt. V. Stockton. Scrapped 6/12/44.*

259: *This P-51D-20-NA, 44-72160, KI-K was the aircraft Cole was shot down in on 25/2/45. It carries black ETO bands on horizontal surfaces, black codes, and 55th FS triangle on an overall NMF finish. Group nose markings are black and white, name is red with yellow outline.*

260: *P-51D-5-NA flown by Burford during July/August 1944. NMF with OD*

on top surfaces. Early Group Mustang markings, black ETO bands on horizontal surfaces. Crew Chief S/Sgt. K.D.McKenzie.

261: *This P-51D-5-NA 44-13541, KI-M, 'Olivia de', was McKeon's assigned aircraft and the one he was lost in. It wears the early Group markings, but is NMF overall with no OD on upper surfaces. The name, codes and 55th FS triangle are black, as are the ETO bands on wing and tail horizontal surfaces. The actress Olivia de Havilland was a personal friend of his.*

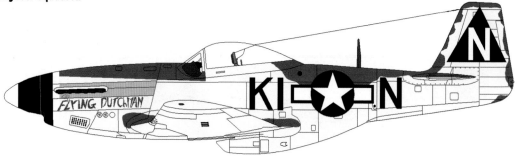

262 Capt. Earl W. Hower ('Pop'), Lebanon, Pennsylvania. To 55th FS 2/8/43. Flt. CO 18/9/44 to 30/9/44. To USA 1/10/44, tour complete.

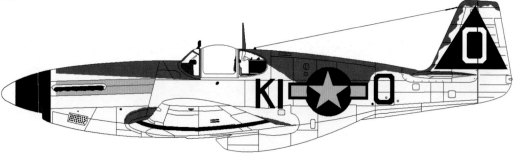

263 1st Lt. Edwin E. Wasil ('Ed'), Chicago, Illinois.

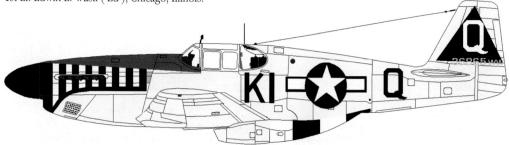

264 43-6865, P-51B-7NA, was a war-weary machine used by the 55th FS OTU.

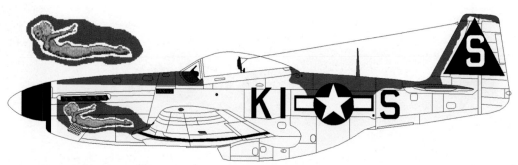

265 1st Lt. Walter Mullins ('Moon'), Fort Worth, Texas. To 55th FS 14/6/44. Flt. CO 9/10/44 to 18/10/44 when he was killed on a training flight, crashing into the North Sea.

1/72 Scale

262: P-51D-5-NA 44-13799 was Hower's mount in August 1944. OD top surfaces, NMF undersides, black codes and Squadron triangle. 'N' on tail is white. Name in red on nose. No bands or stripes.

263: P-51C-10-NT 43-25031 became Wasil's aircraft in August/September 1944 after change to Mustangs. NMF undersides, OD top surfaces. Black ETO bands on horizontal surfaces. Codes and Squadron symbol black. Star and bar' greyed out' on fuselage only. Aircraft has a Malcolm hood. See 232.

264: 43-6865, P-51B-7-NA, was a war-weary used by the 55th FS OTU. NMF

overall with black codes and 55th FS triangle, on which the individual code 'Q' is repeated in white. Full black and white piano keys, with all-black spinner signifying an OTU aircraft. Note serial and WW on tail in yellow.

265: Mullins was lost in this P-51D-5-NA, 44-13859. Upper surfaces of wings, tail and fuselage are OD, undersides in NMF. Early Group Mustang scheme of black and white markings on nose. Code 'S' is repeated on vertical tail in white on black 55th FS triangle. The beautiful nude appeared on both sides of the aircraft. Black ETO bands on wings and horizontal tail surfaces.

55th Fighter Squadron

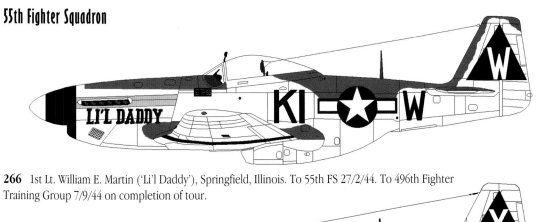

266 1st Lt. William E. Martin ('Li'l Daddy'), Springfield, Illinois. To 55th FS 27/2/44. To 496th Fighter Training Group 7/9/44 on completion of tour.

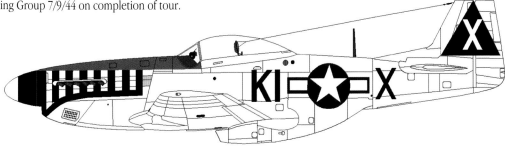

267 Capt. Mont J. Ryan ('Baldy'), Long Beach, California. To 55th FS 19/9/44. Flt. CO 7/3/45 to end of war.

268 1st Lt. William J. McGee ('Maggie'), Peekskill, New York. Joined 55th FS 28/10/44 until MIA 20/2/45. POW.

77th Fighter Squadron

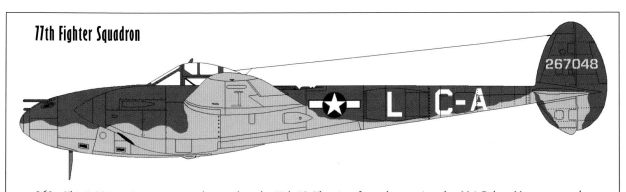

269 This P-38H-5-LO was a very early arrival on the 77th FS. The aircraft was later assigned to Maj. Robert Montgomery, the 77th FS's first combat CO.

1/72 Scale

266: This P-51D-5-NA, serial unknown, was Martin's aircraft in July/August 1944. Early nose markings in black and white, black codes, ETO bands and Squadron triangle. OD upper surfaces over NMF undersides. Name black, outlined red.

267: Feibelkorn's aircraft was passed to the 55th FS after he left the 77th FS and assigned to Ryan. Written off in a take-off crash 12/6/45. It wore no bands or stripes, and had codes and 55th triangle in black added. See 291.

268: P-51D-5-NA 44-13905 was the aircraft assigned to McGee. He was shot down in it on 20/2/45. Extremely worn finish, with all white areas greyed out. Invasion stripes on undersides of wings and fuselage, codes and 55th FS triangle in black, as is the name 'Joe' on the canopy rail. Upper surfaces OD, which is unusual in combination with the piano key group markings.

269: This P-38H-5-LO wears the standard OD and Grey scheme as applied by Lockheed at the factory, with the serial on the vertical tail surfaces in yellow. The squadron codes are incorrectly applied, but would be repainted. See 280.

77th Fighter Squadron

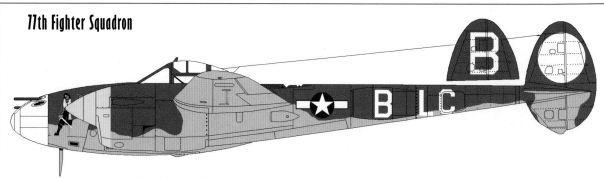

270 Colonel Barton M. Russel ('Barney'), Billings, Montana. Assigned to 20th FG July 1937. Served in many capacities in 77th FS, up to Squadron CO from May 1941 to 1/8/42. Group Executive Officer 1/8/42 to 17/1/43. Group CO 17/1/43 to 2/3/44, then to USA tour complete. Claimed half an FW 190 in the air, on 14/1/44.

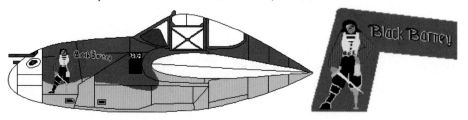

271 Colonel Barton M. Russel ('Barney'), Billings, Montana.

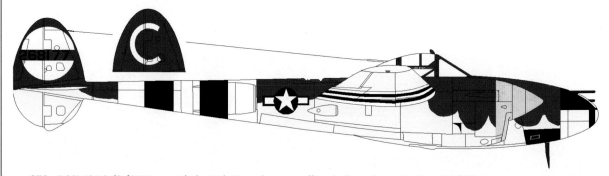

272 P-38J-10-LO 42-68177 was with the 77th FS until written off in a belly landing at Sudbury 22/6/44, due to engine trouble.

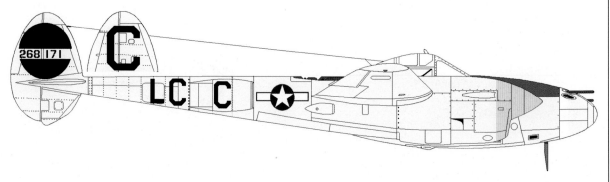

273 1st Lt. Alvin F. Clark ('Little Alvin'), Los Angeles, California. To 77th 7/12/43. Brought down by ground explosion, crashed near Reims, 12/8/44, evaded & returned. To USA 4/10/44. Claimed 1.5 Bf 109s and 1 FW 190 in the air. **1/72 Scale**

270/271: P-38J-10-LO 42-67888 'Black Barney' was Col. Russel's assigned aircraft in February 1944. OD and NG scheme, white codes and 77th FS circle, yellow Group colours, NMF nose cone with white band to simulate droopsnoot.

272: P-38J-10-LO 42-68177 was with the 77th FS until written off in a belly landing at Sudbury 22/6/44, due to engine trouble. It had arrived in overall NMF finish but was given a coat of dark green on top surfaces, the undersides remaining unpainted. Aircraft carries full invasion stripes on wings and tail booms.

273: This P-38J-10-LO 42-68171 was Clark's aircraft prior to D-Day. NMF overall, codes and serial in black, as is the 77th Squadron circle, yellow Group colours on spinner and cowl fronts, droopsnoot simulation on nose.

77th Fighter Squadron

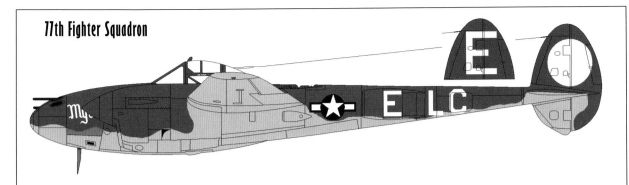

274 Capt. James Madison Morris ('Slick'), Detroit, Michigan. Joined 77th FS 8/10/42 until POW 7/7/44. He scored 7.33 aerial victories plus 2.8 ground strafing credits. 4 kills in the air on 8/2/44, 2 Bf 109s and 2 FW 190s.

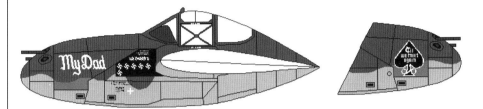

275 Capt. James Madison Morris ('Slick'), Detroit, Michigan.

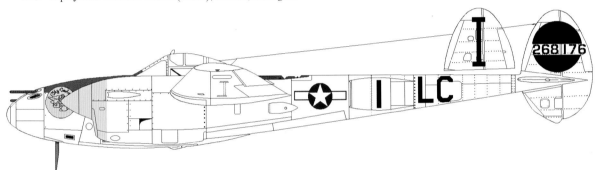

276 1st Lt. Walker L. Whiteside ('Whitey'), Claremont, California. Joined 77th FS 17/11/43. Flt. CO 14/6/44 to 6/8/44. KIA on 6/8/44, shot down by fighters and crashed near Hennickendorf in P-51D-5-NA 44-13792, LC-X. Claimed 1 Bf 109 and half an Me 210 in the air.

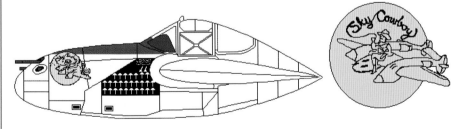

277 1st Lt. Walker L. Whiteside ('Whitey'), Claremont, California.

1/72 Scale

274/275: *P-38J-10-LO 42-67717 'My Dad/ Till We Meet Again' was Morris's aircraft in February 1944. He scored one kill in this aircraft, a Bf 110 on 24/ 2/44 near Schweinfurt. Aircraft is in the standard OD and Grey scheme, with white codes and Squadron symbol. Artwork and mission detail in black and white.*

276/277: *P-38J-10-LO 42-68176, LC-I, Whiteside's aircraft in May 1944. NMF overall, black codes, serial and Squadron circle symbol. Yellow Group colour on forward cowlings and spinners. White mission tally on black panel,* *mostly umbrellas, representing top cover missions. Artwork is black on yellow. Aircraft lost in takeoff crash 12/7/44, Lt. Richard Robbins being seriously hurt in the accident.*

77th Fighter Squadron

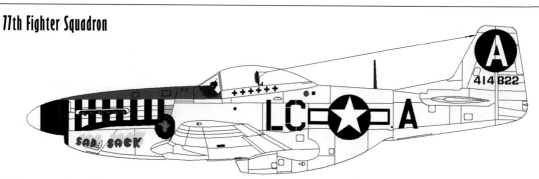

278 Maj. Merle J. Gilbertson ('Jakie'), Flora, North Dakota. To 77th FS 9/2/43. Flt. CO 1/1/44 to 26/8/44. Squadron Operations Officer 26/8/44 to 29/9/44, and again from 1/1/45. Flew 2 tours. Claimed 2.8 kills in the air and 4 on the ground.

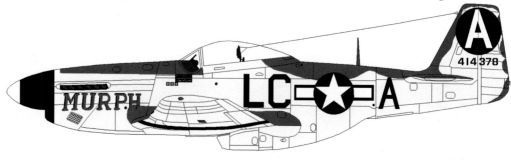

279 Maj. Maurice R. McLary ('Mac'), Pendleton, Indiana.

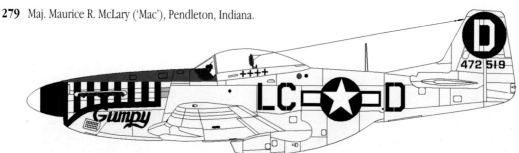

280 Col. Robert P. Montgomery ('Monty'), Bethlehem, Pennsylvania. To 77th FS August 1940. Served in various positions, including CO. Shot down 11/2/44 and evaded through Spain, returning on 21/9/44. Group CO 15/12/44 to end of war. Claimed 2 Bf 109s, 1 FW 190 and 1/3 FW 200 in the air and 3 ground kills.

281 1st Lt. Reps D. Jones, Miami Springs, Florida. To 77th FS 18/9/44. Flt CO 15/2/45 to 3/4/45. Assistant Squadron Operations Officer 4/4/45. Promoted Capt. 21/3/45. Claimed 1 Bf 109 and 1 FW 190 in the air and 4 FW 190 and 1 Bf 109 ground kills.

1/72 Scale

278: P-51D-10-NA 44-14822 'Sad Sack' was Gilbertson's last mount during his second tour. Aircraft NMF overall with the piano key markings in black and white, black codes, serial and squadron symbol. Tip of spinner is NMF, name is red with black outline and yellow shadow. 6 black cross kill marks on canopy rail. No stripes or bands carried. See 282.

279: P-51D-5-NA 44-14378 was McLary's aircraft August 1944, as CO of 77th FS. Top surfaces OD, undersides NMF. Early type black/white nose markings, black codes, serial, and ETO bands on horizontal wing and tail sur-

faces. Individual code A repeated in white on black 77th circle on tail. Name is red with black shading. Aircraft lost on 1/11/44, Lt. Denis J. Alison being KIA, probably shot down by Me 262 jet, near Zuider Zee. See 242, 248-251.

280: P-51D-20-NA 44-72519 'Gumpy' was Montgomery's last aircraft with the Group in early 1945. NMF overall with black codes and serial, individual code repeated in white on black circle on tail. Piano key markings on nose in black and white. Four black cross victory markings on canopy rail. Name black with red outline.

77th Fighter Squadron

282 Maj. Merle J. Gilbertson ('Jakie'), Flora, North Dakota. End of his first tour, September 1944.

283 P-51D-10-NA 44-14843 of the 77th FS, assigned pilot unknown, but a busy aircraft, used by Feibelkorn to destroy 4 aircraft and damage another on 28/9/44, and by Gilbertson to down Bf 109s on 5/8/44 and 16/8/44.

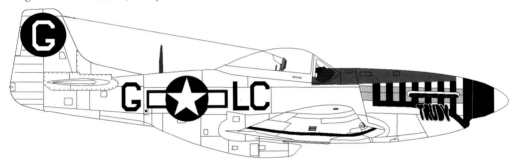

284 P-51D assigned to 77th FS, pilot and serial unknown.

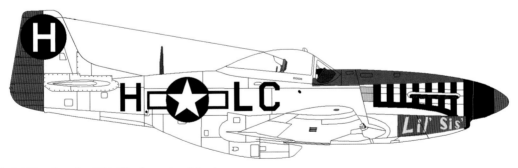

285 P-51D assigned to 77th FS, pilot and serial unknown.

1/72 Scale

281: P-51D-10-NA 44-14823 'Miss Miami' was Jones's aircraft in early 1945. Named after his hometown, NMF overall with black/white Group nose markings, black codes and serial, F in white on black circle on tail. Name is black. 7 black crosses in white circles on canopy rail. No ETO or D-Day bands carried. Aircraft scrapped 9/45. See 278.

282: P-51D-5-NA, 44-13637, was named 'Smoky'. Early Mustang nose markings, OD top surfaces, NMF undersides. Black codes, serial and circle, white G on tail. Very abbreviated D-Day stripes under rear fuselage only, black

ETO bands on wings and tail surfaces, Machine lost 2/1/45, Capt. T. Hambledon evaded and returned.

283: P-51D-10-NA 44-14843 of the 77th FS, assigned pilot unknown. The aircraft wears standard late war Group markings, without stripes or bands. Name is red on yellow.

284: P-51D LC-G. Codes and Squadron symbol in black, ETO bands on horizontal surfaces of wings and tail, spinner tip remains NMF. Name 'Trudy' is black outlined in yellow.

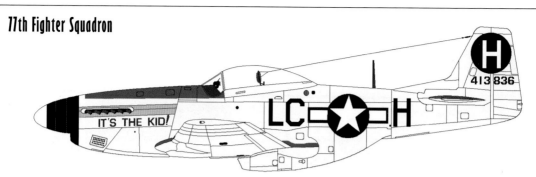

286 1st Lt..Frederick H. Alexander ('The Kid'), Seattle, Washington. To 77th FS 28/3/44 until 17/10/44, then to USA tour complete. Claimed 2 Bf 109s in the air and 6 ground kills.

287 P-51D-5-NT 44-11217, pilot not known. Flew with 77th FS.

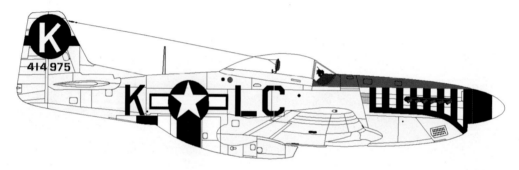

288 1st Lt. Robert E. Murrell ('Bobby'), Highland Park, Michigan. To 77th FS 29/9/44 until KIA 19/2/45. Hit trees and crashed near Detmold. Claimed one victory in the air, an FW 190 on 2/12/44 in LC-H, 44-11354.

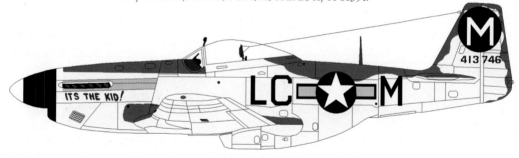

289 1st Lt. Frederick H. Alexander ('The Kid'), Seattle, Washington.

1/72 Scale

286: *Alexander's later aircraft was this P-51D-5-NA 44-13836. Top of wings and tail only in OD otherwise NMF overall. Black codes and serial, and 77th FS circle, individual code H in white. Early Group black and white nose markings, name on both sides of cowling in red. See 289.*

287: *P-51D-5-NT 44-11217, pilot not known. Flew with 77th FS. Standard late war Group markings, bar under individual code J indicates second J in Sqdn. Remains of D-Day stripes under fuselage only, very worn and dirty. Black ETO bands on wing and horizontal tail surfaces.*

288: *This P-51D-15-NA was Murrel's aircraft in November 1944. NMF overall with black and white group markings on nose. White K on black 77th FS circle on tail. Half D-Day stripes on lower fuselage only. Strangely, the black ETO band remains on the vertical tail only*

289: *P-51D-5-NA 44-13746 assigned to Alexander in August 1944. OD top surfaces, NMF undersides, code and serial in black. Individual code M in white on black 77th circle. Early Group P-51 markings in black and white. Name in red on both sides of the nose cowling. See 286.*

77th Fighter Squadron

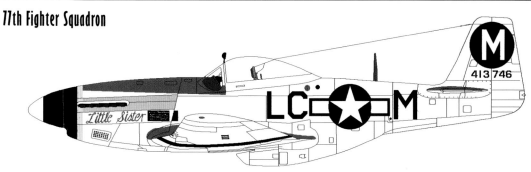

290 Capt. Paul J. McCully ('P.J.'), Los Angeles, California. Joined 77th FS 22/4/44 until he returned to the USA tour complete, 5/12/44. Flt. CO 9/11/44 until 5/12/44.

291 1st Lt. Ernest Charles Feibelkorn ('Feeb'), Lake Orion, Michigan. To 77th FS 9/1/44 until 5/12/44, when returned to USA tour expired. Top scorer in 20th Group with 9 air and 2 ground victories. KIA in Korea on 6/7/50. Capt. from 10/11/44.

292 Capt. Merle B. Nichols ('Nick'), Bellevue, Washington. Joined 79th FS 3/8/43. Flt. CO 1/1/44 to 15/5/44 when tour complete. Returned to USA until 2/8/44, then to 20th HQ as Tactical Inspector until 18/9/44. To 77th FS 19/9/4. Squadron Operations Officer 19/9/44 to 17/12/44. CO from 18/12/44. Completed 2 tours. Claimed 1 FW 190, 1 Bf 109 and 1 Bf 110 in the air, plus 3 damaged.

293 Capt. Ted E. Slanker ('Butcher Boy'), Portland, Oregon. To 77th FS 13/7/44. Flt. CO 5/12/44 to 17/12/44. Assistant Operations Officer 18/12/44 to 19/1/45. Asst. Group Operations Officer from21/4/45 to end of war. Claimed 1 FW 190 in the air, 1 Me 210 on the ground. Gained nickname after a low flying incident during training in the USA which caused a cattle stampede, resulting in some dead cows.

1/72 Scale

290: P-51D-5-NA, 44-13746 was McCully's aircraft in October 1944. OD on upper surfaces of wings and horizontal tail but not on fuselage. Undersides all NMF. Early style Group nose markings, but the aft band is yellow instead of white, a holdover from P-38 days. Codes, serial and Squadron disc in black. 'Little Sister' on nose is red. Black ETO bands on wings and tail.

291: Feibelkorn's P-51D-5-NT 44-11161 at the end of his tour, late 1944. He scored 3.5 victories in it. Aircraft has very reduced D-Day stripes under fuselage, black ETO bands on wing and tail surfaces. Codes, serial and circle in

black. Piano keys on nose black and white, name 'June Nite' red with yellow detail. 11 swastika kill marks on canopy rail. Whole aircraft is well worn.

292: P-51D-15-NA 44-14891 was Nichol's aircraft as CO of the 77th FS, early 1945. Name yellow with black shading on a red panel. Black ETO bands on wings and horizontal tail surfaces, standard late war Group markings.

293: Slanker's assigned aircraft in early Group markings as worn on the P-51. NMF overall with codes, serial and tail disc in black. Black ETO bands on wing and horizontal tail surfaces. See 294.

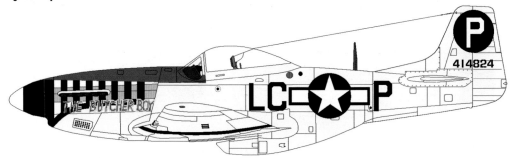

294 Capt. Ted E. Slanker ('Butcher Boy'), Portland, Oregon.

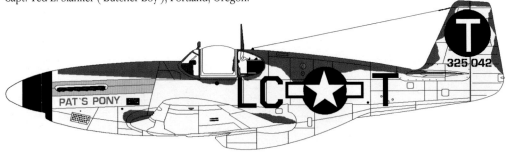

295 1st Lt. John D. MacArthur ('Squeakie'), Hollywood, California. To 77th FS 20/4/44 until 17/10/44 when he returned to USA, tour complete.

296 Capt. Lowell E. Einhaus ('Lefty'), Austin, Minnesota. To 77th FS 11/8/44. Flt. CO 18/12/44 to 22/2/45 tour complete. Claimed 6 FW 190s, all on ground.

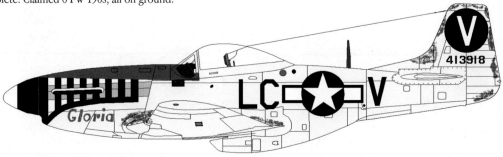

297 1st Lt. Baxter M. Phillips, Laurel, Maryland. Joined 77th FS 14/11/44 until end of war. His sole claim was a half share in a Bf 110 damaged on the ground.

1/72 Scale

294: *This P-51D-10-NA was Slanker's assigned aircraft, here in later updated Group markings. The aircraft is NMF overall with codes and serial in black, as is the 77th FS disc on the tail. The name was repainted as seen when the piano keys were added. Black ETO bands on wings and horizontal tail. See 293.*

295: *P-51C-10-NT 43-25042 LC-T 'Pat's Pony' flown by MacArthur in autumn 1944. OD top surfaces, NMF undersides. Early Group P-51 markings on nose, black codes and serial, name in red. Aircraft was later named 'Mary Ann'*

but pilot at that time is not known.

296: *P-51D-5-NA 44-13918 was Einhaus's aircraft in October 1944. Top surfaces OD, undersides NMF. Early style P-51 nose markings in black and white. Black codes, serial and squadron symbol. No bands or stripes carried.*

297: *This P-51D-5-NA was Phillip's aircraft in late 1944 and early 1945. It has been retro-fitted with a fin fillet, and carries the standard group markings of the period, but shows well worn remnants of the earlier Olive Drab upper surfaces.*

77th Fighter Squadron

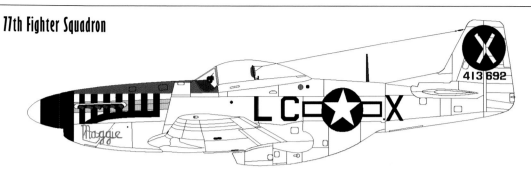

298 Lt. Cartheledge L. Huey Jr ('Hooey'), Fairfield, Alabama. Joined 77th FS 28/10/44 and served to end of war. Flt. CO from 12/4/45.

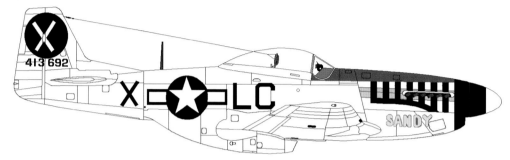

299 Lt. Cartheledge L. Huey Jr ('Hooey'), Fairfield, Alabama.

300 1st Lt..Henry J. Piatkiewicz ('Pat'), West Allis, Wisconsin. Joined 77th FS 18/12/44 to end of war. Destroyed 1 FW 44 in the air.

301 War-weary P-51B-10-NA, 42-106476, was inherited from the 359th FG, where it served as IV-H of the 369th FS. It was used by Lt. J. J. Kelly of that unit to destroy a Bf 109 on 24/12/44, represented by the kill mark under the windshield.

1/72 Scale

298: P-51D-5-NA 44-13692 assigned to Huey in early 1945. 'Maggie' on port nose in red with yellow outline was his girlfriend, 'Sandy' on starboard side was the wife of Crewchief T/Sgt. Bartram, in yellow with red outline. Aircraft NMF overall, no D-Day or ETO bands. The piano keys have not been filled in with white, and the code X on the 77th FS's disc symbol is NMF and quite roughly applied. Tip of spinner is white.

299: Starboard side of Huey's aircraft 44-13692.

300: This P-51D-10-NA was Piatkiewicz's assigned aircraft. He scored his

only victory in it on 20/2/45. It survived the war. On 14/1/45 Lt. John Stark used it to destroy a Bf 109, shared with Merle Gilbertson. Completely standard Group markings for early 1945. Name is yellow on a red panel.

301: 42-106476 is NMF overall, with black codes, serial and 77th FS disc on tail. Bar under Z indicates it is the second aircraft in the squadron with that code. WW on the tail indicates it is a restricted war-weary aircraft. Piano key Group markings lack the white infill, and the all-black spinner means it belongs to the squadron OTU. No bands or stripes carried.

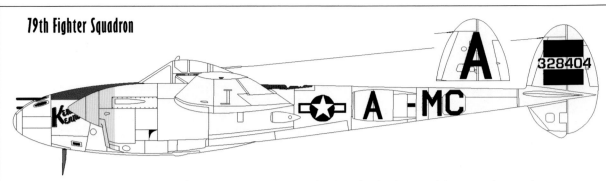

302 Maj. Delynn E. Anderson ('Andy'), Stearns, Kentucky. Joined 79th FS 6/3/43. Flt. CO 5/4/43 to 3/12/43. Squadron Operations Officer 19/3/44 to 10/5/44, Squadron CO 10/5/44 to 27/9/44, then to USA tour complete. He had 2 ground kills and a fifth share in an He 177 in the air. He was shot down and KIA in Korea in 1950.

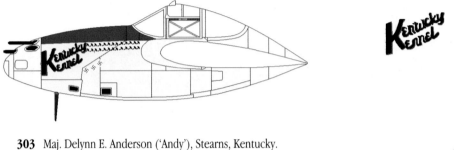

303 Maj. Delynn E. Anderson ('Andy'), Stearns, Kentucky.

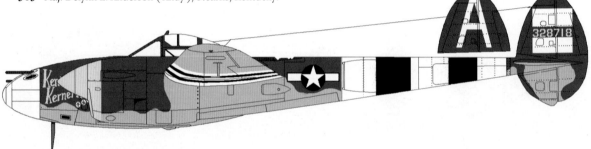

304 Maj. Delynn E. Anderson ('Andy'), Stearns, Kentucky.

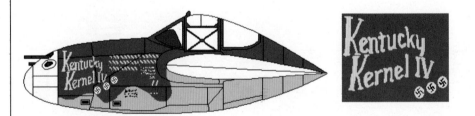

305 Maj. Delynn E. Anderson ('Andy'), Stearns, Kentucky.

1/72 Scale

302/303: Second of the 'Kernels' was this P-38J-15-LO 43-28404, flown for about a month in April/May 1944, until written off in a crash landing with Lt. Al Learned at the controls. Markings similar to previous aircraft, but code changed to MC-A on promotion to Squadron CO. Name now blue with red shading. See 336.

304/305: Last of the P-38 'Kernels' was this P-38J-15-LO 43-28718. Locally sprayed OD (or RAF Dark Green) on uppersurfaces. Undersides probably remained NMF but may have been finished gray, with codes and Squadron

symbol in white. Yellow Group colours and serial presentation, the name and mission details also being yellow. Aircraft has droopsnoot simulation on nose. Anderson flew this aircraft through May, June and July 1944 until the arrival of the Mustang.

79th Fighter Squadron

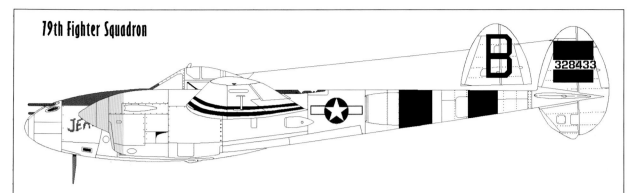

306 1st Lt. James D. Bradshaw ('Brad'), Lake Worth, Florida. Joined 79th FS 2/8/43. Assistant Squadron Operations Officer 14/5/44 to 17/8/44, then to USA, tour complete.

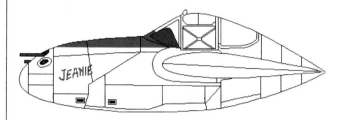

307 1st Lt. James D. Bradshaw ('Brad'), Lake Worth, Florida.

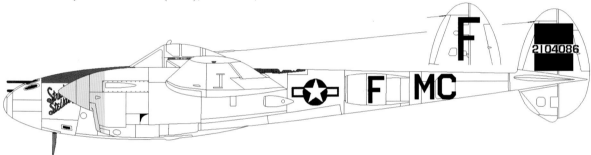

308 Maj. R. C. Franklin, Star Route, Mojave, California. To 79th FS 23/2/44 until 14/5/44 as CO, then transferred to HQ 8th Fighter Command. Claimed 1 Bf 110, 1 Bf 109, one fifth of an He177 in the air and one ground kill.

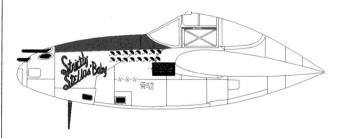

309 Maj. R. C. Franklin, Star Route, Mojave, California.

1/72 Scale

306/307: *P-38J-15-LO, 43-28433, assigned to Bradshaw during June 1944. Aircraft lost 19/6/44, crash-landed on return from operation by Lt. Roger Peterson. NMF overall with full D-Day stripes, yellow group markings, black serial, code B, and 79th FS square on tail. Bradshaw's wife's name 'Jeanie' on nose is red. Crew Chief Sgt. J. Strickler, Asst. Crew Chief Cpl. C.W. Weaver, Armourer Sgt. S. K. Ballew, Radio Sgt. L. Nelberger.*

308/309: *P-38J-15-LO 42-104086 MC-F 'Strictly Stella's Baby' was Franklin's machine while CO of the 79th FS. Stella was his wife's name. Aircraft is NMF overall, black codes, serial, and 79th FS square. Yellow group colours on spinners and forward cowlings. 3 black swastika kill marks. Name is red with black detail.*

79th Fighter Squadron

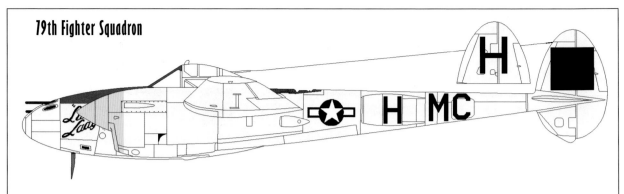

310 1st Lt. Arthur W. Heiden ('Ace'), Burton, Nebraska. To 79th FS 12/2/44. Claimed half a Bf 110 in the air and half an He 111 on the ground. Completed tour of 300 hours and returned to USA 17/12/44.

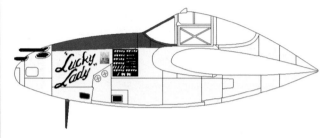

311 1st Lt. Arthur W. Heiden ('Ace'), Burton, Nebraska.

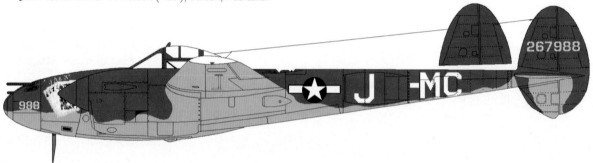

312 Maj. Carl E. Jackson, Los Angeles, California. Joined 20th FG 6/8/43. Assistant Group Operations Officer 6/8/43 until 30/1/44. 79th FS CO 31/1/44 until downed by mechanical failure 20/2/44 and became POW. Claimed 3 air kills, all FW 190s.

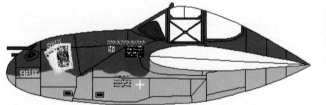

313 Maj. Carl E. Jackson, Los Angeles, California.

1/72 Scale

310/311: This P-38J-10-LO, 42-67427 was Heiden's assigned aircraft in April 1944. It was later re-coded to H-bar and was written off 23/4/44 when it was crash landed on return from operations at Podington by Lt. Vernon Beesley. It is in NMF finish overall with black codes, serial and 79th FS square on tail, yellow Group marking on forward cowlings. Name is yellow with black detail. Photo is a pin-up of actress Larraine Day who corresponded with the crew. They were crewchief T/Sgt. Max Pyles, assistant Clyde Birdwell and John Cavalier with Armourer Sgt Charles Fink.

312/313: This P-38J-10-LO 42-67988 was Jackson's assigned aircraft as Squadron CO during February 1944, and the aircraft he was lost in. It has the standard OD and NG finish, with white codes, yellow serial. Lockheed Construction number in grey on nose cone,2499, overpainted with last three of serial in yellow. Name 'Jack' above playing cards is red with yellow shading. One swastika kill mark, and twelve umbrellas denoting top cover missions.

79th Fighter Squadron

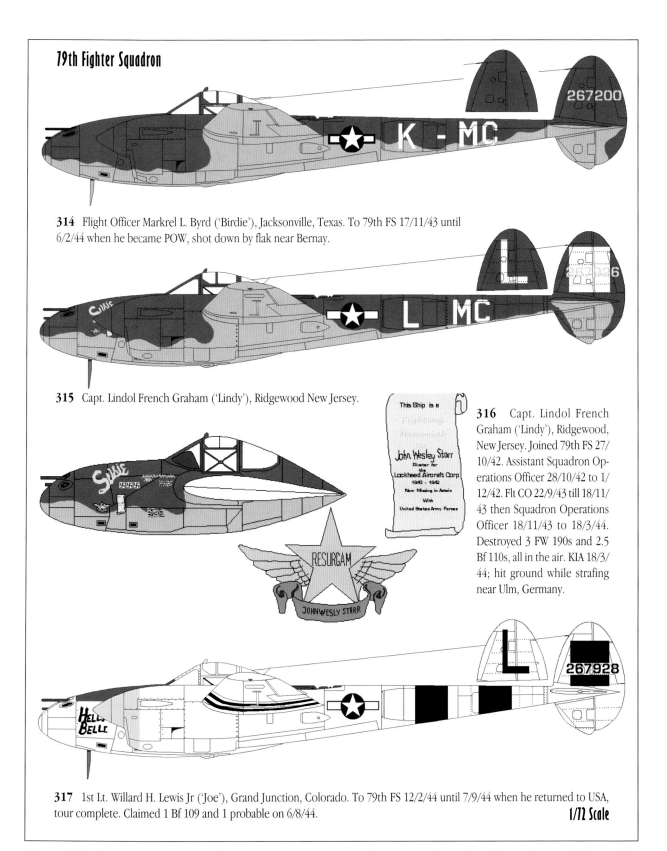

314 Flight Officer Markrel L. Byrd ('Birdie'), Jacksonville, Texas. To 79th FS 17/11/43 until 6/2/44 when he became POW, shot down by flak near Bernay.

315 Capt. Lindol French Graham ('Lindy'), Ridgewood New Jersey.

316 Capt. Lindol French Graham ('Lindy'), Ridgewood, New Jersey. Joined 79th FS 27/10/42. Assistant Squadron Operations Officer 28/10/42 to 1/12/42. Flt CO 22/9/43 till 18/11/43 then Squadron Operations Officer 18/11/43 to 18/3/44. Destroyed 3 FW 190s and 2.5 Bf 110s, all in the air. KIA 18/3/44; hit ground while strafing near Ulm, Germany.

317 1st Lt. Willard H. Lewis Jr ('Joe'), Grand Junction, Colorado. To 79th FS 12/2/44 until 7/9/44 when he returned to USA, tour complete. Claimed 1 Bf 109 and 1 probable on 6/8/44.

1/72 Scale

314: This P-38J-5-LO 42-67200 was assigned to F/O Byrd when it was written off on 10/1/44. Battle damaged and with one engine feathered, he ran off the runway on landing, wiping out the undercarriage. Standard OD and NG scheme with white codes, and serial in yellow.

315/316: P-38J-10-LO 42-67926 MC-L 'Susie' was Graham's aircraft in February 1944 and the aircraft in which he was killed. OD and NG, codes and squadron symbol in white. Serial and name in yellow. 3 Black swastikas on white squares for his three FW 190 kills on 29/1/44. The memorial scroll ap-

peared on several Lockheed aircraft, in memory of ex-Lockheed employees missing or KIA with the armed forces.

317: P-38J-10-LO 42-67928 MC-L flown by Lewis during May/June/July 1944. NMF overall, with full invasion stripes, Group yellow markings on front of engines. The name, 79th FS square, and code 'L' are in black. See 318 and 355.

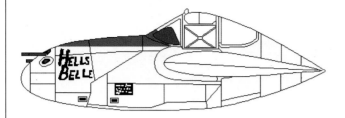

318 1st Lt. Willard H. Lewis Jr ('Joe'), Grand Junction, Colorado.

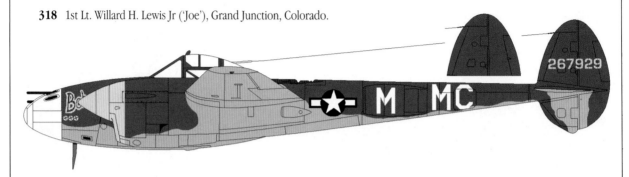

319 Lt. Col. Robert J. Meyer ('Bob'), Buffalo, New York. To 79th FS 30/7/43. Flt. CO 18/11/43 to 27/9/44. Squadron Operations Officer 27/9/43 to 8/12/44. Squadron CO 9/12/44 to4/4/45. Then to USA on completion of second tour. Claimed 3 FW 190s in the air plus a probable Me 410.

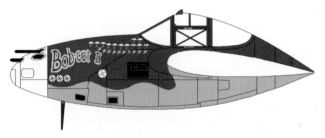

320 Lt. Col. Robert J. Meyer ('Bob'), Buffalo, New York.

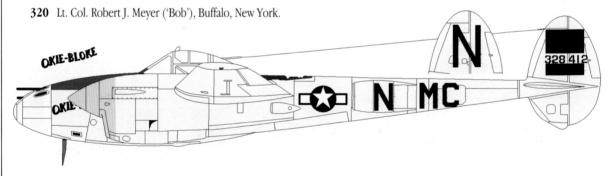

321 Maj. William W. Smith ('WW'), San Antonio, Texas. To 55th FS 5/11/42. Squadron Operations Officer 11/42 to 6/43. Transferred out because of injuries received in flying accident, June 1943. Re-joined 79th FS 16/5/44. Squadron Operations Officer 14/6/44 to 15/8/44, then back to 55th FS as Operations Officer 15/8/44 until 10/4/44, then to USA tour completed. Claimed 2 Bf 109s in the air.

1/72 Scale

318: P-38J-10-LO 42-67928 MC-L flown by Lewis during May/June/July 1944. NMF overall, with full invasion stripes, Group yellow markings on front of engines. The name, 79th FS square, and code 'L' are in black. See 317.

319/320: This P-38J-10-LO 42-67929 was flown by Meyer in May 1944, until it was lost 25/5/44 to flak, with 2nd Lt. Harry J.Watson Jr who became a POW. The aircraft had been re-coded MC-R in the meantime. It is in OD and NG scheme with droopsnoot simulation and yellow Group colours on spinners and cowl fronts. Name 'Bobcat II' is red with yellow outline.

321: This P-38J-15-LO 43-28412 was Smith's aircraft in May 1944. NMF overall with codes and serial in black, as is 79th FS square on the tail surfaces. Yellow Group colours on cowlings and spinners. Name 'Okie Bloke' is black. See 322 and 371.

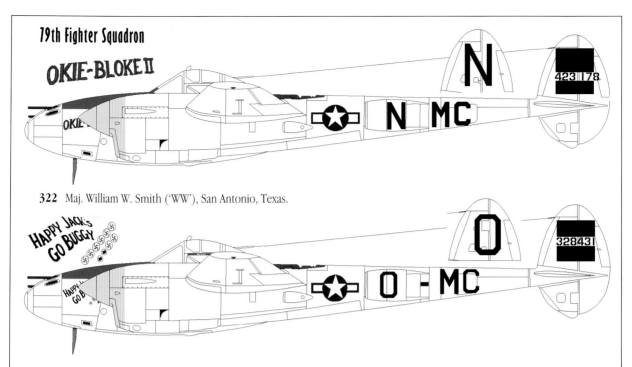

79th Fighter Squadron

322 Maj. William W. Smith ('WW'), San Antonio, Texas.

323 Capt. Jack M. Ilfrey ('Happy Jack'), Houston, Texas. To 79th FS 20/4/44. Squadron Operations Officer 14/6/44 until 27/9/44. Squadron CO 27/9/44 until tour completed 9/12/44, when he returned to USA. Previous tour with 94th FS, 1st FG in North Africa. He scored 5.5 air kills with the 1st FG and 2 with the 20th FG, all in P-38s.

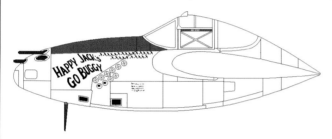

324 Capt. Jack M. Ilfrey ('Happy Jack'), Houston, Texas.

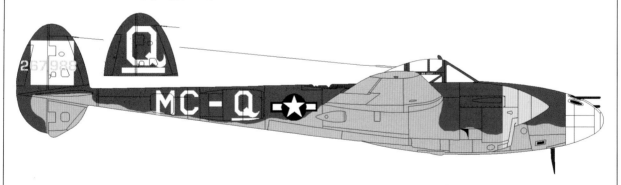

325 1st Lt. Woodrow W. Williams ('Woody'), Houston, Texas. To 79th FS 28/3/44 until injured on combat mission 27/7/44. He was then hospitalized, returning to USA 23/11/44.

1/72 Scale

322: Smith's second P-38 with the 79th FS was this J-15, 44-23178, which he flew during June and July 1944, up to the time the group changed to P-51s. It carried the same markings as his previous aircraft, but the name was now red with some detail in black. See 321 and 371.

323/324: P-38J-15-LO 43-28431 MC-O was Ilfrey's aircraft shown as in May/June 1944 prior to D-Day. Aircraft is NMF overall, with yellow Group colours on cowlings. Droopsnoot simulation, black codes and Squadron square, serial also in black. He destroyed 2 Bf 109s in this aircraft on 24/5/44, and

was shot down in it on 13/6/44, becoming an evader.

325: P-38J-10-LO 42-67988 was William's assigned aircraft until it was lost on 8/5/44 at the end of a combat mission, when it bellied in owing to undercarriage problems and crash-landed at Wittering airfield. It is in a factory applied OD and ND finish, with codes and Squadron symbol in white. Serial and Group colours on front of cowlings, yellow. Usual droopsnoot simulation on nose. Aircraft possibly named 'Li'l One', but it is not known if this was painted on.

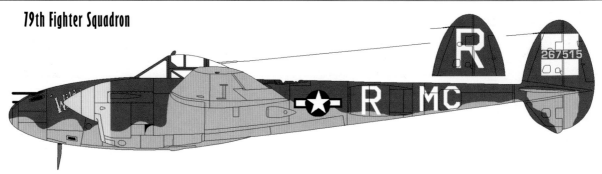

326 Capt. Merle B. Nichols ('Nick'), Bellevue, Washington. Joined 79th FS 3/8/43. Flt. CO 1/1/44 to 15/5/44 when tour complete. Returned to USA until 2/8/44, then to 20th FG HQ as Tactical Inspector until 18/9/44. To 77th FS 19/9/4. Squadron Operations Officer 19/9/44 to 17/12/44. Squadron CO from 18/12/44. Completed 2 tours. Claimed 1 FW 190, 1 Bf 109 and 1 Bf 110 in the air, plus 3 damaged.

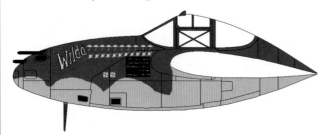

327 Capt. Merle B. Nichols ('Nick'), Bellevue, Washington.

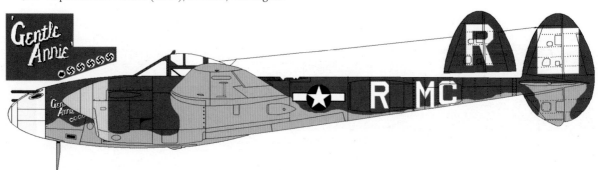

328 Col. Harold J. Rau ('Hal'), Hempstead, New York. Assigned as Group CO 20/3/44, until 25/6/44, when he returned to the USA on leave. He took over as CO again on 27/8/44 until 18/12/44, when he returned to the USA tour expired. He scored 1 air and 4 ground victories.

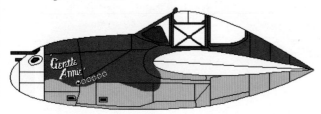

329 Col. Harold J. Rau ('Hal'), Hempstead, New York.

1/72 Scale

326/327: P-38J-10-LO 42-67515 'Wilda' was Nichols' aircraft in May 1944. OD and NG scheme, yellow Group markings and serial, white codes and Squadron symbol. Name is yellow with black shading. Mission marks are yellow, 2 black swastika kill marks on white squares. This machine was later transferred to 474th FG, Ninth Air Force. Crew Chief T/Sgt. Joseph Gall, Assistants Sgt. George Gunther and Cpl. Winston Ranger, Armourer Sgt. Joseph Ryan. See 292.

328/329: 43-104308 is the P-38J-15-LO flown by Rau in April 1944. The air-craft is OD and NG, with Group markings in yellow on spinners and first 12' of cowlings. 79th FS square symbol and codes in white. Droopsnoot simulation in polished metal with white band. See 330, 331, 366.

79th Fighter Squadron

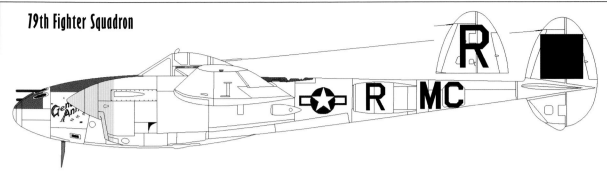

330 Col. Harold J. Rau ('Hal'), Hempstead, New York.

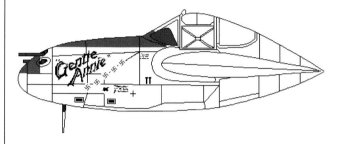

331 Col. Harold J. Rau ('Hal'), Hempstead, New York.

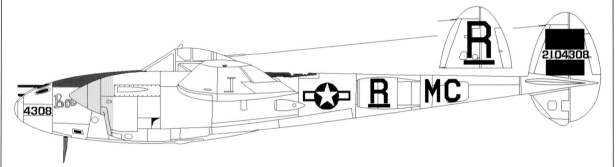

332 Lt. Col. Robert J. Meyer ('Bob'), Buffalo, New York.

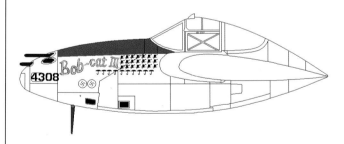

333 Lt. Col. Robert J. Meyer ('Bob'), Buffalo, New York.

1/72 Scale

330/331: P-38J-10-LO 42-69166 flown by Rau in June 1944, just before he went home on leave. He flew this older model for only about a month. It is in NMF overall with yellow Group markings and codes and Squadron markings in black. Note the droopsnoot simulation partly overpainted. See 328, 329, 366.

332/333: 'Bobcat III' was P-38J-15-LO 42-104308 and was assigned to Meyer to replace the second Bobcat. He flew this plane until his tour was complete. NMF overall with standard Group and 79th FS markings, codes and serial in black. The name is again red with yellow outline. See 319, 320 and 362.

79th Fighter Squadron

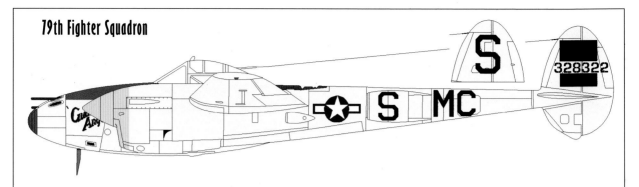

334 1st Lt. John L. Armstrong ('Jack'), Los Angeles, California. Joined 79th FS 28/3/44. Lost due to mechanical failure, 28/8/44. Crashed near Bruchweiler, in P-51 44-13791 'Guardian Angel', and became POW.

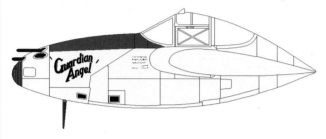

335 1st Lt. John L. Armstrong ('Jack'), Los Angeles, California.

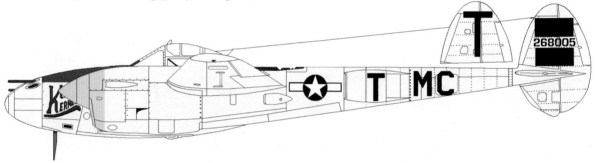

336 Maj. Delynn E. Anderson ('Andy'), Stearns, Kentucky.

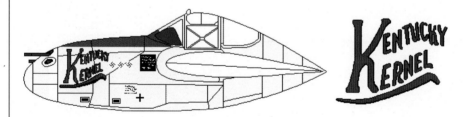

337 Maj. Delynn E. Anderson ('Andy'), Stearns, Kentucky.

1/72 Scale

334/335: P-38J-15-LO 43-28322, MC-S, flown by Armstrong up to the changeover to Mustangs. NMF overall with black codes and serial, and 79th FS square symbol. Yellow Group colours on forward cowls and spinners. Aircraft is unusual in that it lacks the droopsnoot simulation, and has a red tip to the nose. Name is black with red detail. Crewchief T/Sgt. Leonard Kerzinski, Asst. Sgt. Chester Wilde, Armourer Sgt. C.F. Lawler.

336/337: Anderson's first 'Kentucky Kernel' was this P-38J-10-LO 42-68005, which he flew during March and April 1944. NMF overall, black codes and

79th FS square marking, yellow Group colours and has droopsnoot simulation. Name is red with blue shading. 3 swastika kill marks. Aircraft written off 26/4/44 in crash landing at Kingscliffe with Lt. Harry Watson as pilot. See 302-305.

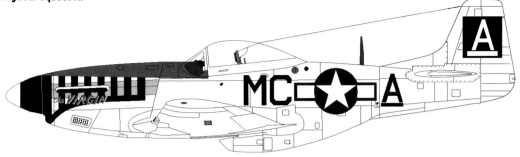

338 1st Lt. Kenneth H. Schons ('Virgin'), Chicago, Illlinois. To 79th FS 14/11/44 until end of war.

339 Capt. Melbourne G. Ingebrigtsen ('Ingy'), Portland, Oregon. Joined 79th FS 8/9/44. Flt. CO 1/2/45 to 3/5/45 when he completed his tour and returned to USA. Claimed 1.5 He 115s on water.

340 1st Lt. Frank E. Strock ('Frankie'), Leavitsburg, Ohio. Joined 79th FS 14/11/44, to end of war. Claimed 3 He 111s, all on ground.

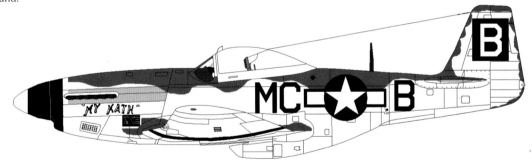

341 1st Lt. Kenneth A. Skinner ('Shaky'), Chicago, Illinois. With 79th FS 14/11/44 until end of war.   **1/72 Scale**

338: Schons' P-51D-5-NT, 44-11219, in January 1945. Aircraft is NMF overall, with Group piano keys in black and white. Black codes and 79th FS square. Bar under A indicates second use of that code letter in the squadron at the time. Name red with yellow shading. No stripes or bands carried.

339: Ingebrigtsen's P-51D-5-NA 44-13752, 'Miss (U) Louise', was the first of three similarly named Mustangs. It has the early Group P-51 scheme of OD upper surfaces, but has been updated with the piano key nose markings. Codes and square are black, name is red with yellow shading.

340: P-51D, serial not known, flown by Strock during his tour. Standard late Group Mustang scheme, no stripes or bands, codes and Squadron symbol in black. 'Butch' is red and yellow.

341: P-51D-5-NA 44-13660, 'My Kath', was Skinner's aircraft in November 1944. It has the early Group nose markings, black codes and squadron symbol. Name is black with yellow detail. Black ETO bands on horizontal wing and tail surfaces.

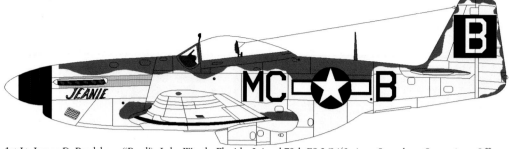

342 1st Lt. James D. Bradshaw ('Brad'), Lake Worth, Florida. Joined 79th FS 2/8/43. Asst. Squadron Operations Officer 14/5/44 to 17/8/44, then to USA, tour completed.

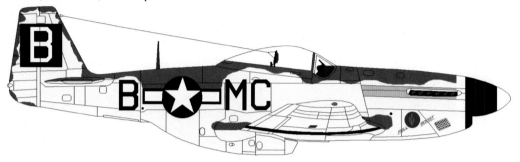

343 1st Lt. James D. Bradshaw ('Brad'), Lake Worth, Florida.

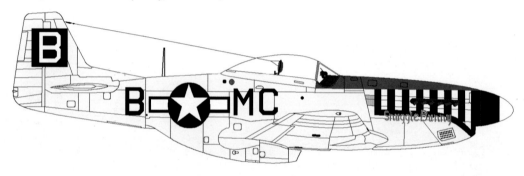

344 Capt. Robert R. Phipps Jr ('B.T.'), Shavertown, Pennsylvania. Joined 79th FS 14/6/44. Flt. CO 7/11/44 until 20/12/44 when he returned to USA, tour completed.

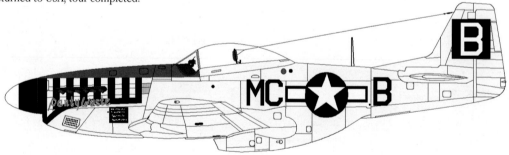

345 Capt. Robert R. Phipps Jr ('B.T.'), Shavertown, Pennsylvania.

1/72 Scale

342: P-51D-5-NA 44-13660 was Bradshaw's assigned Mustang until he went home in August 1944. OD top surfaces, NMF undersides. Early Group markings in black and white, codes in black and individual letter 'B' superimposed in white on black Squadron square. Name 'Jeanie' is black with yellow detail. Black ETO bands on wings and horizontal tail. Same ground crew took care of his P-51 and P-38.

343: Starboard side of of Bradshaw's 44-13660. 'Full Boost' is red, with red hand, middle digit extended, on a blue circle.

344: P-51D-5-NA 44-13660 was assigned to Capt. Phipps in November 1944. Names 'Panty Waste' on port side nose and 'Snuggle Bunny' on starboard, are both red with yellow outline. No ETO or D-Day stripes carried. Aircraft is NMF overall, Group piano key markings in black and white, black codes, white 'B' on black square on tail.

345: Port side view of 44-13660 in November 1944 after it was taken over by Phipps.

79th Fighter Squadron

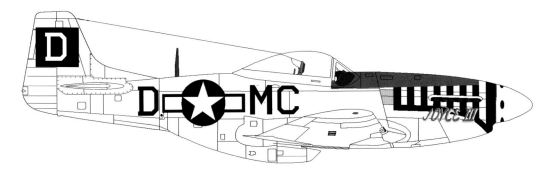

346   Capt. William A. Cameron ('Willie'), Redondo Beach, California. Joined 79th FS 28/3/44. Asst. Squadron Operations Officer 19/8/44 to 12/11/44 then to USA, tour complete.

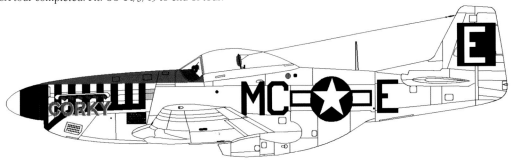

347   1st Lt. Robert R. Dufresne ('Duffie'), Ferndale, Michigan. Joined 79th FS 18/9/44 until 24/4/45 then to USA tour completed. Flt. CO 14/3/45 to end of tour.

348   1st Lt. Donald M. Barnard ('Barney'), Evanston, Wyoming. Joined 79th FS 18/1/45 to end of war.

Capt. Thomas J. Daniel ('Danny'), El Centro, California. To 79th FS 146/44. Flt. CO 28/10/44 to 7/11/44. Assistant Squadron Operations Officer 7/11/44 to 5/12/44. To USA 9/1/45, tour completed.

1st Lt. Walter E. Bullers ('Bud'), Mayport, Pennsylvania. To 79th FS 18/9/44. To USA 8/4/45 tour complete. Claimed 1 He 115 on water, 1 Bf 110 on ground.

1/72 Scale

346: P-51D-5-NA 44-13846 'Soar Lassie II' flown by Cameron in July/August 1944. OD topsides, NMF undersides, black codes, ETO bands, and 79th FS square with 'C' repeated in white thereon. Black and yellow nose colours, a holdover from P-38 days were worn for a brief period. Name is yellow with red shading. C/Chief T/Sgt. Stanley Lecznar, Amourer Cpl. John Henderson.
347: P-51D-10-NA, 44-14844, was Dufresne's assigned aircraft in February 1944. It was written off in a belly landing at base on 26/2/45 by Capt. J.K. Taylor of Westerly, Rhode Island, two days after Dufresne left to return home.

Aircraft is NMF overall with codes and Squadron square in black. Piano keys black and white but spinner is all natural metal. Name 'Joyce III' is red with yellow outline.
348: P-51D-10-NA 44-14365 assigned to Daniel, then to Bullers, then to Barnard in early 1945. Aircraft lost 23/7/45 when Lt. R. Crawford crashed on a training flight. NMF overall, codes and square black. Black/white Group markings on nose. Name 'Corky' red with yellow detail, carried by Barnard, previously named 'Danny Boy' by Daniel, then ' Buds Comet' by Bullers.

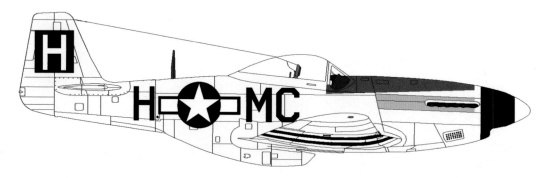

349 1st Lt. Robert E. Campbell ('Bob'), Ada, Oklahoma. To 79th FS 25/5/44 until tour completed 3/10/44 then returned to USA. Destroyed 2 Bf 109s in the air.

1st Lt. David Stewart ('Stew'), Dallas, Texas. Joined 79th FS 20/11/44. Claimed 7 ground kills: 3 Bf 110s, 2 FW 190s, 1 Bf 109 and 1 He 111. Shot down by flak in this machine 10/4/45 near Zossen, Germany. POW.

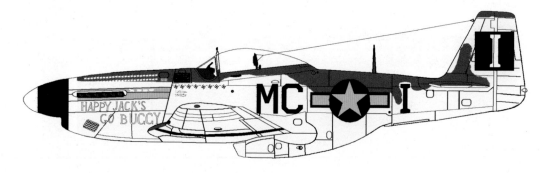

350 1st Lt. Arthur W. Heiden ('Ace'), Burton, Nebraska.

351 Capt. Jack M. Ilfrey ('Happy Jack'), Houston, Texas.

1/72 Scale

349: P-51D-5-NA 44-13751 was flown by Campbell at the end of his tour and passed to Stewart after he left. Aircraft is as flown by Campbell in August 1944, in the early Group Mustang markings. D-Day stripes on lower surfaces only, OD upper surfaces, NMF lower. Codes and Squadron symbol in black. Name is red with yellow shading.
350: Heiden's P-51D-5-NA, 44-13620, coded MC-H. It wears the early Group Mustang scheme with D-Day stripes on lower surfaces. Aircraft lost 12/8/44 to flak, Lt. Paul Denbo being KIA when it crashed near Peche. See 310.

351: P-51D-5-NA 44-13761 flown by Ilfrey when he rejoined the group after evading in June 1944. The upper surfaces of wings, tail, and fuselage are OD, all other surfaces NMF. Black ETO bands are carried on wings and horizontal tail. Codes and Squadron square symbol in black, with individual code 'I' repeated in white on the fin/rudder. Early black and white group markings on nose. Name is yellow with red outline. Top cover, sweep, loco-busting mission tally on nose in white. 8 black swastikas on white circles. Note greyed-out fuselage insignia. See 323, 324, 352.

79th Fighter Squadron

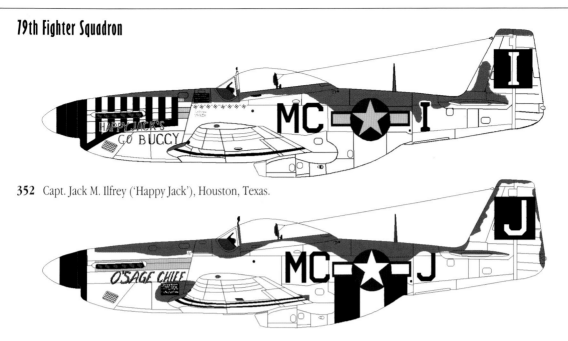

352 Capt. Jack M. Ilfrey ('Happy Jack'), Houston, Texas.

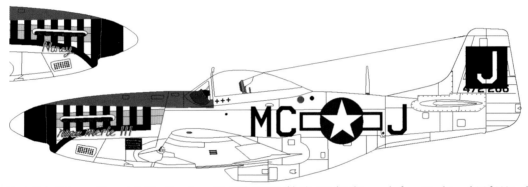

353 Capt. Harold O. Binkley ('Bink'), Hominy, Oklahoma. To 79th FS 15/5/44. Flt. CO 27/9/44. To 9/12/44 tour completed. Binkley was a full-blooded Osage native American. He claimed 1 Bf 109 and 1 FW 190.

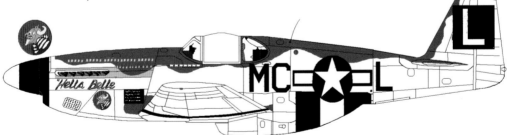

354 Capt. Dale N. Jones ('Jonesie'), Chariton, Iowa. To 79th FS 8/9/44. Flt. CO 4/1/45 to end of war He claimed 1 Bf 109 in the air and 1 He 111 on the ground. His father flew B-26s from England. This is the only recorded instance of a father and son flying in combat simultaneously.

355 1st Lt. Willard H. Lewis Jr ('Joe'), Grand Junction, Colorado.

1/72 Scale

352: *Ilfrey's P-51 with later up-graded markings in November 1944, when he finished his tour. Group black and white piano keys added to nose, covering most of the mission tally previously carried. Name re-painted in black with yellow outline. OD upper surfaces retained. See 323, 324, 351.*

353: *P-51D-5-NA 44-13855 was Binkley's aircraft in November 1944. OD on top, NMF on all undersides. D-Day stripes on undersides of wings and fuselage only. Early black/white Group marking on nose. Name red with black shading. Codes and 79th FS square black. Single kill marking on cowling.*

354: *P-51D-20-NA 44-72266 was Jones' last aircraft. NMF overall, no bands or stripes. Codes, serial and square, black. Name now 'Nina Merle III'; 'Nancy' on starboard side. Aircraft written off 12/6/45 in crashlanding. See 381.*

355: *P-51C-10-NT 43-25054 'Hells Belle', August 1944. Top surfaces OD, NMF below. Early Group black/white nose markings, black codes and square, white code 'L' superimposed. Black ETO bands on horizontal surfaces, and ¹/₂ D-Day stripes under rear fuselage only. Crew Chief of this long-lived aircraft was Tex Schrader. Aircraft later passed to 1st Lt. Keith C. Price. See 318.*

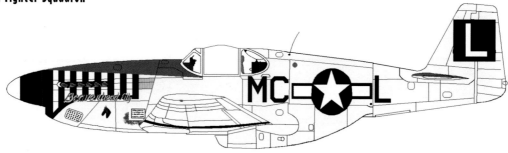

356 1st Lt. Keith C. Price ('Casey'), Lima, Montana. To 79th FS 14/6/44. Completed tour and returned to USA 9/1/45. Claimed 1 FW 190 and 1 damaged.

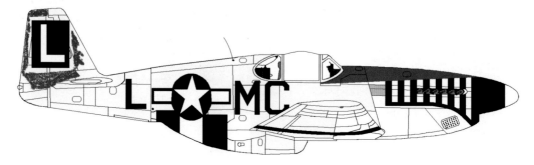

357 1st Lt. Robert M. Scott ('Scotty'), Hays, Kansas. To 79th FS 14/11/44 until end of war. Flt. CO 18/4/45.

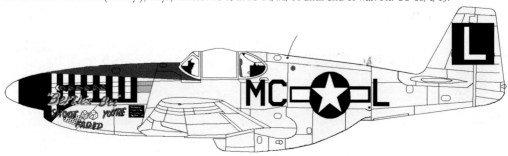

358 1st Lt. Robert M. Scott ('Scotty'), Hays, Kansas.

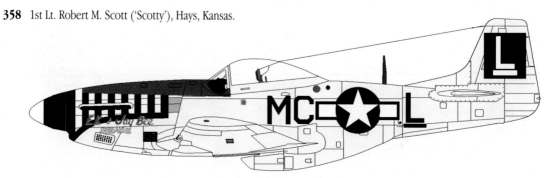

359 1st Lt. John Bennett Lee ('General'), Sealston, Virginia. To 79th FS 28/10/44 until end of war. Flt. CO from 23/4/45. Claimed 1 Ju 52 destroyed on ground.

1/72 Scale

356: *P-51C 43-25054 MC-L was renamed 'Beaverhead Filly' by Price. The OD has gone from top of fuselage but remained on wings and tail. Group nose markings updated and D-Day stripes removed from November 1944. She next passed to 1st Lt. Robert M. Scott. See 355, 357-358.*
357: *In December 1944, though the OD was removed from the top of the fuselage, the remnants were still visible on the vertical tail, starboard side only. Tex Schrader crewed MC-L through all her three 'lives'.*
358: *In January 1945 Scott flew her as 'Berties Bet'/'Shoot Youre Faded'. The*

OD has gone from the upper surface of wings and tail, as have the ETO bands. This aircraft flew some 700 combat hours all told, and was finally written off on 21/8/45 when belly landed by Lt. Donald M. Barnard.
359: *P-51D-15NA 44-15198 MC-L bar 'E.K. and Jay Bee./ Suzanne' was Lee's aircraft in November 1944. NMF overall with codes and Squadron square in black. No bands or stripes are carried. Names are red and yellow.*

79th Fighter Squadron

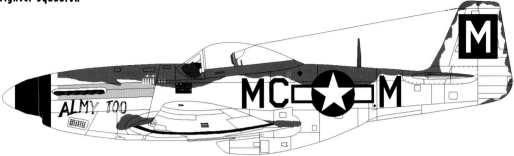

360 1st Lt. George W. Merriman ('Georgie'), Beaver Falls, Pennsylvania. Joined 79th FS 12/2/44. Flt. CO 19/8/44 to 7/9/44 when he completed his tour and returned to USA

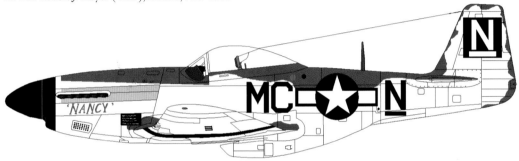

361 Lt. Col. Robert J. Meyer ('Bob'), Buffalo, New York.

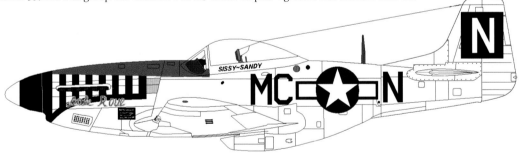

362 Lt. Col. John P. Randolph ('Jack'), Schertz, Texas. Assigned 20th FG 27/7/44. Deputy Group Commander 28/8/44 to 9/11/44, then to 359th FG as group CO. Claimed 1 Bf 109 in the air plus 4 ground kills with the 20th FG.

363 Capt. Clifford Kies ('88'), Austin, Texas. To 79th FS 11/8/44, Flt. CO from 27/12/44 to 20/2/45 when he was wounded by flak. Made it home but his combat days were over. Sent to USA. He claimed 1 He 111 on the ground.

1/72 Scale

360: *P-51D-5-NA 44-13667 'Almy Too' was Merriman's aircraft at the end of his tour. NMF undersides, with OD top surfaces. Black ETO bands on horizontal surfaces. Mission marks on cowl in yellow, name black with red detailing, appears to be flaking off. Aircraft later recoded MC-T. Crew Chief T/Sgt. James Mulligan, Asst. Sgt James Adams, Armourer Sgt. Clyde Chadwick.*
361: *During his second tour, Meyer flew P-51D-20-NA, 44-72402 as his final wartime mount. Standard Group piano key marking and 79th FS square on the tail. Three swastika kills marked on the canopy rail. Crew Chief T/*

Sgt. Keli, assisted by Cpl. Walker, with armourer Sgt. 'Pop' Roy.
362: *P-51D-5-NA 44-13541 'Nancy' assigned to Randolph in August 1944. OD top surfaces, NMF undersides. Black ETO bands on wings and horizontal tail surfaces, black codes and square. Early group nose colours in black and white, name is red.*
363: *P-51D-5-NT 44-11195 was Kies's mount when he was wounded. Name 'Little Roue' in red and yellow. 'Sissy' and 'Sandy' on canopy frame, codes and square are black. Black ETO bands on horizontal tail surfaces only.*

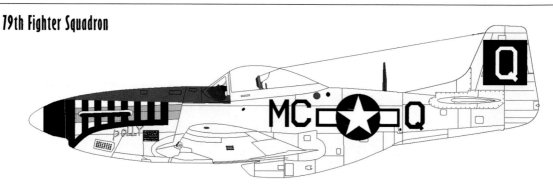

364 1st Lt. Joseph E. Shelton ('Joe'), Kansas City, Missouri. To 79th FS 14/11/44 until end of war.

365 Col. Harold J. Rau ('Hal'), Hempstead, New York.

366 1st Lt. Richard H. Black ('Pinky'), Centralia, Illinois. To 79th FS 12/2/44. Assistant Squadron Intelligence Officer 7/2/45 to 28/5/45. To USA 28/5/45 tour complete. Claimed 1 Bf 109 destroyed in the air.

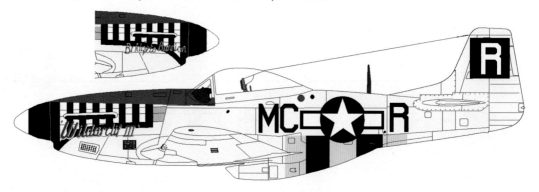

367 Capt. Darrel A. Beschen ('Gopher'), Dubuque, Iowa. To 79th FS 19/9/44. Flt. CO 1/3/45 to end of war. Destroyed 1 Bf 109 in the air and 1.5 He 111s on the ground.

1/72 Scale

364: *'Polly', P-51D-5-NA 44-13653 was Shelton's a/c at the end of the war. NMF overall, standard Group markings, no stripes or bands.*
365: *Rau's P-51D-5-NA, 44-13337, from 27/8/44 when he returned to take over as CO again, the day Col. Cy Wilson was lost. NMF overall with black ETO bands on wings and horizontal tail. Early Group P-51 nose markings in black and white, code 'R' repeated on vertical tail surfaces. See 328-331.*
366: *P-51D-5-NA 44-13535 was Black's aircraft in late 1944. Top of fuselage, wings and tail OD, all other surfaces NMF. Black codes, 79th FS square and*

ETO bands on underside of wings and tail. D-Day stripes on lower fuselage only. Name 'Black's Bird' red with yellow detail. Whole aircraft very worn.
367: *P-51D-10-NA 44-14337 'Wildarclif III / Bridgets Bunnion' was Beschen's assigned aircraft in late 1944 early 1945. NMF overall, with black codes, serial and 79th FS square symbol. Black ETO bands on horizontal surfaces, very dirty, worn D-Day stripes remain under fuselage only. Names both sides are red with yellow shading. Crewchief T/Sgt. Jim Douglas, Asst. P.F.C. George Fregone, Armourer Sgt. Luther Ghent.*

79th Fighter Squadron

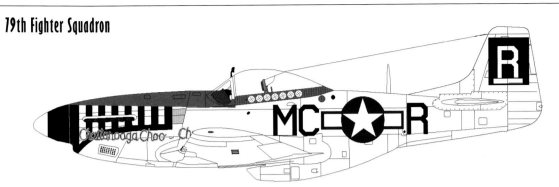

368 1st Lt. Edward F. Pogue ('Pogie'), Chattanooga, Tennessee. Joined 79th FS 14/11/44. Flt. CO from 27/4/45. Destroyed 4 He 111s, 1 Bf 109, 1 Bf 110, all on ground.

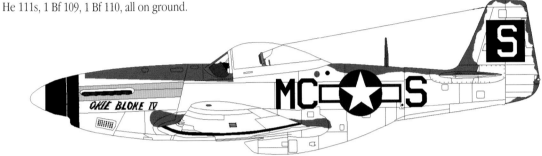

369 Maj. William W. Smith ('WW'), San Antonio, Texas.

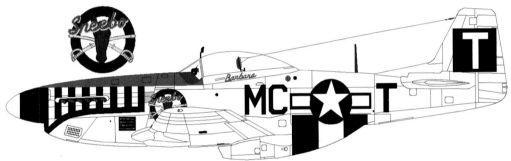

370 1st Lt. Donald A. Sass ('DA'), Milwaukee, Wisconsin. To 79th FS 28/9/44 till end of war. Flt. CO 1/3/45 to end of war Promoted Capt. 26/4/45. Ex-cavalry officer.

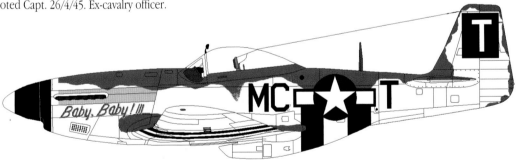

371 1st Lt. James H. Baldwin ('Baldy'), Los Angeles, California. Joined 79th FS 27/2/44, completed tour and returned to USA 17/8/44.

1/72 Scale

368: Pogue's P-51D-5-NA 44-13535 in April 1945. Late war Group markings, no stripes or bands carried, codes and Squadron symbol black. Red canopy rail shows 7 kills. 'Chattanooga Choo Choo' is red with yellow detailing.
369: Smith's P-51D-5-NA, 44-13791, his last aircraft with 79th FS. Early Group P-51 markings, OD top surfaces and NMF below. Black ETO bands on horizontal wing and tail surfaces. Name black and yellow. Later flown as 'Guardian Angel' by Lt. John L. Armstrong, lost in it 28/8/44, POW. See 321-322.
370: P-51D-5-NA 44-13667 MC-T was assigned to Sass in October/November

1944. NMF overall, with D-Day stripes on lower fuselage only. No ETO bands carried. Named 'Sneebo' after his horse, while serving as a cavalry officer. 'Barbara' in red on canopy rail. Front of spinner NMF.
371: 44-13876 'Baby Baby! III', Baldwin's assigned P-51D-5-NA from the changeover to the end of his tour in August 1944. Early Group Mustang markings, with OD top over NMF undersides. D-Day stripes on undersides of wings and fuselage. Codes and square are black, name red with yellow shading. Crew Chief T/Sgt. Harry Keli, Asst. Sgt. Ed Roy, Amr. Sgt. James Walker.

79th Fighter Squadron

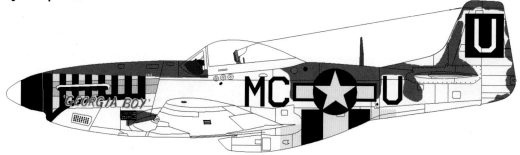

372 1st Lt. Thomas M. Gardner ('Tom'), Atlanta, Georgia. Joined 79th FS 7/7/44. Flt. CO 18/12/44 to 15/1/45, then to USA tour complete.

373 Capt. James N. Reichard ('Reich'), Tulsa, Oklahoma. To 79th FS 12/6/44. Flt. CO 7/11/44 to 31/12/44. Assistant Squadron Operations Officer 1/1/45 to 13/3/45. Assistant Group Operations Officer 14/3/45 to end of war. Claimed .5 FW 190 in the air.

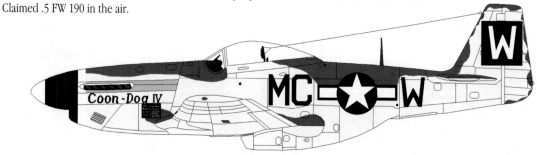

374 1st Lt. Zell M. Wyman ('Zelbert'), Ionia, Michigan. To 79th FS 29/5/43. Flt. CO 27/9/44 to 12/10/44 then to 67th FW.

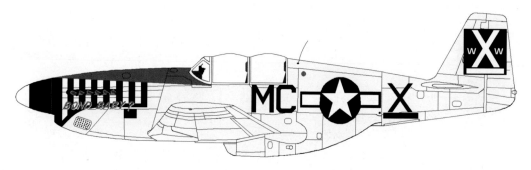

375 1st Lt. Wallace E. Lowman ('Lucky'), Los Angeles, California. Assigned 55th FS 28/10/44. Promoted Capt. 27/5/45. Flt. CO 17/4/45.

1/72 Scale

372: *P-51D-5-NA 44-13873 was Gardner's aircraft in early 1945. It has OD top surface, NMF undersides, D-Day bands on lower fuselage only. Codes and Squadron symbol black. White areas of star and bar, D-Day stripes and Group markings have been greyed out, although spinner tip is white. Name 'Georgia Boy' is red with yellow outline.*

373: *P-51C-10-NT 43-25064 as flown by Reichard in August 1944. OD top surfaces, NMF undersides. Black codes and 79th square. Early P-51 nose markings in black and white, D-Day stripes on lower surfaces only. Mission*

tally in yellow on cowling, one swastika kill mark under canopy. Name red.

374: *Wyman's P-51D-5-NA 44-13661 in August 1944. OD top surfaces, NMF undersides, black codes, name and square. Early style nose markings.*

375: *A war weary P-51B or C, 'Bond Baby?', converted to a two-seater. Named for war-bond competition in which the prize was a trip in the rear seat to any UK destination. Won by Sgt. Ed Beck, who was flown to Northern Ireland by Lt. Lowman. NMF with black codes and 79th square, black and white piano keys, X and WW on tail in white. No ETO or D-Day stripes.*

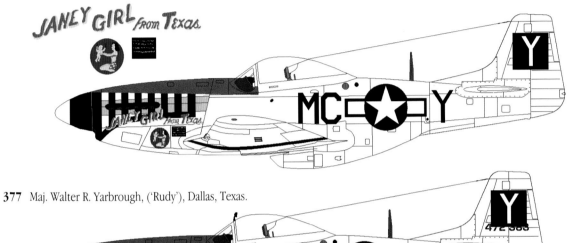

376 Capt. Charles R. Hamme, Morristown, Pennsylvania. Assigned 79th FS 7/7/44. Flt. CO 5/12/44 to 6/1/45. Completed tour and transferred to HQ Base Air Depot Area 6/1/45.

377 Maj. Walter R. Yarbrough, ('Rudy'), Dallas, Texas.

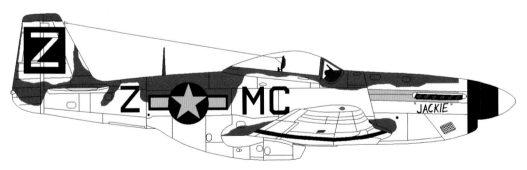

378 Maj. Walter R. Yarbrough, ('Rudy'), Dallas, Texas. Joined 79th FS 30/9/44. Flt. CO 30/10/44 to 8/12/44. Squadron Operations Officer 9/12/44 to 3/4/45. Squadron CO 4/4/45 to end of war.

379 P-51D, serial unknown, 79th FS. Pilot assignment not known.

1/72 Scale

376: P-51D-5-NA 44-13753 'Kitty and Bunny' was Hamme's assigned aircraft. It carries standard Group markings on NMF finish overall, with codes and Squadron square symbol in black. Black ETO bands are carried on wings and horizontal tail surfaces. Name is red with yellow shadow detail.
377: P-51D, MC-Y, serial unknown, assigned to Yarbrough in late 1944. NMF overall, with black codes, serial and Squadron symbol. Black ETO bands on horizontal surfaces. Name is red with yellow shading.
378: This P-51D-20-NA 44-72383, MC-Y, was flown by Yarbrough in April/

May 1945. Markings basically as previous aircraft, but no ETO bands carried, girlie art is absent, and name is slightly different. This aircraft went to the Swiss air force after the war, becoming J-2029 in that air force.
379: This P-51D, serial unknown, has the early Group P-51 markings, with the top surfaces in OD and undersides NMF. Individual letter 'Z' is repeated in white on 79th FS black square on tail. Black ETO bands on horizontal wing and tail surfaces. Name 'Jackie' is black. Pilot assignment not known.

79th Fighter Squadron

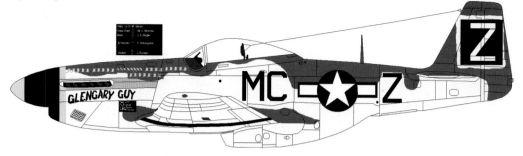

380 Capt. Glenn M. Webb, Santa Monica California. To 79th FS 22/4/44 as Lt., promoted Capt. 4/10/44. Flt. CO 7/9/44/ until 11/11/44, when he returned to USA, tour complete.

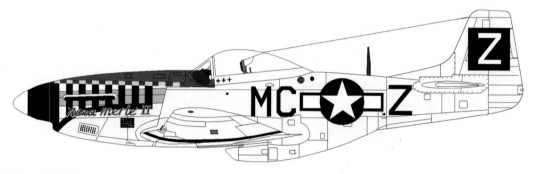

381 Capt. Dale N. Jones ('Jonesie'), Chariton, Iowa.

1/72 Scale

380: P-51D-5-NA 44-13760 flown by Webb in August/ September 1944. Name is black with red shading and is his name plus those of his two sons, Gary and Guy. All upper sufaces of wings, tail and fuselage are OD, rest of aircraft is NMF. Black ETO stripes are carried on wings and horizontal tail. Nose markings are black and yellow, a carry-over from the yellow Lightning markings. Code 'Z' on tail is white.

381: This P-51D-5-NT 44-11244, MC-Z, was Jones's aircraft in February 1945. NMF overall with black codes and ETO bands on horizontal surfaces, Group piano keys in black and white. Name 'Nina Merle II' is red with yellow outline. Aircraft lost when it crashed near Darfeld, 24/2/45, with Lt. Leonard M. Wright, fate not known. See 354.

Left: Newly-delivered P-38J-10-LO, 42-67757, of the 38th FS, 55th FG, somewhere over England in January 1944. Finish is entirely standard for the period with no personal markings visible. The meaning of the small yellow or red 'P29' on the rudder is unknown. CG-C was lost on 31 January 1944 while being flown by 2nd Lt. David D. Fisher, who was shot down by fighters and killed in the ensuing crash near Venlo, Holland. It may just have survived long enough to receive the white Squadron triangle on the fins.

Above: *Nine-victory ace Major Edward B. Giller poses his P-51D-15-NA, 44-14985, for the camera in early 1945. Named 'The Millie G' and coded CY-G, the yellow and green nose colours of the 343rd Fighter Squadron, 55th Fighter Group are clearly visible. On the natural metal finish of the wings, the type identity bands are in black, whereas on the Olive Drab 41 of the tailplane they are in white. Although the curving red dividing line between the natural metal and Olive Drab on the fuselage is clear, the red prancing stallion on the yellow rudder is almost lost in the light reflection. See colour profile 479.*

THE 55TH FIGHTER GROUP

Pursuit to Defend

When the 55th Fighter Group arrived at Nuthampstead on 16 September 1943 they found the base was still under construction and a sea of mud, consequently the men soon christened it 'Mudhampstead'. They received their first four P-38s on 27 September 1943. Others swiftly followed, and the group became operational on 15 October 1943.

These early P-38s were H models, mostly H-5s but with a few H-1s among them. All were camouflaged in standard factory-applied Olive Drab upper surfaces over Neutral Gray undersides. The 'star and bar' national insignia was carried on the outside of each tail boom immediately aft of the wing trailing edge; on the upper port wing and below the starboard wing. The tail boom insignia were 25 inches in diameter, those on the wings 30 inches diameter. Some of the earliest arrivals had red-bordered insignia.

The aircraft serial, minus its first digit, was displayed on the outer surfaces of each vertical tail, in 9 inch yellow digits.

Squadron codes were allocated at the start of operations: CG for the 38th, CL for the 338th and CY for the 343rd squadrons, which they kept throughout the war. They were applied to the P-38s on the outside of each boom immediately aft of the radiator housing, with the individual aircraft letter on the radiator housing itself. They were in white

18 inch high letters, applied by stencil, and it appears to have been rare for the stencil breaks to have been painted in within the 55th FG.

To improve recognition of identity, from January 1944 a geometric symbol was painted, 30 inches high, on the outer sides of the vertical tails. The 38th FS used a triangle, the 338th FS a disc, and the 343rd FS a square. An aircraft's individual code letter was also repeated on the inner vertical tail surfaces, again 30 inches high. The symbols covered the serial numbers on the tail, and these were very often not reinstated.

From the beginning of 1944, the Group began receiving P-38 J models, at first in the same colours and markings as the -H models, but from February 1944, they began arriving in natural metal finish. All the codes and markings were then applied in black. A few of these 'silver' Lightnings were sprayed within the unit with a coat of Olive Drab or RAF Dark Green on the top surfaces.

From April 1944, the 'Droopsnoot' simulation markings were ordered, but many of the 55th Group's aircraft appear not to have had this, and of those that did, at least some were over-sprayed with Olive Drab or RAF Dark Green from early summer onwards.

In March 1944, the Eighth Air Force issued a system of colours to identify each Group, that allocated to the 55th being yellow/white checks. These were to be applied to the first 12 inches of both engine cowlings, with the spinners banded yellow and white, but this was never carried out, the Group carrying on without colours.

The 55th FG carried out the first Droopsnoot operation ever flown, on 10 April 1944; the 343rd FS escorting the 38th FS and 338th FS who carried bombs. These were dropped on the signal from Bombardier 1st Lt. William Stroud who was flown in the Group's Droopsnoot aircraft by Capt. Jerry Ayers. The target was Coulomiers airfield, and during the strafing after the bomb run, they lost their CO, Col. Jack Jenkins, who was downed by flak to become a POW. He had previously led the Group when they became the first fighter group over Berlin, on 3 March 1944.

On 15 April 1944, Capt. Gerald Brown became their first ace. The next day the 55th FG moved base to Wormingford, where they saw out the war. On 22 April 1944 Capt. Robert L. Buttke became the second and last P-38 ace within the Group.

The P-38s received D-Day stripes from 5 June 1944, in line with all other groups. These covered the codes on the tail booms, and they were not reinstated.

On 18 July, the Group officially became P-51-equipped, and flew their first Mustang operation on 21 July 1944.

The majority of the first Mustangs received were D-5-NA models, although there were a few Bs and Cs as well.

These first arrivals had black type recognition markings on the spinners and first 12 inches of the cowling and D-Day stripes on the undersides only. To this scheme the group added Olive Drab vertical fins, rudders and aft upper fuselage. On the vertical tail surfaces they applied their squadron geometric symbols in white, 30 inches across at the widest point. Codes were added in black, either side of the fuselage star, in RAF fashion, with the squadron code always forward, individual aircraft letter aft. This style of the tail markings lasted only 2 or 3 weeks, the symbols then being removed or over-painted, but in several cases the Olive Drab fin and rudder remained.

During the first week of August the Group at last added some colour, in the form of green-yellow-green banded spinners, and two rows of 6 inch checks in green and yellow immediately behind the spinner. In the words of one pilot: "This lifted everyone's spirits, in case they needed lifting, as it gave us an identity".

The green used was very dark, probably the available camouflage shade, US Medium Green 42, or RAF Dark Green. It has been illustrated somewhat lighter in this book, purely to show that it is green, and avoid confusion with any of the other Groups' colours.

From autumn 1944 several 343rd FS Mustangs were painted Olive Drab or Dark Green on all fuselage surfaces aft of the wing trailing edge and the upper surfaces of the horizontal tail. The colour swept up from the trailing edge in an arc to the anti-glare panel under the windshield. A 6 inch wide red stripe separated this Olive Drab area from the natural metal nose area. Wings and the underside of the tail remained in natural metal finish. Codes were applied in the usual way, but in white instead of black. Where ETO bands were applied, they were also in white on tailplane upper surfaces. Several 343rd FS aircraft also had a rearing 'mustang' on the rudder, some on the fin, most in red, but sometimes in black.

In November 1944, rudder colours were introduced: dark green for the 338th FS and yellow for the 343rd FS. The 38th Squadron did not paint their rudders until March 1945, when they were painted red.

During September 1944, the 338th FS had also added a further 6 inch wide band aft of the nose checker-board, in solid dark green. This band and the Squadron rudders were in the same dark green shade as that used in the Group nose colours.

The final embellishment added to the 55th Fighter Group's aircraft was a 4 inch wide red stripe bordering the anti-glare area and around and below the canopy. This first began to appear on 343rd FS aircraft in December 1944, and was then applied to all Group aircraft from March 1945.

The 55th were not given to conformity when it came to painting instructions. Their use of various theatre markings for example was haphazard to say the least. For modelling, photos are really indispensable. Unfortunately, there is a comparative dearth of published and available information on this Group, which was a hard working, businesslike outfit, but with none of the great aces or famous leaders of some of the other Groups.

Right: *Well-worn P-38H-1-LO 42-66718 of the 343rd Fighter Squadron, 55th Fighter Group, coming in to land at its home base of Nuthampstead in late 1943. Note the blue and white ying-yang marking on the wheel hub. The aircraft arrived on the unit in October but was transferred to the 554th Fighter Training School in December. See colour profile 465.*

Centre right: *Major Edward B. Giller of the 343rd Fighter Squadron, 55th Fighter Group in his P-51D-15-NA, 44-14985 on a bright day early in 1945. Named* The Millie G, *the aircraft shows the most distinctive phase of the 343rd's markings. Note the well-worn type identity bands on the wings. See colour profile 479.*

Lower right: *Texan Col. Jack S. Jenkins' P-38H-5-LO, 42-67074, the first of four* Texas Rangers, *seen at Nuthampstead in October 1943. The national insignia on the tailboom still retains the red surround which should have been replaced by Insignia Blue in August. Sgt. Robert Sand created the 'cowboy' artwork on the nose which was painted on a panel and was transferred from aircraft to aircraft. See colour profiles 390-393.*

38th Fighter Squadron

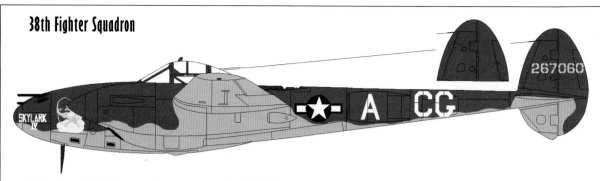

382 Maj. Mark K. Shipman. Flew a tour with the 14th FG in the Mediterranean before joining the 55th FG as Flt. CO, then CO 38th FS. Claimed 2.5 air kills (1.5 air kills with 55th FG) and 2 damaged. With 55th FG 4/43 until 2/44.

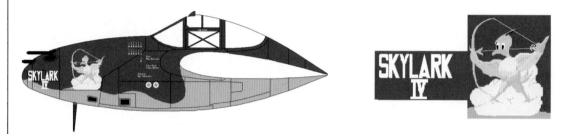

383 Maj. Mark K. Shipman.

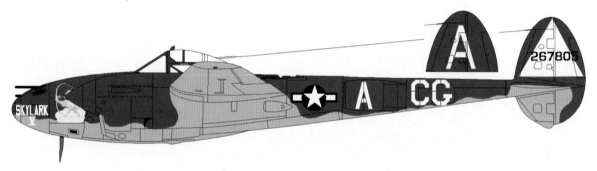

384 Maj. Mark K. Shipman.

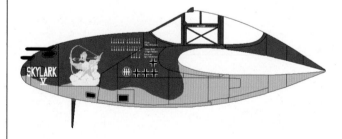

385 Maj. Mark K. Shipman.

1/72 Scale

382/383: 'Skylark IV', P-38H-5-LO 42-67060, flown by Shipman at the start of 1944. OD and NG scheme. White codes, yellow serial. Two swastika kill marks, yellow brooms for fighter sweeps, several with red umbrella superimposed to indicate top cover sweeps.

384/385: P-38J-10-LO 42-67805 'Skylark V', February 1944. OD and NG, white codes and 38th FS triangle. Black serial. One Italian and four German kill marks, many more missions markings. Gun door carrying art was switched from previous aircraft.

38th Fighter Squadron

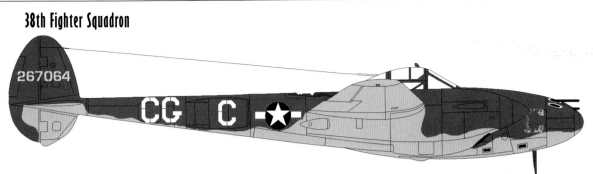

386 P-38H-5-LO 42-67064 of 38th FS in early 1944. Pilot unknown. Aircraft lost in an accident in January 1944.

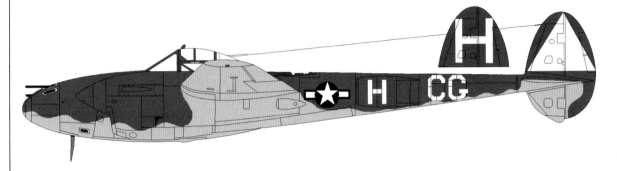

387 P-38J of 38th FS, spring 1944. Serial not displayed, pilot not known.

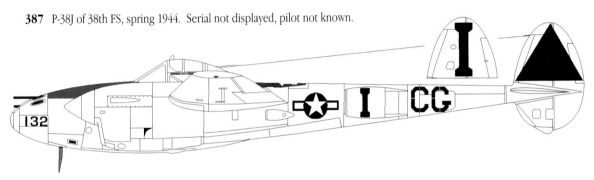

388 P-38J-10-LO 42-68132 of 38th FS Spring 1944. Pilot assignment not known.

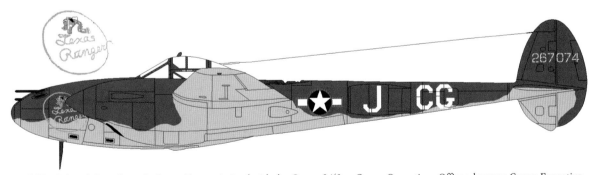

389 Col. Jack S. Jenkins, De Leon, Texas. Arrived with the Group 9/43 as Group Operations Officer, became Group Executive Officer. CO from 6/2/44 until 10/4/44 when he was lost to flak near Coulommiers, became POW.

1/72 Scale

386: P-38H-5-LO 42-67064 of 38th FS in early 1944. OD and NG with white codes and yellow serial. Remains of overpainted 'C' can be seen on nose. Pilot unknown. Aircraft lost in an accident January 1944.

387: P-38J of 38th FS, spring 1944. Serial not displayed, pilot not known. OD and grey scheme, codes and Squadron symbol in white.

388: P-38J-10-LO 42-68132 of 38th FS Spring 1944. NMF overall, with codes and 38th triangle in black. Last 3 of serial in 9 inch high digits on nose, also in black. Pilot assignment not known.

389/390: Jenkins flew four P-38s with the Group, all named 'Texas Ranger'. First of the four was this P38H-5-LO 42-67074. OD and NG scheme, with white codes and yellow serial. Star and bar still outlined in red in October 1943, two months after this should have been replaced by blue. Personal insignia on gun door was removed from aircraft to aircraft and was therefore the same on all, originally painted on by propeller specialist Sgt. Bob Sand. This aircraft was written off in a crash landing at Debden 13/11/43, owing to battle damage. Crew Chief T/Sgt Causey, Armourer Sgt. Valentine.

38th Fighter Squadron

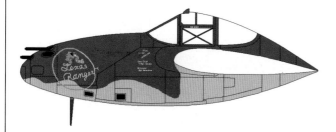

390   Col. Jack S. Jenkins, De Leon, Texas.

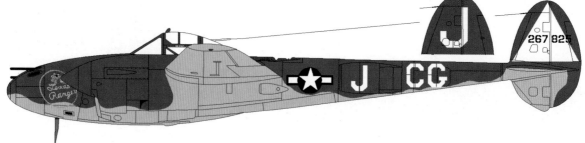

391   Col. Jack S. Jenkins, De Leon, Texas.

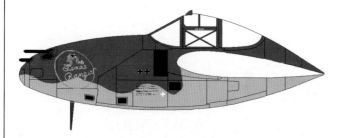

392   Col. Jack S. Jenkins, De Leon, Texas.

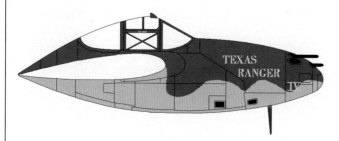

393   Col. Jack S. Jenkins, De Leon, Texas.

1/72 Scale

391/392/393: Fourth and last of the 'Rangers' was this P-38J-10-LO 42-67825, this being the aircraft Jenkins was shot down in. OD and NG with white codes and Squadron triangle. Serial has been repainted in black, and black panels added to the nose for crew details not yet added. Two crosses for his two aerial kills. 'Texas Ranger IV' on starboard side of nose in yellow. The mission on which he was lost was also the groups first 'Droopsnoot' mission. The same ground crew cared for all of his aircraft.

38th Fighter Squadron

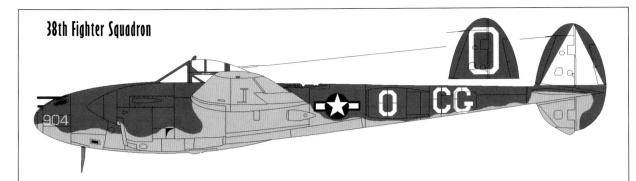

394 Lt. Willard L. Kreft. With 38th FS from 4/43 until 5/44. Claimed a half share in an FW 190 destroyed in the air, shared with Maj. Milton Joel on 3/11/43.

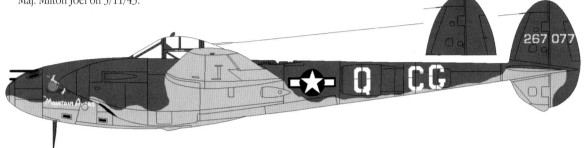

395 Capt. Jerry H. Ayers. With 38th FS from 5/42 until 5/44. Claimed 1 Bf 109 destroyed in the air on 29/11/43. His career was curtailed by ear problems.

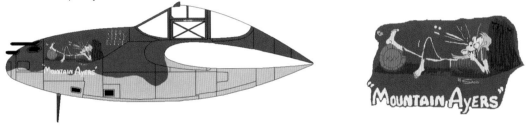

396 Capt. Jerry H. Ayers. With 38th FS from 5/42 until 5/44.

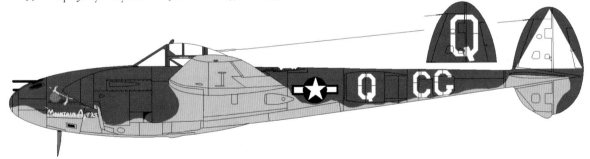

397 Capt. Jerry H. Ayers. With 38th FS from 5/42 until 5/44.

1/72 Scale

394: P-38J-10-LO, 44-267904, flown by Kreft early in 1944. It wears the standard OD and grey scheme, with white codes and Squadron triangle marking. Although the serial has not been repainted on the fin, the 'last three' are carried on the nose in yellow figures, 9 inches high.

395/396: P-38H-5-LO 42-67077 as flown by Ayers in December 1943. Standard OD and NG scheme with white codes and yellow serial. Nose art, 'Mountain Ayers', painted by Sgt. Bob Sand, was carried on the gun door, so that it could be transferred to later aircraft easily. Mission marks are yellow brooms,

some with red umbrellas superimposed, for top-cover escort missions.

397: Ayers' later aircraft was this P-38J-5-LO 42-67277, in March 1944. Again in the standard OD and grey finish. Now with the white triangle of the 38th FS added, and the individual aircraft code letter on inner vertical tail surfaces, 30 inches high.

38th Fighter Squadron

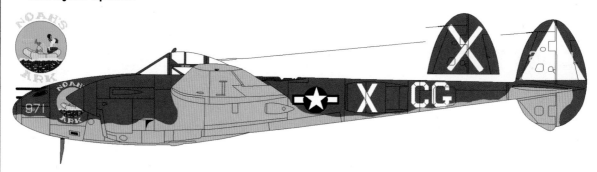

398 Lt. Noah R. Tipton, Calderwood, Tennessee. Joined 38th FS 12/43 until 21/5/44, when he was downed by ground fire to become a POW. Claimed 1 air and 1 ground victory.

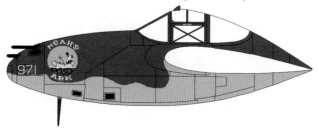

399 Lt. Noah R. Tipton, Calderwood, Tennessee.

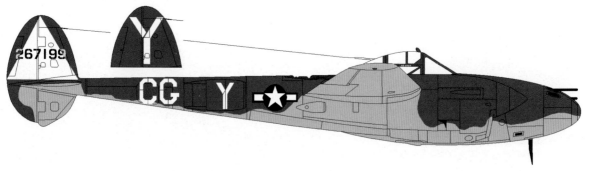

400 P-38J-5-LO 42-67199 of 38th FS, March 1944. Pilot unknown. This aircraft was transferred to the 496th FTG and lost in an accident in May 1944.

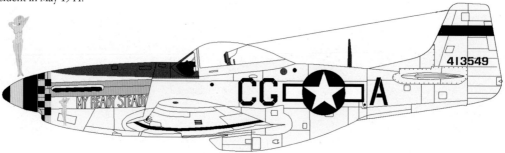

401 Capt. Donald H. Snell. With 38th FS from 2/44 until 9/44. Became Squadron CO. Claimed 1 FW 190 in the air.

1/72 Scale

398/399: P-38J-10-LO 44-26971 'Noah's Ark' flown by Tipton in April/May 1944. Aircraft crash-landed at RAF Manston 24 April 1944 by 1st Lt. William R. Monty. It is in standard OD and NG finish, with white codes and 38th FS triangle. Serial not repainted on tail but 'last three' on nose in yellow 9 inch high digits.

400: P-38J-5-LO 42-67199 of 38th FS, March 1944. Standard OD and NG scheme, with white codes and Squadron triangle. Serial has been re-painted in black over the triangle, and individual code 'Y' repeated in white on

inner faces of tail, 30 inches high. Pilot unknown.

401: P-51D-5-NA 44-13549 flown by Snell. NMF with standard green/yellow nose colours, black codes, serial and ETO bands. Name 'My Ready Steady' is yellow with black outline. Vargas girl pin-up varnished on ahead of name.

38th Fighter Squadron

402 Capt. Merle M. Coons, Gresham, Oregon. Joined 38th FS 6/44 until 12/44 then returned to USA. Claimed 3 Bf 109s and 2 FW 190s in the air, plus a probable Bf 109. All victories in P-51s.

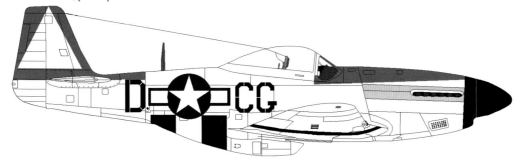

403 1st Lt. Edwin B. Lawrence, Tennessee. To 38th FS from 6/44 until 14/10/44. KIA on this date. During a formation takeoff for a mission he was caught in his leader's propwash, hit a tree and was killed in the subsequent crash.

404 1st Lt. Alfred E. Carr Jr, Slidell, Louisiana. To 38th FS 9/44 to 20/2/45 when he was downed by flak and became a POW. Claimed 1.5 ground victories in January 1945.

405 1 Lt. Arthur L. Thorsen. To 38th FS from 2/44 until 10/44. Claimed 1 FW 190 in the air.   **1/72 Scale**

402: P-51D-10-NA 44-14068, 'The Worry Bird', was Coon's assigned Mustang in November 1944. NMF overall with black ETO bands on wings and horizontal tail surfaces. D-Day stripes under rear fuselage only. Three kill flags ahead of windscreen. Standard Group colours on nose. Aircraft passed to Lt. Carr, who named it 'Little Joe', when Coon went home. Crew Chief S/Sgt. Duncan, Asst. C/Chief Sgt. Holderman, Armourer Cpl. Weens. See 404.

403: Lawrence was killed in this P-51D-5-NA, 44-13701, shown in the first markings applied to the Group's Mustangs. NMF overall with black depot-

applied type recognition markings on the nose. Black ETO bands on horizontal tail and wings. D-Day stripes under rear fuselage only. Vertical tail and top of rear fuselage are OD and the 38th FS triangle symbol is white. This style of markings lasted only 2 or 3 weeks. Black codes.

404: 44-14068 while flown by Lt. Carr. Code and artwork changed, all stripes and bands removed. Lost 20/2/45 when Carr baled out near Stuttgart.

405: P-51D-5-NA 44-13747 flown by Thorsen September 1944. NMF with black codes, serial and ETO bands on wings and horizontal tail.

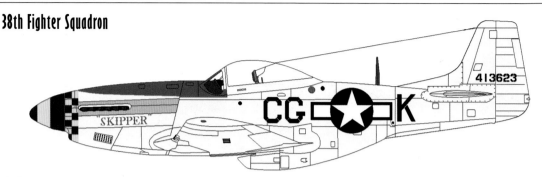

406 2nd Lt. David G. Elliott, San Francisco, California. To 38th FS 5/44 to 10/8/44 when he was downed by the explosion of a train he had bombed. He evaded and returned to England on 27/8/44 then to USA.

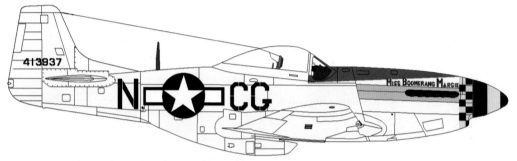

407 Capt. Lester Earls ('Buck'), with 38th FS 12/43 to 9/44.
Lt. David F. Jewell Jr, 38th FS 7/44 to 3/45. Claimed 1.5 air victories plus .5 ground.

408 Capt. McCauley Clark, served with 38th FS 8/44 to 1/45, then to 55th FG Headquarters until end of war. Claimed 2 FW 190s and 2.5 Bf 109s in the air, plus 1 damaged. He served 2 tours.

409 Capt. John Dave Landers ('Firewall'), Wilson, Oklahoma. Served a tour with 49th FG in the Pacific, shot down 2 Bettys, 2 Zeros and 2 Oscars. After serving in Training Command in USA he joined the 38th FS on 27/4/44, until 9/44 when he went to 357th FG. Claimed 1 FW 190 and 3 Me 410s in the air while with the 55th FG, all in P-38Js. Later CO of 78th FG. **1/72 Scale**

406: P-51D-5-NA 44-13623 'Skipper' was Elliott's Mustang and the aircraft he was lost in. NMF with standard nose colouring, black codes and serial. Name is red. No bands or stripes carried.

407: P-51D-5-NA 44-13937 'Miss Boomerang Margie', flown by Earls, then passed on to Jewell. NMF with no stripes or bands. Black codes and serial, yellow/green nose colours and name, which was on both sides of nose.

408: On his second tour, Clark flew this P-51D-25-NA, 44-72784. Black codes and serial. Five swastika kill marks ahead of different artwork. Green/

yellow Group nose markings.

409: P-51D-5-NA 44-13823 flown by Landers in July 1944. Aircraft is NMF overall, with OD vertical tail. D-Day stripes on lower surfaces of wings and aft fuselage. Six Japanese and 7 German kill flags for his air and ground credits at the time. 'Big Beautiful Doll' is red with black outline, and was on both sides of the cowling. Aircraft was lost 20 February 1945, 1st Lt. Albert M. Koenig baled out near Ettlebruck, Luxembourg, after flak damage, returning to unit in 3 days.

38th Fighter Squadron

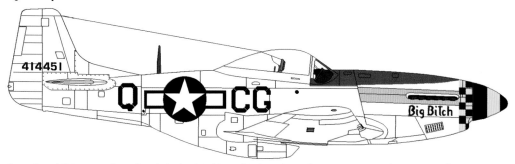

410 Capt. Donald E. Penn. Served with 38th FS 8/43 until 3/45. Claimed 2 air victories and 1 on ground.

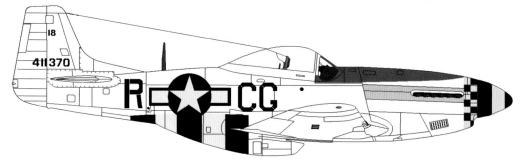

411 Lt. Robert L. Sill, Fort Dodge, Iowa. To 38th FS from 9/44 to 20/2/45 when he was shot down and KIA by flak near Nuremburg, Germany.

412 Capt. McCauley Clark, served with 38th FS 8/44 to 1/45. Then to 55th FG Headquarters until end of war. Claimed 2 FW 190s and 2.5 Bf 109s in the air, plus 1 damaged. He served 2 tours.

413 Capt. Oscar B. Clifton. With 38th FS 4/44 until 10/44. 1 ground victory.

1/72 Scale

410: Penn's aircraft in early 1945 was P-51D-10-NA 44-14451 'Big Bitch'. NMF with standard Group nose colours, black codes and serial, name green. No bands or stripes.

411: P-51K-1-NT 44-11370 was Sill's assigned aircraft and the one in which he was KIA. NMF with standard Group nose markings, black codes and serial, and '18' on fin, significance unknown. Remaining D-Day stripes under rear fuselage have had the white stripes greyed out, as also the fuselage insignia. Note D-Day stripes in reversed colours.

412: This P-51D-10-NA 44-14296 was Clark's aircraft during his first tour, in September-October 1944. NMF with standard Group nose colours, it has a black ETO band on vertical tail only. Black codes and serial, 3 black swastika kill marks, pilot's name on canopy frame is also black.

413: P-51D-5-NA 44-13723, 'One Musthang', Clifton's assigned aircraft in September-October 1944. NMF with no bands or stripes. Group green and yellow nose colours. Black codes and serial. Crew Chief T/Sgt. Maurice Pailly.

38th Fighter Squadron

414 Lt. Billy Clemmons. To 38th FS 8/44 until 4/45. Claimed 3.5 air kills plus .5 on the ground. Flew 62 missions.

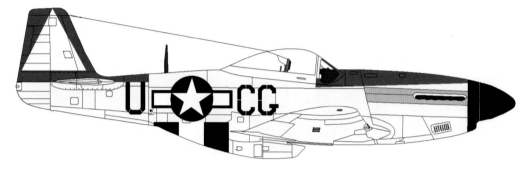

415 1st Lt. Robert M. Littlefield, San Francisco, California. Shot down by flak, 13/8/44 attacking a bridge at Barentin, France. Evaded and returned, then to USA.

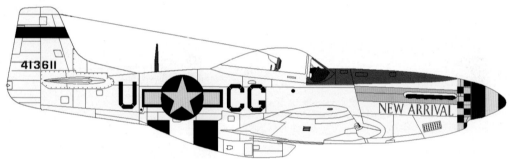

416 1st Lt. Clifford C. Sherman. To 38th FS 5/44 until 10/44. Claimed 3.5 Bf 109s and 1 FW 190 in the air.

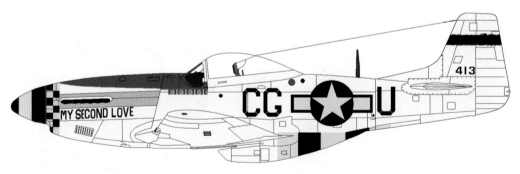

417 1st Lt. Clifford C. Sherman.

1/72 Scale

414: *P-51D-15-NA 44-15492 was Clemmons aircraft in April 1945. NMF with red edge to anti-glare panel and around canopy. Group nose colours in yellow/green, and red rudder of 38th FS which was painted on from March 1945. Eight kill marks on canopy are probably for the aircraft rather than the pilot.*

415: *P-51D-5-NA, 44-13577, in which Littlefield was lost, as it appeared in July 1944. NMF with OD on vertical tail surfaces and upper rear fuselage, 38th FS triangle on tail in white. Black codes, nose and spinner. D-Day stripes under rear fuselage only. No ETO bands.*

416: *P-51D-5-NA 44-13611 'New Arrival' was Sherman's aircraft in August/ September 1944. NMF with standard group nose colours. Black codes, serial and ETO band on vertical tail only. D-Day stripes under rear fuselage, star and bar is greyed out, name is red.*

417: *P-51D-5-NA of 55th FS, possibly same aircraft as above.*

38th Fighter Squadron

418 Lt. Dudley M. Amoss, Greenwich, Connecticut. To 38th FS from 8/44 until 21/3/45 when he was shot down by ground fire, and became POW. Claimed 5.5 air kills plus 1.5 on ground.

419 Capt. Earl R. Fryer, Boyertown, Pennsylvania. Joined 38th FS 5/44 until KIA on 8/11/44. Hit while strafing a train and killed in crash-landing near Renkum, Holland. Claimed 3 Bf 109s and 1 FW 190 in the air plus one ground kill.

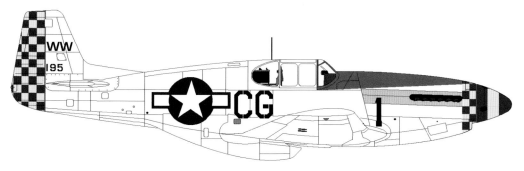

420 Trainer P-51B-1-NA 43 -12195 as used by 38th FS 11/44.

421 Trainer P-51B, CG-3, serial unknown, as it had not been re-painted, in use in early 1945.　　　**1/72 Scale**

418: P-51D-15-NA 44-15123 'Queenie' was the aircraft Amoss was shot down in. NMF with black codes and serial, yellow/green Group nose colours. Name in red.

419: P-51D-5-NA 44-13084 'Spunk Town' was Fryer's aircraft most of his tour, and in which he was KIA. Shown in July 1944, it wears the earliest Mustang scheme, and still has the black depot-applied nose colouring. Vertical tail and aft upper fuselage in OD. D-Day stripes under rear fuselage, otherwise overall NMF. Name is black on red arrowhead panel. Codes black.

420: P-51B-1-NA 43 -12195 as used by 38th FS in November 1944. NMF overall with Group green/yellow nose, black codes and serial, and 'WW' for 'War Weary' on fin. The green and yellow checks on rudder signified a training aircraft. No stripes or bands carried.

421: P-51B, CG-3, serial unknown, as it has not been re-painted, in use in early 1945. Nose and rudder in Group colours, black codes and 'WW' on fin. No bands or stripes. Whole aircraft is well-worn looking. Fitted with Malcolm hood and fin fillet.

338th Fighter Squadron

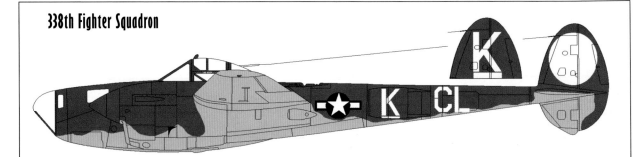

422 1st Lt. William Stroud, Bombardier. Came to the 55th after completing a tour on B-17 bombers. Was flown by various pilots on several missions in the Group's droopsnoot aircraft, including the first ever, on 10/4/44, to Coulommiers airfield.

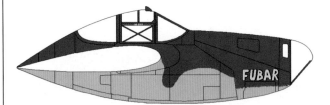

423 1st Lt. William Stroud, Bombardier.

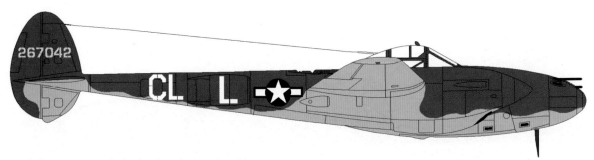

424 P-38 H-5-LO 42-67042 of 338th FS early 1944.

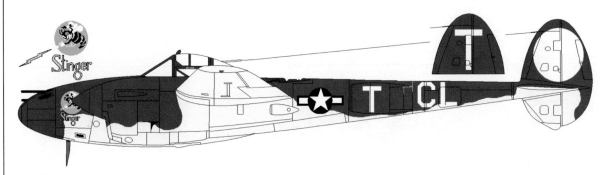

425 Lt. Thomas D. Schank, Greeley, Colorado. With 338th FS from April 1944 to October 1944. Claimed 5 air kills, 1 in P-38 and 4 in P-51. All were Bf 109s.

1/72 Scale

422/423: P-38J-10-LO 42-67704 droopsnoot aircraft 'Fubar' as used by the 55th FG from April 1944. OD and NG with white codes and 338th FS circle. Name is yellow with black outline and is a contemporary abbreviation for 'F****d Up Beyond All Recognition'. It was later transferred to the 56th FG and then to the Mediterranean.

424: P-38 H-5-LO 42-67042 of 338th FS early 1944. Among the earliest aircraft received by the Group, it is in standard OD and NG scheme with serial in yellow and newly applied codes in white.

425: P-38J-15-LO 42-104106, 'Stinger', was Schank's mount in May/June 1944. It has received a coat of OD on top surfaces, over the original NMF in which it was received. Codes and Squadron circle are white. 'Droopsnoot' simulation has been painted out, also with OD, and lightning bolt obliterated from artwork on port side only. Art is identical both sides and handed to face forward. See 426, 440.

338th Fighter Squadron

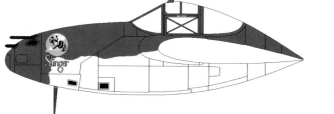

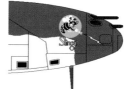

426 Lt. Thomas D. Schank, Greeley, Colorado.

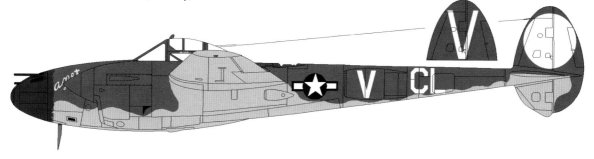

427 Maj. Thomas Ace White, Hillsboro, Oregon. Flew a tour with the 82nd FG in the Mediterranean, prior to joining the 338th FS in 1943, until July 1944 when he returned to the USA, tour complete. He scored 6 air victories in the Mediterranean but did not add any while with the 55th FG.

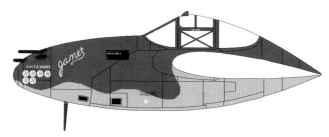

428 Maj. Thomas Ace White, Hillsboro, Oregon.

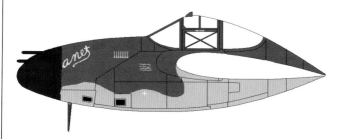

429 Maj. Thomas Ace White, Hillsboro, Oregon.

1/72 Scale

426: P-38J-15-LO 42-104106, 'Stinger', was Schank's mount in May/June 1944. It has received a coat of OD on top surfaces, over the original NMF in which it was received. Codes and Squadron circle are white. Droopsnoot has been painted out, also with OD, obliterating the lightning bolt from artwork on port side only. Art is identical both sides and handed to face forward. See 425, 440.

427: This P-38J was White's assigned aircraft in June 1944. OD and NG with white codes and Squadron circle symbol. See 432, 433.

428: This P-38J was White's assigned aircraft in June 1944. OD and NG with white codes and Squadron circle symbol. Pod shows victory markings and name 'Janet' as originally applied.

429: This P-38J was White's assigned aircraft in June 1944. OD and NG with white codes and Squadron circle symbol. The droopsnoot simulation was later added, and this in turn was over sprayed with fresh OD paint. Serial not displayed.

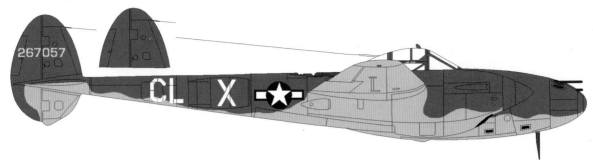

430 1st Lt. Delbert Blount, hospitalised 31/1/44, severely wounded in left arm. Re-joined group, then lost on 21/7/44 in P-51D 44-13807, crashed near Kempten, Germany, engine trouble. He became a POW.

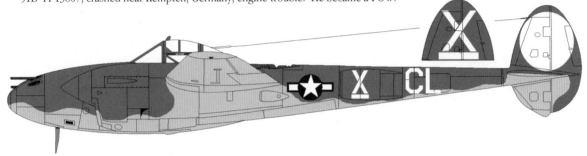

431 P-38J with 338th FS, serial unknown, lost in a crash landing near Wormingford in early 1944. Bar under X signifies more than one aircraft with this code within the squadron.

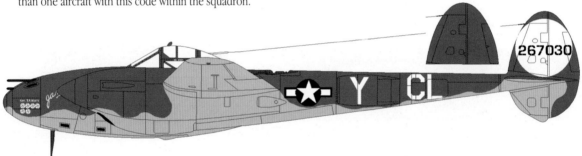

432 Maj. Thomas Ace White, Hillsboro, Oregon.

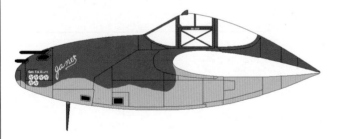

433 Maj. Thomas Ace White, Hillsboro, Oregon.

1/72 Scale

430: P-38H-5-LO 42-67057 of 338th FS, December 1943. OD and grey scheme, white codes, serial in yellow. Aircraft was written off after crash-landing at Leiston due to battle damage 31/1/44.

431: P-38J with 338th FS, serial unknown, lost in a crash landing near Wormingford in early 1944. OD and grey scheme with codes and squadron symbol in white. Bar under X signifies more than one aircraft with this code within the squadron.

432/433: This P-38H-5-LO 42-67030 was flown by White in early 1944. It is in

standard OD and grey scheme, with white codes and circle symbol of the 338th FS, on which the serial has been repainted in black Six swastikas on white circles on nose represent his victories with the 82nd FG. Pilot's name above them in white and the name 'Janet' is yellow. Code 'Y' has not been repeated on inner tail surfaces. See 427-429.

338th Fighter Squadron

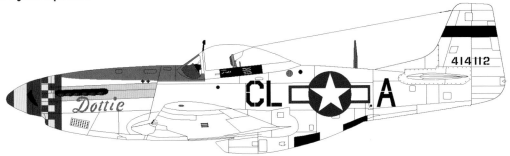

434 P-51D-10-NA 44-14112 'Dottie' in late 1944, pilot assignment not known.

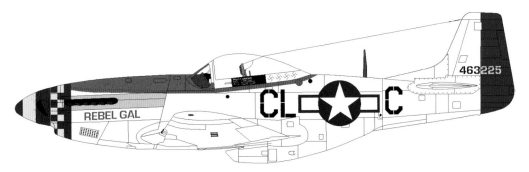

435 P-51D-10-NA 44-14223 was Col. Righetti's aircraft, shown after he relinquished it. New pilot unknown.

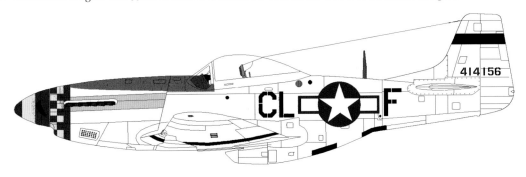

436 Lt. Archie S. Dargan. With 338th FS from 1/45 until 9/45. Claimed 2 FW 190s in the air and one ground kill.

437 Capt. Samuel D. Gevorkian. With 338th FS from 6/44 till 8/8/45, when he was killed in a flying accident in Southern Germany. Claimed 2 Bf 109s and 6 ground kills.

1/72 Scale

434: *P-51D-10-NA 44-14112. NMF overall, with the Group nose colours plus the green band of the 338th FS behind the checks. Remains of D-Day stripes under rear fuselage only. Black codes, serial and ETO band on vertical tail only. Black panel on canopy frame with crew details in white. Name is red. 2 kill crosses on cowl, later increased to 4.*

435: *P-51D-10-NA 44-14223. NMF with no bands or stripes, partial green band aft of Group nose colours, with green rudder of 338th FS. Black codes and crew panel on canopy frame, serial black on fin, yellow on rudder.*

436: *P-51D-20-NA 44-63225 'Rebel Gal' was Dargan's aircraft in March/April 1945. NMF, no stripes or bands, solid green band aft of Group nose markings, green rudder of 338th FS. Codes black, serial black and yellow. Red name and border around canopy and anti-glare panel. Black panel on canopy carries crew names in white. Four swastikas on canopy frame.*

437: *P-51D-10-NA 44-14156, as flown by Gevorkian, late 1944. NMF overall, black ETO bands, codes and serial Minimal D-Day stripes under rear fuselage only. Green and yellow nose markings with 338th FS solid green band.*

338th Fighter Squadron

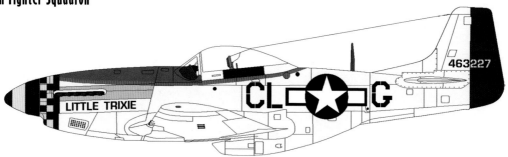

438 Capt. Carroll D. Henry, with 338th FS 9/44 to 6/45. Claimed 1.5 aerial kills plus 5 on the ground. Often flew as Lt.Col. Righetti's wingman.

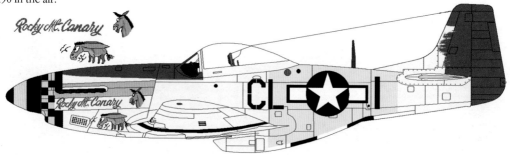

439 Lt. Col. Wendell J. Kelly, HQ 55th FG from 6/44 until 11/44. Previous service with 367th FG, Ninth Air Force. Claimed 1 FW 190 in the air.

440 Lt. Thomas D. Schank, Greeley, Colorado. He flew this aircraft from 7/44.

441 1st Lt. Russell C. Haworth, Wichita Falls, Texas. In 338th FS 7/44 until 12/44. Shot down 4.5 Bf 109s and half a DFS 230 in the air. 'Krazy Kid', P-51D-5-NA 44-13642, was Haworth's aircraft for most of his tour.

1/72 Scale

438: Henry's P-51D-20-NA, 44-63227, April 1945. NMF, no bands or stripes. Black codes and name 'Little Trixie'. Serial black on fin, yellow on dark green 338th FS rudder. Nose colours backed by Squadron green band. Red edging to anti-glare panel and around cockpit.

439: Kelly's assigned P-51D-5-NA 44-13607, September 1944. Maintained by 338th FS, has 338th's green stripe aft of Group colours on nose. D-Day stripes under rear fuselage, ETO bands on wings and horizontal tail, codes and serial, black. 'Mary Bell III' red with black outline. Single swastika kill mark.

440: Schank's P-51D-5-NA 44-13668. 'Rocky Mountain Canary' is local slang for a mule. NMF, black ETO bands on horizontal surfaces. D-Day stripes left on extreme fuselage underside only, where they have been removed is still discoloured. Remains of early OD tail markings peeling off. See 425, 426.

441: 44-13642. NMF with remains of OD tail as first applied to Group's P-51s. Dark green rudder and nose band. ETO bands (on wings only) and codes black. Name red on yellow. Finish well worn. Crew Chief Sgt. Clark, Asst. Crew Chief Sgt. Gallego, Amr. Cpl. Todey.

338th Fighter Squadron

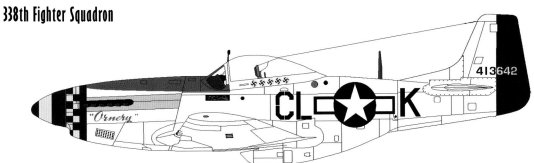

442 1st Lt. Leedom Kirk John, Coatesville, Pennsylvania. With 338th FS 12/44 until 9/45. Claimed 5 ground victories, including 3 FW 200s on 16/4/45.

443 Lt. Robert E. Black, was with 338th FS 3/45 until 7/45.

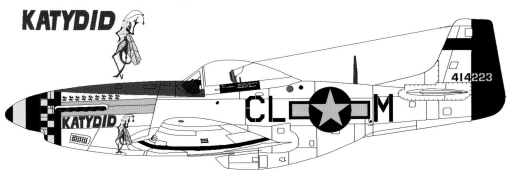

444 Lt. Col. Elwyn Guido Righetti ('Eager El'), Luis Obispo, California. Joined 55th HQ 22/10/44, flew with 338th FS and became Squadron CO 26/11/44. Group CO 22/2/45 until KIA on 17/4/45 near Dresden. Shot down by flak while strafing an airfield and then probably murdered by civilians. No trace ever found. He claimed 7.5 air and 27 ground victories and died on his 30th birthday.

445 1st Lt. Walter J. Konantz, Lamar, Missouri. With the 338th FS from 1944 to 4/45. Claimed 4 air victories. His brother Harold served in the same squadron.

1/72 Scale

442: *John's P-51D-5-NA 44-13642, 'Ornery', April 1945. NMF, Group nose colours, with 338th FS green band and rudder. Black codes, serial black and yellow, name red. Crew Chief S/Sgt. Robert W. Clark.*

443: *Black's assigned P-51K-5-NT 44-11639, 'The Grim Reaper'. NMF with black codes, serial black and yellow. Squadron green nose band, rudder and name. Red edge to anti-glare panel and around canopy.*

444: *Righetti's P-51D-10-NA 44-14223 in early 1945. Named after his wife, Cathryn. NMF overall, with Group nose markings, rudder in 338th FS green.*

Black ETO bands on wings and tail surfaces. Black codes and panel on canopy frame, with crew names in yellow. Grasshopper is green and yellow, name green. Nine kill markings are broken black swastikas on yellow discs. Crew Chief T/Sgt. Easton, Asst Sgt. Hunter, Amr Sgt. Robinson.

445: *P-51D-10-NA 44-14278, Walter Konantz' first assigned aircraft. He kept it only a short time, scored first victory in it 11/9/44. NMF with D-Day stripes under rear fuselage only. ETO bands on wings and tail. Group nose colours, with 338th FS green band. Name in red, both sides of cowling. See 449, 450.*

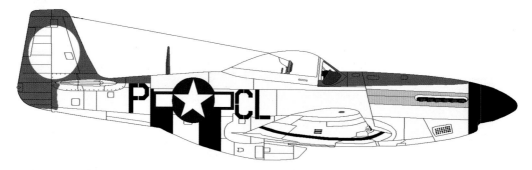

446 Lt. Col. John L. McGinn, Minnesota. Served a tour with the 347th FG in the Solomons area before coming to the 55th FG. Credited with 3 Zekes and a probable. Scored 1 Bf 109 and 1 FW 190 with the 338th FS, plus 2 damaged Bf 109s.

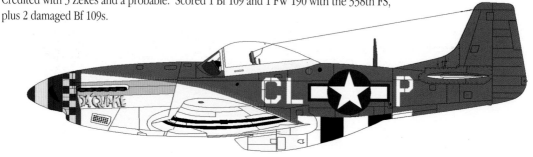

447 Lt. Col. John L. McGinn, Minnesota. This aircraft was bellied in on a beach at Cap Ferret, France, 26/8/44, by 1st Lt. Sam Gevorkian, where it stayed until recovered for the Musée de l'Air, 3/5/81.

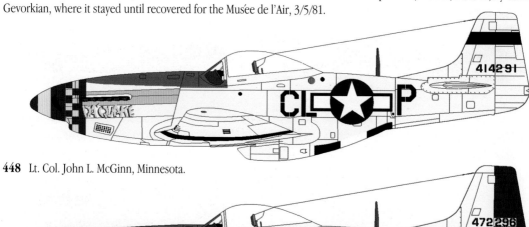

448 Lt. Col. John L. McGinn, Minnesota.

449 Last of McGinn's aircraft, passed to Lt. Walter Konantz when McGinn went home, tour completed. Ground crew for McGinn and Konantz were Crew Chief S/Sgt. James C. Seibert, Asst. Sgt. Ted Alexander, and Amr Cpl. 'Pops' Spaulding

1/72 Scale

446: P-51D-5-NA 44-13740, McGinn's first such assigned, but crashed before first mission in P-51s. Earliest Group Mustang scheme: NMF, aft fuselage and vertical tail in OD with 338th FS circle symbol. Black nose, codes and ETO bands on wings and horizontal tail. D-Day stripes under rear fuselage only. Name probably not applied. Aircraft repaired, then to 359th FG as CV-A.
447: McGinn's next P-51D-5-NA 44-13954. Red-bordered OD and NMF scheme as used by 343rd FS. D-Day stripes on lower wings and fuselage, Group green and yellow colours on nose. Checkerboard backed with an 8 inch band of

dark green only on 338th FS aircraft. Name yellow with green shadow.
448: Second 'Da'Quake', P-51D-10-NA 44-14291. NMF overall, black ETO bands on wings and tail, D-Day stripes under rear fuselage. Group colours on nose, with 338th FS green band. Codes and serial black. Lost power 7/10/ 44, 40 miles SW of Leipzig, crashed and burned. Capt. Peter Dempsey POW.
449: P-51D-20-NA 44-72296. NMF overall, black codes and serial. No bands or stripes, Group colours on nose with green 338th FS band. Rudder now painted same dark green. See 445, 450.

338th Fighter Squadron

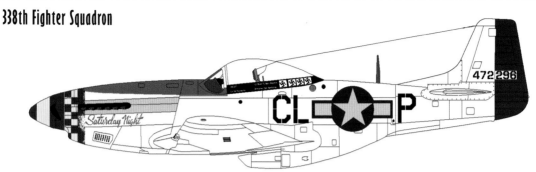

450 1st Lt. Walter J. Konantz, Lamar, Missouri. With 338th FS from 1944 to 4/45. Claimed 4 air victories. His brother served in the same squadron: 2nd Lt. Harold J. Konantz. To 338th FS in 3/45 until shot down in this aircraft by a nervous gunner in a B-17, 7/4/45. Became POW. Flew 7 missions, no claims.

451 1st Lt. Kenneth Lashbrook, with 338th FS 9/44 until 4/45. Claimed 2 Bf 109s and 1 Me 262 in the air.

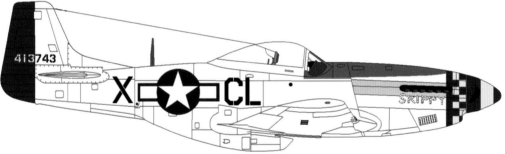

452 Lt. Elmer L. Mercurio ('Buster') served with 338th FS from 5/44 to 11/44.
Capt. William F. McGill was with the 338th FS from 1/45 to 3/5/45 when he was killed in a taxiing accident. Previously flew a tour in the MTO. He was the 55th FG's last wartime casualty.

453 Capt. Darrel S. Cramer, Ogden, Utah. Served with 339th FS, 347th FG in Pacific. Made 2 claims for Japanese kills. Joined 338th FS 7/44 until 2/45, then to HQ until end of war. Claimed 5.5 Bf 109s and 1 FW 190 in the air, flown by Emil 'Bully' Lang, 173-victory Luftwaffe ace, who was KIA. Crew Chief S/Sgt. R.W. Parkhurst, Asst. Crew Chief Sgt. G. Debanardi, Amr. Sgt. T. Jung. **1/72 Scale**

450: *P-51D-20-NA 44-72296, to Walter Konantz in 9/44 until 4/45, then to his brother, Harold. NMF, green rudder and nose band of 338th FS. Group nose colours, greyed out star and bar, whole aircraft well-worn. Name both sides, transferred from 44-14278. Crew names yellow on black canopy rail. See 445, 449.*
451: *Lashbrook's P-51D, serial unknown, in August 1944. NMF with black ETO bands and codes. OD on vertical tail. Heavy discolouring under rear fuselage, where D-day bands removed. Name in Group nose colours.*
452: *P-51D-5-NA 44-13743, assigned to Mercurio until end of tour, then to*

McGill. Destroyed in a taxiing accident April 1945. McGill killed 3 May. NMF with Group nose colours, 338th FS green band and rudder. 'Skippy' red with white polka dots, on both sides.
453: *Cramer's P-51D-10-NA 44-14121 'Mick #5', 9/44. Very worn. NMF, Group nose markings, 338th FS green band and rudder. Black ETO band on fin only. D-Day stripes under rear fuselage only. Dark green panel on lower nose with 'Z' in yellow. Two Japanese, 9 German swastika kill marks. Name red, outlined black. Pilot and crew names on canopy frame in black.*

343rd Fighter Squadron

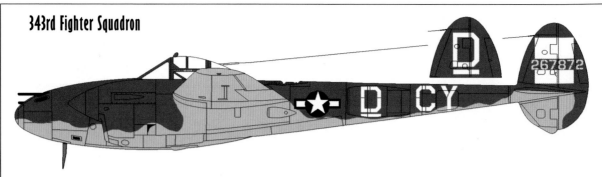

454 Capt. Frank E. Birtciel, Sylvia, Kansas. Joined 343rd FS 8/43 until 4/45. Bailed out 3/4/45 over Belgium, engine seized. Returned to unit in three days. Claimed 5 victories, all on the ground.

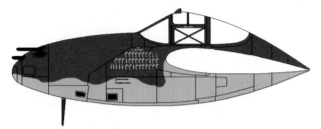

455 Capt. Frank E. Birtciel, Sylvia, Kansas.

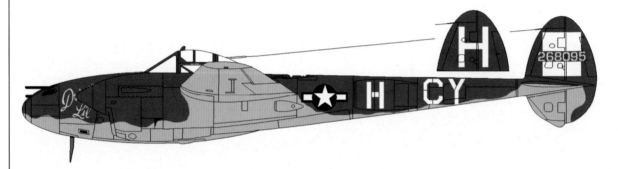

456 1st Lt. Russell W. Erb, with 343rd FS from unknown date until 11/44. He transferred to 354th FG, Ninth Air Force, and was KIA flying a P-47.

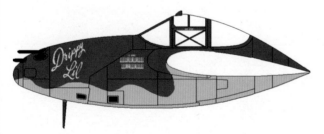

457 1st Lt. Russell W. Erb.

1/72 Scale

454/455: Birtciel flew this P-38J-10-LO 42-67872 in May 1944. OD and NG scheme, with codes and 343rd FS Squadron square symbol in white. Serial and mission tally in yellow.

456/457: P-38J-10-LO 42-68095, 'Drippy Lil' was Erb's assigned aircraft in May 1944. OD and NG scheme, with white codes and 343rd FS square on tail. Serial, name and mission tally in yellow. Aircraft lost when Erb baled out into the North Sea 7/5/44. He was rescued by Air Sea Rescue.

343rd Fighter Squadron

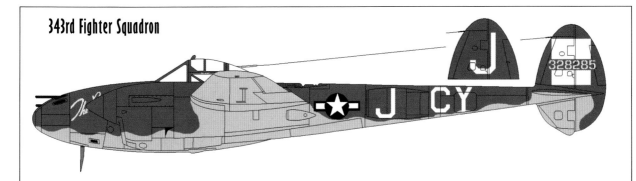

458 1st Lt. James May, left 338th FS to USA 8/44.

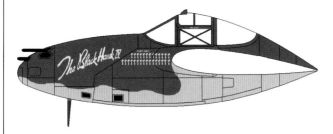

459 1st Lt. James May.

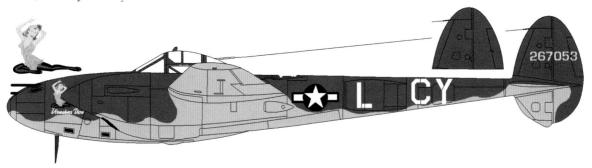

460 Lt. James W. Gilbride, Springfield, Illinois. Joined 55th FG prior to leaving USA until KIA 29/11/43.
Lt. Hugh J. Goudelock. 343rd FS 11/43 until 5/44, then to USA.

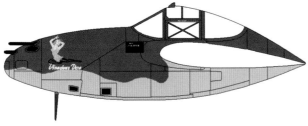

461 Lt. James W. Gilbride, Springfield, Illinois.
Lt. Hugh J. Goudelock.

1/72 Scale

458/459: *P-38J-15-LO 43-28285 'The Blackhawk IV' flown by May in May 1944. OD and NG, white codes and Squadron symbol. Serial, name and mission tally in yellow.*
460/461: *P-38H-5-LO 42-67053 'Vivacious Vera' was the first aircraft received by the Group, at Nuthamstead, on 15/9/43. It was assigned to Gilbride, who named it after his wife. After Gilbride was lost it passed to Goudelock who wrote it off in a crash landing at Ludham, Norfolk, 13/12/43, after returning on a single engine from his only mission in it, to Kiel, and running out of* *fuel. Aircraft completed 18 missions. Standard OD and NG scheme, codes white, serial yellow.*

343rd Fighter Squadron

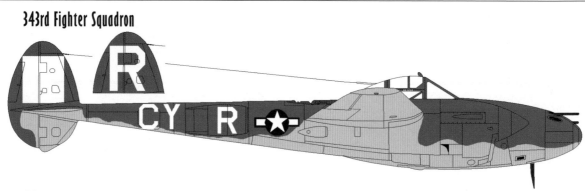

462 Maj. Eugene E. Ryan. To 343rd FS 2/43 until 4/45 then to 338th FS to end of war. Claimed 3 air and 1.5 ground victories.

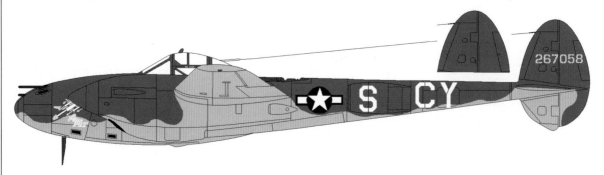

463 Capt. Kenneth J. Sorace, Brooklyn, New York. With 55th FG before they left USA until 14/6/44, when he was shot down by a Bf 109, and baled out, becoming an evader. Spent time with Maquis, returned to UK on 12/9/44, then to USA on 1/10/44.

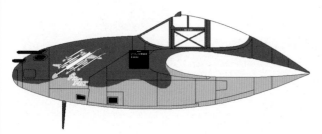

464 Capt. Kenneth J. Sorace, Brooklyn, New York.

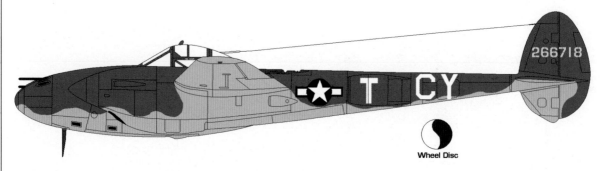

Wheel Disc

465 P-38H-1-LO, one of the original aircraft received by 55th FG in 10/43.

1/72 Scale

462: P-38J CY-R flown by Ryan in May/June 1944. Damaged in a night crash-landing off the runway 10/6/44. OD and grey scheme with white codes and squadron square symbol.

463/464: P-38H-5-LO 42-67058 'Pitter Pat' was Sorace's assigned aircraft in February 1944. It was handed over to the 1st FG in the MTO in that month. Standard OD and NG scheme, white codes and yellow serial.

465: P-38H-1-LO, one of the original aircraft received by the 55th FG in October 1943. Standard OD and grey scheme, with white codes and yellow serial.

Blue/white ying-yang pattern on inner wheel discs. This aircraft went to 554th Fighter Training School in December 1943, as B9-T.

343rd Fighter Squadron

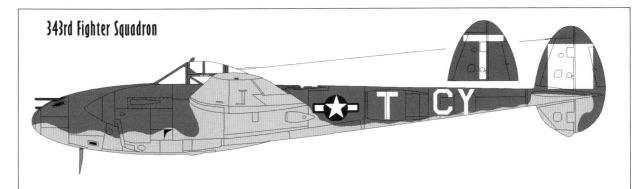

466 P-38J of 343rd FS in 5/44. Serial number and assigned pilot unknown.

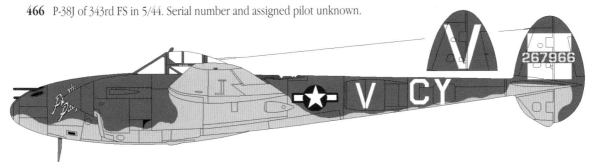

467 1st Lt. William H. Allen, Torrance, California. With 343rd FS 5/44 to 10/44. Claimed 5 trainers in the air over Göppingen airfield, on 5/9/44 to become an 'ace in a day'. No other claims in 89 missions, 270 combat hours.

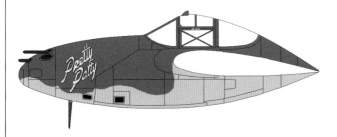

468 1st Lt. William H. Allen, Torrance, California.

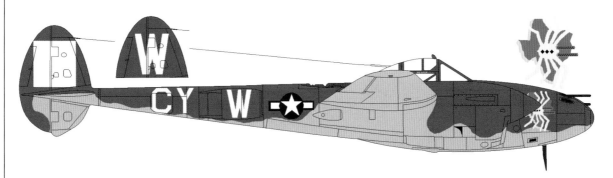

469 Maj. Dallas W. Webb ('Spider'), served with 343rd FS from 2/43 until 4/44, then to HQ 55th FG. Claimed 1 Me 210 and 1 Bf 109 destroyed in the air.

1/72 Scale

466: P-38J of 343rd FS in May 1944. OD and NG with white codes and Squadron symbol. Aircraft crashlanded near RAF Manston after sustaining battle damage over Europe. Serial and pilot unknown.

467/468: This P-38J-10-LO 42-67966 'Pretty Patty' was Allen's aircraft in May 1944. OD and NG with white codes and Squadron symbol. Serial yellow, name is yellow with black shading.

469/470: P-38J CY-W, serial not displayed, flown by Webb March/April 1944. OD and NG, white codes and Squadron symbol. Spider emblem is superim-

posed on a green, yellow-shadowed, map of Texas.

343rd Fighter Squadron

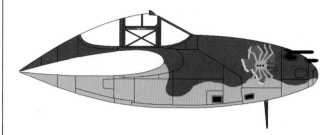

470 Maj. Dallas W. Webb ('Spider').

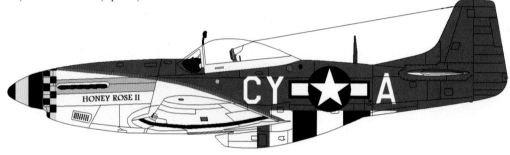

471 Lt. Edward J. Dvorak

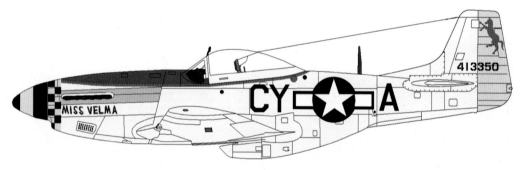

472 Capt. Frank E. Birtciel, Sylvia, Kansas. Joined 343rd FS 8/43 until 4/45. Bailed out 3/4/45 over Belgium after engine seized. Returned to unit in three days. Claimed 5, all on the ground.

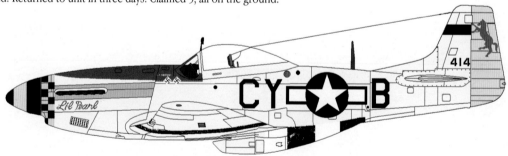

473 Lt. Donald L. Mercier. With 343rd FS 6/44 until12/44. Claimed 1.5 Bf 109 and 1 He 111 in the air. Aircraft shot down by Bf 109s west of Koblenz 25/12/44 with Lt Robert A. Maxwell, who became POW.

1/72 Scale

471: *Dvorak flew this P-51D-5-NA, serial unknown, autumn 1944. Wears the 343rd FS scheme of OD aft fuselage over NMF with a dividing red stripe. Group green and yellow colours on nose and spinner. White codes, black ETO bands on wings and under horizontal tail. D-Day stripes under rear fuselage only. Lacks the Squadron yellow rudder. Name is green with yellow outline.*

472: *P-51D-5-NA 44-13350 was Birtciel's final machine. Passed to Ray Allen who named it 'Merrimack'. NMF overall, standard Group nose markings,*

343rd FS yellow rudder with red prancing horse. Red outline to anti-glare panel and canopy. Black codes and serial. Name green with yellow outline. See 474.

473: *Mercier's P-51D-10-NA 44-14384 'Lil Pearl' in August 1944. NMF with standard Group nose colours, yellow rudder with 343rd FS red horse. Black codes, serial and ETO bands.. D-Day stripes under rear fuselage. Name in red, port side only. Two swastika kill marks. Crew Chief Sgt. Bill Newman.*

343rd Fighter Squadron

474 Capt. Frank E. Birtciel, Sylvia, Kansas.

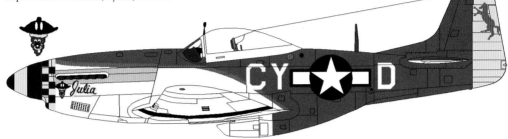

475 1 Lt. David M. Fry. To 343rd FS 6/44 until 13/9/44 when he baled out near Kassel, Germany, after engine failure, POW. Claimed 1 He 111 on the ground.

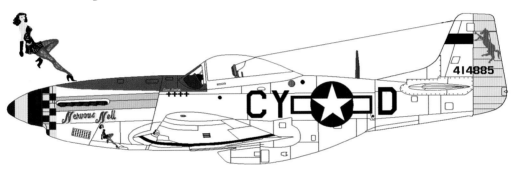

476 Capt. Douglas A. Parker. With 55th FG HQ 7/44 until 9/44, then to 343rd FS until end of war. Claimed 1 Bf 109 in the air plus several ground kills.

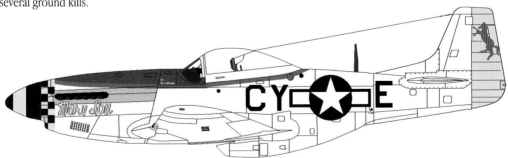

477 Lt. Wayne R. Erickson, with 343rd FS from 1/45 until 7/45. Claimed 1 destroyed plus 2 damaged, all on the ground.

1/72 Scale

474: 44-14561, 'Miss Velma', Birtciel's aircraft in late 1944. Group colours on nose and spinner, 343rd FS yellow rudder with red stallion. White codes, name green with yellow detail. OD aft fuselage and top surface of horizontal tail with red border. NMF forward fuselage and wings. White ETO bands on upper horizontal tail, black on underside, none on wings. See 472.

475: Fry was lost in his P-51D-5-NA 44-13374, 'Julia', 13/9/44. 343rd FS OD and NMF. Group nose colours, yellow rudder, red horse, white codes. Black ETO bands on wings and under tail surfaces, white on top surfaces. Crew

Chief Sgt. Bill Krejny.

476: Parker's assigned P-51D-15-NA 44-14885. NMF, black ETO bands, codes and serial. Standard Group nose colours, 343rd FS rudder. Name green, yellow detail. Four black crosses with white outline ahead of windscreen, pilot's name in white above. Vargas pin-up is a print, varnished on.

477: P-51D, serial unknown, flown by Erickson 3/45-4/45. NMF, Group nose colours, 343rd FS rudder. Red border to anti-glare panel and cockpit. Name yellow with green outline. Pilot's name in white ahead of cockpit.

343rd Fighter Squadron

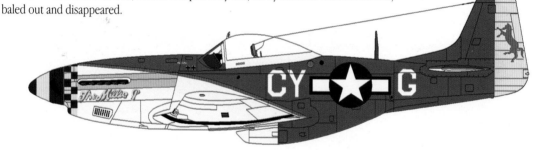

478 Capt. Robert Buttke, Sacramento, California. With 343rd FS 3/43 until 4/45. Claimed 5.5 aerial victories, 5 in P-38s and .5 in a P-51. Aircraft lost 17/4/45, 2nd Lt. Philip A. Erby KIA, hit by flak over Kamenz airfield, baled out and disappeared.

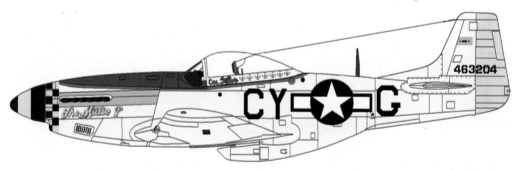

479 Maj. Edward B. Giller, Jacksonville, Illinos. To 343rd FS 2/43 until 6/45. Claimed 3 air and 6 ground victories.

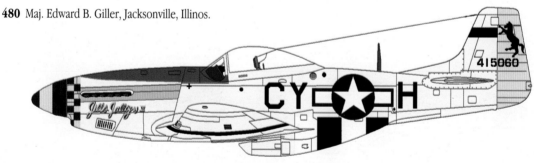

480 Maj. Edward B. Giller, Jacksonville, Illinos.

481 Maj. Paul E. Hoeper. With 343rd FS from 2/43 until 6/44, and from 9/44 to 11/44, then on to HQ. Claimed 1 Me 210 in the air and 1 Me 262 destroyed on the ground. Aircraft lost 21/2/45 with 2nd Lt. George E. Eichhorn, downed by flak, train strafing near Nuremburg. POW.

1/72 Scale

478: *Buttke's P-51D-15-NA 44-15025, early 1945. NMF, black ETO bands. Group nose colours, yellow 343rd FS rudder with red stallion. Five black crosses under windshield. Name red, black details, pilot's name on canopy rail in red. Named 'Beautiful Lavenia' after Crew Chief Robert Pinson's wife.*
479: *Giller's P-51D-15-NA 44-14985 in 2/45. OD and NMF 343rd FS scheme, with red stripe. Group nose colours, yellow 343rd FS rudder with red stallion. Black ETO bands on wings and underside of horizontal tail, white codes and bands on tail topside surfaces. Pilot's name in white ahead of*

windscreen, above 2 black, white-outlined crosses. Crew Chief Sgt. James T. Marine, Asst. C/chief Sgt. McGee.
480: *Giller's last 'Millie G', P-51D-20-NA 44-63204. Crashlanded post-war at Kaufbeuren airfield, 14/9/45. NMF, no stripes or bands, 55th FG nose colours and 343rd FS yellow rudder. Red border to anti-glare panel and canopy.*
481: *Hoeper's P-51D-15-NA, autumn 1944. NMF, 55th FG nose markings, yellow 343rd FS rudder. Black codes, serial, stallion and ETO bands. D-Day stripes under fuselage only. Name yellow with green shadows. See 482.*

343rd Fighter Squadron

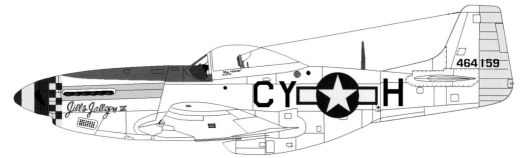

482 Maj. Paul E. Hoeper.

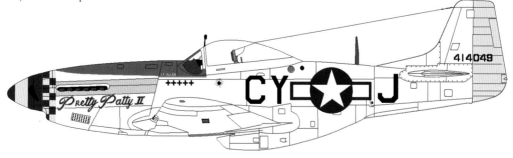

483 1st Lt. William H. Allen, Torrance, California.

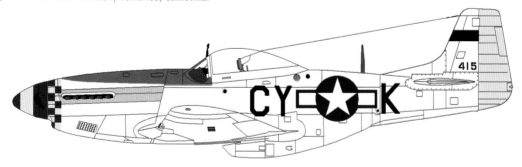

484 Lt. John McCabe. Served with 343rd FS from 9/44 until 4/45, then to USA, tour completed.

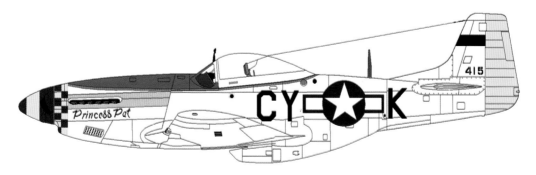

485 Lt. Edward H. Geary. With 343rd FS 2/45 until 7/45. Claimed 2 ground victories and 2 damaged.

1/72 Scale

482: P-51D-20-NA 44-64159, 'Jill's Jalopy VII' was Hoeper's aircraft with HQ but still maintained by 343rd FS for him. Colours as previous aircraft but no bands or stripes and stallion. Aircraft lost 9/4/45 when 2nd Lt. Richard K. Abel collided with a 4th FG P-51 while strafing near Munich, Germany and was KIA. See 481.

483: Allen's P-51D-5-NA 44-14049 'Pretty Patty II' in September 1944. NMF with Group green/yellow nose markings, and 343rd FS yellow rudder. Black codes and serial. Name is squadron green with yellow detailing. Five white-outlined

black crosses under windshield. Crew Chief S/Sgt. J.C. Ruzicka. See 467,468.

484: This P-51D, complete serial unknown, was flown by McCabe until March 1945, and then passed on to Lt. Geary. It is NMF with Group nose colours and yellow rudder of the 343rd FS. Black ETO band on fin only. Codes and serial black. See 485.

485: When McCabe went home, CY-K passed to Geary, who named it 'Princess Pat'. Aircraft is marked as before, with addition of the name and a red stripe bordering the anti-glare framing and cockpit.

343rd Fighter Squadron

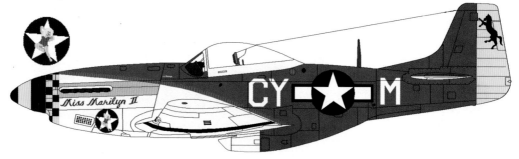

486 Lt. Richard Ozinga. Aircraft lost 24/12/44 in mid-air collision, Lt. Kenneth J. Mix, KIA. Hit P-51D 44-13923 from 357th FG named 'Big Beautiful Doll', previously flown by John Landers while CO of 357th.

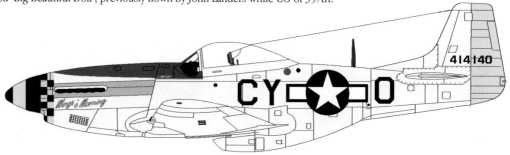

487 Lt. Richard D. Bartlett. With 343rd FS from 5/44 until 11/44, then to USA tour completed. Claimed half share of a Bf 109 destroyed in the air, plus 3 ground kills.

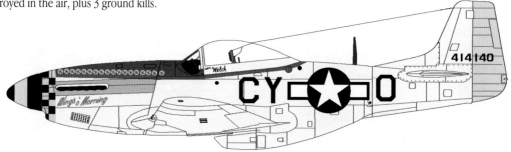

488 Capt. Robert E. Welch, Brown City, Missouri. With 343rd FS from 9/44 until 9/45. Claimed 5 Bf 109s and 1 FW 190 destroyed in the air, plus 12 ground kills.

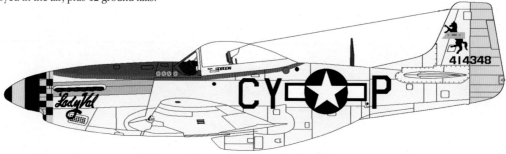

489 Capt. Vincent P. Gordon. Joined 343rd FS 10/44 until 7/45. Claimed 4 victories, all on the ground. **1/72 Scale**

486: P-51D-5-NA 44-13837 'Miss Marilyn II', Ozinga's aircraft in late 1944. 343rd FS OD/NMF scheme with red stripe. Group nose markings, yellow rudder with stallion in black. Black ETO bands on wings and under horizontal tail. Name in green, yellow outline, white codes.

487: P-51D-10-NA 44-14140 'Wings o' Morning' flown by Bartlett at the end of his tour. NMF, standard Group nose colours with 343rd FS yellow rudder. Codes and serial black, name green and yellow. To Welch when Bartlett left. See 488.

488: 'Wings o' Morning' as flown by Welch in April 1945. Markings as before, now with red border to anti-glare panel and around canopy. 18 swastikas on yellow circles along nose, representing his 6 air and 12 ground victories. 'Capt. Welch' on canopy frame in black.

489: 'Lady Val', P-51D-10-NA 44-14348, flown by Gordon in April 1944. NMF, no bands or stripes. Group nose colours and yellow Squadron rudder. Red edge around anti-glare panel and canopy. Name and rampant stallion are black. Rear-warning radar aerials fitted on fin, over horse.

343rd Fighter Squadron

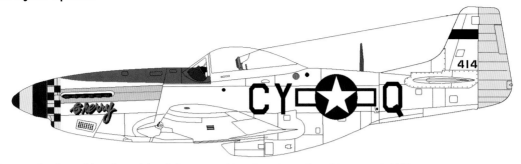

490 Lt. Richard D. Gibbs. Claimed 4 air kills, an FW 190 and Ju 88 Mistel, and 2 FWs on 17/4/45.

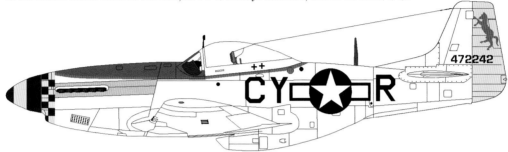

491 P-51D-20-NA 44-72242 of 343rd FS in March 1945, pilot unknown.

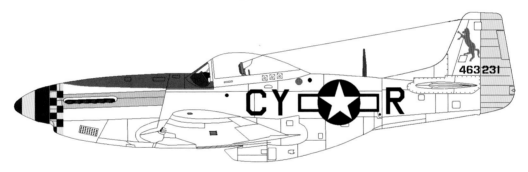

492 Maj. Eugene E. Ryan.

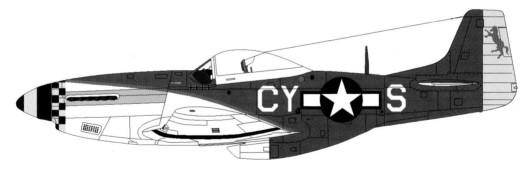

493 Capt. William Henry Lewis, New Jersey. Scored 7 air victories, plus one damaged.

1/72 Scale

490: *Gibbs's P-51D-10-NA 44-14175 'Cherry', spring1945. NMF overall, no stripes or bands except on vertical fin. Group markings on nose and spinner, 343rd FS yellow rudder, name red with black shading.*

491: *P-51D-20-NA 44-72242 in March 1945, pilot unknown. NMF, usual Group nose colours, yellow 343rd FS rudder with red stallion, black codes and serial. Red border to anti-glare panel and around canopy. Two crosses on canopy frame.*

492: *Ryan's P-51D-20-NA 44-63231 April 1945. NMF, standard Group nose markings, 343rd FS yellow rudder, red stallion on fin. Codes and serial black. 3 swastika kill marks on canopy frame. See 462.*

493: *P-51D-5-NA 44-13907, Lewis's first aircraft with 55th FG. Wears 343rd FS August/September 1944 OD/NMF scheme with red stripe. Green and yellow group markings on nose and spinner. Yellow rudder, stallion red. Codes white, 4 black kill crosses below windshield. Serial not repainted on tail. Black ETO bands on wings and underside of tail, white on upper tail surfaces. See 494, 495.*

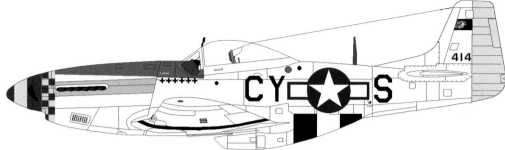

494 Capt. William Henry Lewis, New Jersey.

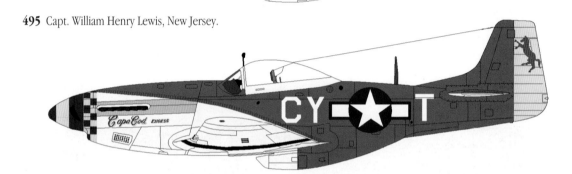

495 Capt. William Henry Lewis, New Jersey.

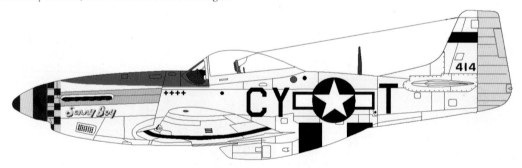

496 Capt. Chester E. Coggeshall Jr, Hyannis, Massachusetts, 343rd FS. Claimed 1 ground kill on 16/4/45, then shot down by ground fire on the same mission which was the last one of his second tour. It was later found he survived the crash only to be murdered by civilians, who were later tried and hanged.

497 Lt. Ted E. Hoffman. With 343rd FS 7/44 until 3/45. Claimed 4 air kills on 5/9/44, unidentified trainers.

1/72 Scale

494: Lewis's aircraft in early 1945 was P-51D-15-NA, 44-14907. NMF overall, Group markings on nose and spinner, yellow rudder for 343rd FS. Black codes and ETO bands on wings and tail. D-Day stripes below rear fuselage only. Serial has not been repainted on rudder. Six black kill crosses under windshield. Whole aircraft is of worn appearance. See 493, 495.
495: 44-14907 in April 1945. Now with stripes and bands removed, serial repainted and red edge to anti-glare panel and around the canopy. Score of 7 kills indicated by white-outlined black crosses on canopy rail. See 494.

496: Coggeshall's assigned P-51D-15-NA, 44-15608 on his second tour in which he was lost. OD and NMF scheme of the 343rd FS. Yellow rudder, standard Group nose markings. Black ETO bands on wings and tail undersides, white on tail upper surfaces. Stallion is red, codes white, serial not displayed.
497: P-51D-10-NA 44-14608, 'Sonny Boy', flown by Hoffman, late 1944. NMF overall, black ETO bands on wings and tail. D-day stripes under rear fuselage only. Group nose colours and yellow 343rd FS rudder. Four white-outlined black crosses under windshield. Name is yellow and green.

343rd Fighter Squadron

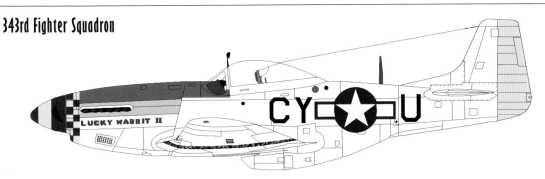

498 Lt. Victor P. Krambo. Joined 343rd FS 9/44, served until shot down on 27/2/45, becoming a POW.

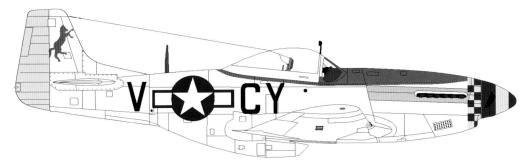

499 Capt. Robert Dean Brown, Lewiston, Idaho. Claimed 1 Bf 109 in the air plus 2 ground kills. Hit by flak at an airfield near Flensburg, Germany, he made it across the Baltic and baled out into Denmark, 20/3/45. Eventually got to Sweden, then to UK. Sent home to USA 4/45.

500 Lt. Grady Morris. With 343rd FS from 12/44 until 19/2/45 when he was shot down by flak and became POW. Claimed 1 FW 190 in the air, 24/12/44.

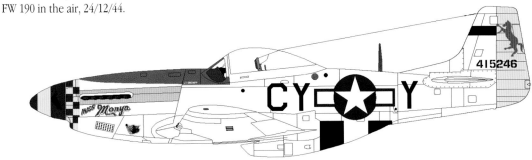

501 Lt. Nick P. Bebaeff. Served with 343rd FS from 6/44 until 1/45. Claimed 1 Bf 109 in the air.   **1/72 Scale**

498: P-51D, serial unknown, flown by Krambo late 1944. NMF with very worn ETO bands on wings only. Group colours on nose and spinner, 343rd FS yellow rudder. Codes black. 'Lucky Wabbit II' green with yellow shading.
499: Brown's P-51D-10-NA 44-14135, which he was flying on 20/3/45. NMF with standard Group nose colours, yellow rudder, red stallion on fin. Black codes, serial not displayed, black ETO bands on horizontal tail surfaces only, none on wings. Red border to anti-glare panel and around canopy.
500: P-51D-10-NA 44-14235 'Lil Jan' assigned to Morris. NMF overall, black

codes and serial, Group colours on nose, yellow 343rd FS rudder. Wolf's head on cowling appeared on several of the squadron's aircraft. Lost 16/4/45, Lt. Patrick L. Moore shot down by flak and KIA south of Munich.
501: Bebaeff's P-51D-15-NA 44-15246 'Miss Manya', late 1944. NMF with yellow rudder of 343rd FS and red horse. Black codes and serial, D-Day stripes under rear fuselage. Name in green and yellow. ETO band on fin only. Wolf's head on cowl, appeared on several squadron aircraft. See 500.

343rd Fighter Squadron

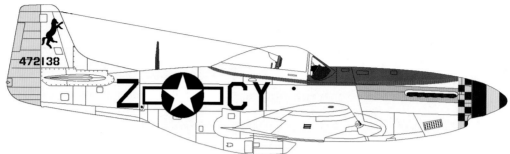

502 Capt. Robert E. Welch, Brown City, Missouri.

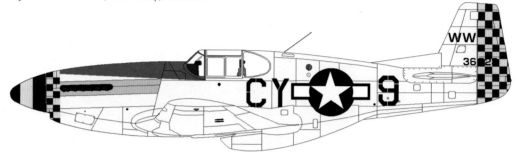

503 Squadron hack P-51B-7-NA 43-6928, in early 1945. Note serial has been wrongly applied as 36528. This aircraft had a second seat in place where the radios and fuselage tank had been removed.

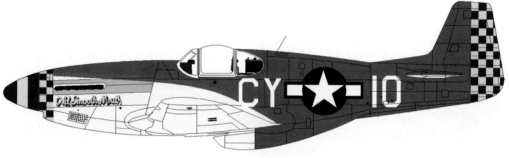

504 P-51C, serial unknown, with the 343rd FS in February 1945.

1/72 Scale

502: P-51D-20-NA 44-72138 was Welch's aircraft in May 1945. NMF with standard Group nose colours, yellow 343rd FS rudder, black codes and serial, horse is black on fin. Red border around canopy and anti-glare panel. No bands or stripes.

503: Squadron hack P-51B-7-NA 43-6928, in early 1945. Note serial has been wrongly applied as 36528. This aircraft had a second seat in place, where the radios and fuselage tank had been removed. Group nose and rudder colours. Black codes, serial and 'WW', no bands or stripes.

504: P-51C, serial unknown, with the 343rd FS in February 1945. Aircraft has the OD and NMF scheme used by the 343rd FS with the addition of the checked rudder of the 'Clobber College'. No bands on wings, but they are present on horizontal tail, in white on OD upper surface. White codes, name 'Old Smooth Mouth' is yellow with green shading.

BIBLIOGRAPHY

The Mighty Eighth, R. Freeman.
The Mighty Eighth War Manual, R. Freeman.
The Mighty Eighth War Diary, R. Freeman.
The Mighty Eighth In Colour, R. Freeman.
Mighty Eighth The Colour Record, R. Freeman.
Mighty Eighth Warpaint and Heraldry, R. Freeman.
The Fight for the Skies, R. Freeman.
Fighter Command, J. Ethell & R. Sand.
Stars & Bars, F. Olynyk.
Aces of the 8th, G. Stafford & W. Hess, Squadron Signal.
Aces & Wingmen, Danny Morris.
Aces & Wingmen II Vols. 1 & 2, D. Morris/W. Hess.
Fighter Units & Pilots of the 8th Air Force Vols.1 & 2, K. Miller.
Osprey *Aircraft of the Aces*, Nos. 1,19 & 24.
Markings of the Aces, 8th US Air Force, Book 1, Theodore R. Bennett.
Escort to Berlin — the 4th Fighter Group in World War II, G. Fry and J. Ethell.
Kingscliffe — History of 20th Fighter Group.
20th Fighter Group, R. Mackay, Squadron Signal.
The 55th Fighter Group Versus the Luftwaffe, J.M. Gray.
Fighters of the Mighty Eighth, W. Hess & T. Ivie.
Fighter Losses of the Mighty Eighth, W.H. Adams, Eighth Air Force Memorial Museum.
American Fighters of WWII, Vols.1 & 2, Hylton Lacy.
Double Nickel, Double Trouble, R.M. Littlefield.
American Eagles USAAF Colours 2, P-38 Lightning, R. Freeman.
P-38 Lightning, Aircam No. 10.
P-38 Lightning at War, J. Christy & J. Ethell.
P-38 Lightning in Action, Nos. 25 & 109 Squadron Signal.
P-38 Lightning, P-38 Pilots Association, Turner Publishing.
P-38 Lightning, Aero Series 19.
P-38 Lightning in World War II Colour, J. Ethell.
The Lockheed P-38, Warren Bodie.
P-47 Thunderbolt, Aircam No. 2.
P-47 Thunderbolt at War, W.N. Hess.
P-47 Thunderbolt in Action, Squadron Signal Nos. 18 & 67.
P-47 Thunderbolt in the ETO, E.R. McDowell, Squadron Signal.
Thunderbolt — A Documentary History, R. Freeman.
P-47 Thunderbolt — The Jug, P-47 Pilots Association, Turner Publishing.
Republic's P-47 Thunderbolt, Seversky to Victory, W.M. Bodie.
P-47 Thunderbolt, Aero Series 6.
Mustang at War, R. Freeman.

P-51B/C Mustang, Aircam No. 5.
P-51D Mustang, Aircam No.1.
P-51 Mustang in Action, Squadron Signal No.45.
P-51 Mustang, L. Davis, Squadron Signal
P-51 Mustang, P-51 Pilots Association, Turner Publishing.
P-51 Mustang in Colour Photos From WWII & Korea, J. Ethell.
P-51 Mustang — A Photo Chronicle, L. Davis.
P-51 Mustang Nose Art Gallery, J. & D. Campbell.
WWII Nose Art in Colour, J. Ethell.
Mustang, R. Gruenhagen.
Fighting Mustang — Chronicle of the P-51, W. Hess.
Planes, Names & Dames, L. Davis, Squadron Signal.
Bent & Battered Wings, L. Davis, Squadron Signal.
Flying Scoreboards, E.R. McDowell, Squadron Signal.
Vintage Nose Art, G. Valant.
Fighter Pilot, Kaplan.
Little Friends, Kaplan & Saunders.
Wings of War, J. Ethell.
War Eagles in Original Colour, J. Ethell & W. Bodie.
The History of Aircraft Nose Art, J. Ethell & C. Simonsen.
Talisman, J. & D. Campbell.
War Paint, Fighter Nose Art WWII & Korea, J. & D. Campbell.
Colours & Markings, Ducimus.

4th Fighter Group

334th Fighter Squadron: QP

Pilot	Serial	Code	Type	Page
Anderson	41-6538	QP-B	P-47	14
Andrews	41-6413	QP-V	P-47	22
Arthur	44-13984	QP-U	P-51D	34
Arthur	44-73304	QP-U	P-51D	34
Ayers	43-6518	QP-K	P-51B	25
Beason	44-14518	QP-P	P-51D	33
Beeson	42-27890	QP-B	P-47	14
Beeson	43-6819	QP-B	P-51B	23
Blanchfield	41-16187	QP-E	P-47	15
Blanchfield	43-36746	QP-E	P-51B	24
Blanchfield	42-106767	QP-E	P-51B	24
Boehle	41-6400	QP-O	P-47	20
Boretsky	44-13984	QP-B	P-51D	29
Bowers	44-63223	QP-S	P-51D	34
Buchanan	44-72155	QP-W	P-51D	35
Castle	42-7881	QP-E	P-47	15
Chatterley	41-6358	QP-G	P-47	16
Clark	BM293	XR-W	Spitfire	13
Clark	41-6195	QP-W	P-47	22
Clark	41-6413	QP-W	P-47	22
Clark	43-6560	QP-W	P-51B	27
Clark	42-106650	QP-W	P-51B	27
Clark	44-13372	QP-W	P-51D	35
Coen	41-6413	QP-V	P-47	21
Daymond	BM510	XR-A	Spitfire	13
Dickmeyer	44-14606	QP-D	P-51D	29
Douglass	41-6404	QP-R	P-47	21
Dyer	44-14323	QP-VV	P-51D	35
France	41-6414	QP-K	P-47	18
France	42-7876	QP-K	P-47	18
France	43-6832	QP-K	P-51B	25
Fraser	43-24825	QP-G	P-51B	25
Hand	44-11661	QP-X	P-51D	35
Helfrecht	44-14110	QP-R	P-51D	33
Hively	41-6576	QP-J	P-47	17
Hively	42-7874	QP-J	P-47	17
Hively	Unknown	QP-J	P-47	18
Hively	43-6898	QP-J	P-51B	25
Hively	44-15347	QP-J	P-51D	30
Hively	44-13306	QP-J	P-51D	30
Hofer	41-6484	QP-L	P-47	19
Hofer	42-106924	QP-L	P-51B	26
Hofer	43-6746	QP-X	P-51B	27
Hollander	41-6538	QP-B	P-47	14
Howard	43-24841	QP-D	P-51B	23
Howe	43-6717	QP-S	P-51B	27
Howe	44-13884	QP-G	P-51D	29
Joyce	44-14271	QP-K	P-51D	31
Kennedy	44-72863	QP-K	P-51D	31
Kinnard	44-14292	QP-A	P-51D	28
Kolter	43-7178	QP-Q	P-51B	26
Lacy	44-11677	QP-P	P-51K	33
Lang	44-13352	QP-Z	P-51D	36
Malmsten	43-6957	QP-M	P-51B	26
McMinn	41-6204	O4	P-47	13
McMinn	41-6204	QP-M	P-47	19
McNabb	41-6484	QP-L	P-47	19
Megura	Unknown	QP-P	P-47	20
Megura	43-7158	QP-F	P-51B	24
Megura	43-6636	QP-N	P-51B	26
Mills	41-6191	QP-Q	P-47	21
Monroe	44-15312	QP-N	P-51D	67
Montgomery	42-7980	QP-H	P-47	16
Montgomery	44-15326	QP-H	P-51D	30
Montgomery	44-72382	QP-H	P-51D	30
Morgan	42-7919	QP-N	P-47	20
Norley	44-15347	QP-O	P-51D	32
Norley	44-72196	QP-O	P-51D	32
Norley	44-73108	QP-O	P-51D	33
Oberhansly	44-11661	QP-X	P-51D	35
O'Reagan	41-6392	QP-X	P-47	22
Payne	44-72381	QP-J	P-51D	31
Pisanos	EN783	XR-K	Spitfire	13
Pisanos	42-7945	QP-D	P-47	14
Priser	41-16187	QP-L	P-47	19
Rafalovich	41-6195	QP-W	P-47	22
Sharp	42-106650	QP-W	P-51B	27
Siems	44-13322	QP-O	P-51D	32
Smith	41-6410	QP-Y	P-47	23
Sobanski	42-7924	QP-F	P-47	15
Sobanski	42-75126	QP-F	P-47	16
Speer	43-6957	QP-M	P-51B	26
Steppe	43-6957	QP-M	P-51B	26
Van Epps	42-8641	QP-I	P-47	17
Voyles	44-14292	QP-A	P-51D	28
Woods	44-72251	QP-A	P-51D	28
Wosniak	44-63583	QP-T	P-51D	34
Unknown	44-14537	QP-A	P-51D	28
Unknown	44-15216	QP-F	P-51D	29
Unknown	44-72346	QP-K	P-51D	31

335th Fighter Squadron: WD

Pilot	Serial	Code	Type	Page
Ackerley	44-72416	WD-P	P-51D	49
Anderson	42-74726	WD-V	P-47	40
Berry	44-14361	WD-K	P-51D	47
Blakeslee	BL766	MD-C	Spitfire	37
Blakeslee	42-7863	WD-C	P-47	38
Blakeslee	43-6437	WD-C	P-51B	42
Blakeslee	42-106726	WD-C	P-51B	42

Pilot	Serial	Code	Type	Page
Blakeslee	42-106726	WD-S	P-51B	44
Blakeslee	44-13779	WD-C	P-51D	46
Bucholz	44-14389	WD-T	P-51D	49
Carpenter	41-6226	WD-I	P-47	39
Cooper	42-106855	WD-Z	P-51B	44
Daley	EN853	AV-D	Spitfire	36
Diamond	44-15615	WD-T	P-51D	49
Eaton	44-14923	WD-U	P-51D	50
Ellington	41-6214	WD-F	P-47	38
Evans	42-74686	WD-E	P-47	38
Evans	41-6206	WD-H	P-47	39
Feidler	43-6579	WD-S	P-51B	43
Goodwyn	43-6718	WD-R	P-51B	43
Goodwyn	42-106726	WD-S	P-51B	44
Green	44-14137	WD-KK	P-51D	47
Green	44-63736	WD-M	P-51D	48
Green	44-14923	WD-U	P-51D	50
Henry	43-6579	WD-S	P-51B	43
Lines	43-7172	WD-H	P-51B	42
Lines	44-13555	WD-O	P-51D	48
Little	43-6770	WD-G	P-51B	43
Lucas	44-11200	WD-F	P-51D	46
Mabie	44-13564	WD-I	P-51D	47
McKennon	41-6582	WD-A	P-47	37
McKennon	43-6896	WD-A	P-51B	41
McKennon	42-106911	WD-A	P-51B	42
McKennon	44-13883	WD-A	P-51D	44
McKennon	44-14570	WD-A	P-51D	44
McKennon	44-63166	WD-A	P-51D	45
McKennon	44-14221	WD-A	P-51D	45
McKennon	44-72308	WD-A	P-51D	45
Norley	44-15028	WD-O	P-51D	48
O'Donnell	44-14557	WD-B	P-51D	45
Perkins	44-13564	WD-I	P-51D	47
Peterson	44-13977	WD-H	P-51D	47
Ross	41-6359	WD-K	P-47	39
Rowles	42-75112	WD-Z	P-47	41
Santos	44-15615	WD-T	P-51D	49
Schlegel	43-6770	WD-O	P-51B	43
Schlegel	42-106464	WD-O	P-51B	43
Shapleigh	42-106464	WD-O	P-51B	43
Smith	42-7936	WD-W	P-47	41
Smith	43-7172	WD-H	P-51B	42
Stanhope	41-6233	WD-O	P-47	40
Wadsworth	43-6437	WD-C	P-51B	42
Willruth	44-15028	WD-Y	P-51D	50
Young	41-6185	WD-S	P-47	40
Unknown	AD511	AV-E	Spitfire	36
Unknown	BM461	AV-F	Spitfire	37
Unknown	EN768	AV-W	Spitfire	37
Unknown	44-73100	WD-B	P-51D	46
Unknown	44-72061	WD-N	P-51D	48
Unknown	44-72416	WD-P	P-51D	49
Unknown	44-14438	WD-U	P-51D	50
Unknown	44-72241	WD-W	P-51D	50
Trainer	43-12193	WD-2	P-51B	51
Trainer	44-36570	WD-3	P-51B	51

336th Fighter Squadron: VF

Pilot	Serial	Code	Type	Page
Bennett	42-7873	VF-J	P-47	55
Bennett	42-106686	VF-T	P-51B	64
Bousefield	44-15613	VF-M	P-51D	70
Carlson	41-6575	VF-E	P-47	54
Davis	44-13317	VF-B	P-51D	67
Davis	44-63233	VF-D	P-51D	68
Dickey	44-13630	VF-R	P-51D	71
Dufour	AB271	MD-E	Spitfire	52
Dufour	41-6575	VF-E	P-47	53
Dunn	42-7933	VF-Y	P-47	59
Emerson	44-13317	VF-B	P-51D	67
Fredericks	43-6362	VF-H	P-51B	61
Fredericks	44-14277	VF-H	P-51D	69
Gentile	BL255	MD-T	Spitfire	52
Gentile	42-8659	VF-T	P-47	58
Gentile	43-6913	VF-T	P-51B	63
Glover	43-12214	VF-C	P-51B	60
Glover	44-14787	VF-B	P-51D	67
Glover	44-64153	VF-B	P-51D	67
Godfrey	42-7884	VF-P	P-47	57
Godfrey	43-6765	VF-P	P-51B	63
Godfrey	42-106730	VF-P	P-51B	63
Godfrey	44-13412	VF-F	P-51D	69
Goodson	42-7959	VF-W	P-47	58
Goodson	43-6895	VF-B	P-51B	59
Goodson	43-24848	VF-B	P-51B	59
Goodson	44-13303	VF-B	P-51D	67
Gover	BL722	MD-B	Spitfire	52
Gover	42-74683	VF-G	P-47	54
Gover	Unknown	VF-J	P-47	56
Griffin	44-14277	VF-H	P-51D	69
Groshong	44-15647	VF-I	P-51D	70
Grove	42-103603	VF-T	P-51B	64
Grove	42-103603	VF-T	P-51B	64
Grove	44-15375	VF-T	P-51D	72
Grove	44-72767	VF-T	P-51D	72
Hagan	44-14317	VF-Y	P-51D	72
Hagan	44-72053	VF-Y	P-51D	73
Hastings	44-73843	VF-E	P-51D	68
Herter	43-7005	VF-N	P-51B	62
Higgins	43-6942	VF-D	P-51D	60
Hileman	44-15191	VF-C	P-51D	68
Hobert	41-6256	VF-I	P-47	55
Hurley	42-106666	VF-O	P-51B	62
Ingalls	43-6997	VF-U	P-51B	62
Ingold	42-74663	VF-H	P-47	55
Joiner	44-13830	VF-R	P-51D	71
Lane	44-13307	VF-J	P-51D	70
Lehman	41-6573	VF-S	P-47	57
McMahon	44-14276	VF-A	P-51D	66
Miley	41-6579	VF-L	P-47	56
Miller	44-14527	VF-S	P-51D	72
Millikan	41-6180	VF-U	P-47	58
Millikan	43-6997	VF-U	P-51B	64
Millikan	43-24769	VF-U	P-51B	65
Murchake	44-64142	VF-G	P-51D	69

Pilot	Serial	Code	Type	Page
Nee	Unknown	VF-N	P-47	57
Norley	43-12416	VF-O	P-51B	62
Patteeuw	43-6840	VF-Z	P-51B	65
Patteeuw	44-13325	VF-ZZ	P-51D	73
Pierini	43-6714	VF-J	P-51B	61
Pierini	44-14277	VF-H	P-51D	69
Peterson	41-6539	VF-F	P-47	54
Peterson	43-696	VF-F	P-51B	61
Quist	44-15054	VF-D	P-51D	68
Quist	44-13961	VF-L	P-51D	70
Raphael	41-6529	VF-M	P-47	56
Simon	42-106673	VF-K	P-51B	61
Smith	42-103602	VF-C	P-51B	60
Sooman	41-6192	VF-D	P-47	53
Sooman	43-6936	VF-D	P-51B	60
Stephenson	41-6573	VF-S	P-47	57
Stewart	44-72181	VF-S	P-51D	71
Tussey	42-106730	VF-P	P-51B	63
Van Wyk	43-24848	VF-B	P-51B	59
Van Wyk	43-6772	VF-X	P-51B	65
Villinger	Unknown	VF-C	P-47	53
Villinger	43-6985	VF-C	P-51B	59
Wehrman	43-7005	VF-N	P-51B	62
Young	44-14276	VF-A	P-51D	66
Unknown	43-6362	VF-H	P-51B	61
Unknown	42-106975	VF-N	P-51B	62
Unknown	43-6975	VF-S	P-51B	63
Unknown	44-73021	VF-F	P-51D	69
Unknown	BL766	MD-C	Spitfire	52
Trainer	Unknown	VF-4	P-51B	64
Trainer	42-103602	VF-5	P-51B	66

20th Fighter Group

55th Fighter Squadron: KI

Pilot	Serial	Code	Type	Page
Bisher	42-67823	KI-N	P-38J	81
Brown	44-11205	KI-A	P-51D	88
Burford	44-13790	KI-L	P-51D	89
Cole	44-72160	KI-K	P-51D	89
Cosgriff	44-14880	KI-H	P-51D	88
Frey	42-67855	KI-W	P-38J	85
Geiger	42-67034	KI-V	P-38H	84
Geiger	42-67860	KI-V	P-38J	84
Hower	44-13799	KI-N	P-51D	90
Iehle	Unknown	KI-B	P-51D	88
Larabee	44-13778	KI-J	P-51D	89
Loehnert	42-67916	KI-S	P-38J	84
Martin	Unknown	KI-W	P-51D	91
McAuley	42-67081	KI-K	P-38H	81
McGee	44-13905	KI-Y	P-51D	91
McKeon	44-13541	KI-M	P-51D	89
McLary	42-68131	KI-V	P-38J	85
McLary	42-67464	KI-Y	P-38J	86
McLary	42-67878	KI-Y	P-38J	87

Pilot	Serial	Code	Type	Page
Mullins	44-13859	KI-S	P-51D	90
Reimensnider	42-68108	KI-Y	P-38J	87
Ryan	44-11161	KI-X	P-51D	91
Schultz	42-67451	KI-R	P-38J	83
Scrutchfield	43-28430	KI-N	P-38J	83
Scrutchfield	42-67505	KI-R	P-38J	82
Serros	42-67756	KI-B	P-38J	80
Wasil	43-28301	KI-O	P-38J	82
Wasil	43-25031	KI-O	P-51C	90
Watson	43-28358	KI-I	P-38J	80
Wilson	43-28393	KI-W	P-38J	86
Unknown	42-67052	KI-Z	P-38H	88
Trainer	43-6865	KI-Q	P-51B	90

77th Fighter Squadron: LC

Pilot	Serial	Code	Type	Page
Alexander	44-13836	LC-H	P-51D	96
Alexander	44-13746	LC-M	P-51D	96
Clark	42-68171	LC-C	P-38J	92
Einhaus	44-13918	LC-V	P-51D	98
Feibelkorn	44-11161	LC-N	P-51D	97
Gilbertson	44-14822	LC-A	P-51D	94
Gilbertson	44-13637	LC-G	P-51D	95
Huey	44-13692	LC-X	P-51D	99
Jones	44-14823	LC-F	P-51D	94
Kelly	42-106476	LC-Z	P-51B	99
MacArthur	43-25042	LC-T	P-51C	98
McCully	44-13746	LC-M	P-51D	97
McLary	44-14378	LC-A	P-51D	94
Montgomery	42-67048	LC-A	P-38H	91
Montgomery	44-72519	LC-D	P-51D	94
Morris	42-67717	LC-E	P-38J	93
Murrell	44-14975	LC-K	P-51D	96
Nichols	44-14891	LC-O	P-51D	97
Phillips	44-13918	LC-V	P-51D	98
Piatkiewicz	44-14692	LC-Y	P-51D	99
Russel	42-67888	LC-B	P-38J	92
Slanker	44-14824	LC-P	P-51D	97
Slanker	44-14824	LC-P	P-51D	98
Whiteside	42-68176	LC-I	P-38J	93
Unknown	42-68177	LC-C	P-38J	92
Unknown	44-14843	LC-G	P-51D	95
Unknown	Unknown	LC-G	P-51D	95
Unknown	Unknown	LC-H	P-51D	95
Unknown	44-11217	LC-J	P-51D	96
Trainer	42-106476	LC-Z	P-51B	99

79th Fighter Squadron: MC

Pilot	Serial	Code	Type	Page
Anderson	43-28404	MC-A	P-38J	100
Anderson	43-28718	MC-A	P-38J	100
Anderson	42-68005	MC-T	P-38J	108
Armstrong	43-28322	MC-S	P-38J	108
Armstrong	44-13791	MC-S	P-51D	117

Pilot	Serial	Code	Type	Page
Baldwin	44-13877	MC-T	P-51D	117
Barnard	44-14365	MC-E	P-51D	111
Barnard	43-25054	MC-L	P-51C	114
Beesley	42-67427	MC-H	P-38J	102
Beschen	44-14337	MC-R	P-51D	116
Binkley	44-13855	MC-J	P-51D	113
Black	44-13535	MC-R	P-51D	116
Bradshaw	43-28433	MC-B	P-38J	101
Bradshaw	44-13660	MC-B	P-51D	110
Bullers	44-14365	MC-E	P-51D	111
Byrd	42-67200	MC-K	P-38J	103
Cameron	44-13846	MC-C	P-51D	111
Campbell	44-13751	MC-F	P-51D	112
Daniel	44-14365	MC-E	P-51D	111
Denbo	44-13620	MC-H	P-51D	112
Dufresne	44-14844	MC-D	P-51D	111
Franklin	42-104086	MC-F	P-38J	101
Gardner	44-13873	MC-U	P-51D	118
Graham	42-67926	MC-L	P-38J	103
Hamme	44-13753	MC-Y	P-51D	119
Heiden	42-67427	MC-H	P-38J	102
Heiden	44-13620	MC-H	P-51D	112
Ilfrey	43-28431	MC-O	P-38J	105
Ilfrey	44-13761	MC-I	P-51D	112
Ilfrey	44-13761	MC-I	P-51D	113
Ingebrightsen	44-13752	MC-A	P-51D	109
Jackson	42-67988	MC-J	P-38J	102
Jones	44-72266	MC-J	P-51D	112
Jones	44-11244	MC-Z	P-51D	120
Kies	44-11195	MC-N	P-51D	115
Lee	44-15198	MC-L	P-51D	114
Lewis	42-67928	MC-L	P-38J	103-4
Lewis	43-25054	MC-L	P-51C	113
Lowman	Unknown	MC-X	P-51B/C	118
Merriman	44-13667	MC-M	P-51D	115
Meyer	412-67929	MC-M	P-38J	104
Meyer	42-104308	MC-R	P-38J	107
Meyer	44-72402	MC-M	P-51D	115
Nichols	42-67515	MC-R	P-38J	106
Phipps	44-13660	MC-B	P-51D	110
Pogue	44-13535	MC-R	P-51D	117
Price	43-25054	MC-L	P-51C	114
Randolph	44-13541	MC-N	P-51D	115
Rau	42-69166	MC-R	P-38J	107
Rau	43-104308	MC-R	P-38J	106
Rau	44-13337	MC-R	P-51D	116
Reichard	43-25064	MC-V	P-51C	118
Sass	44-13667	MC-T	P-51D	117
Shelton	44-13653	MC-Q	P-51D	116
Schons	44-11219	MC-A	P-51D	109
Scott	43-25054	MC-L	P-51C	114
Skinner	44-13660	MC-B	P-51D	109
Smith	43-28412	MC-N	P-38J	104
Smith	44-23178	MC-N	P-38J	105
Smith	44-13791	MC-S	P-51D	117
Stewart	44-13751	MC-F	P-51D	112
Strock	Unknown	MC-A	P-51D	109
Taylor	44-14844	MC-D	P-51D	111

Pilot	Serial	Code	Type	Page
Watson	42-67929	MC-R	P-38J	104
Webb	44-13760	MC-Z	P-51D	120
Williams	42-67988	MC-Q	P-38J	105
Wyman	44-13661	MC-W	P-51D	118
Yarbrough	Unknown	MC-Y	P-51D	119
Yarbrough	44-72383	MC-Y	P-51D	119
Unknown	Unknown	MC-Z	P-51D	119

55th Fighter Group

38th Fighter Squadron: CG

Pilot	Serial	Code	Type	Page
Amoss	44-15123	CG-Z	P-51D	133
Ayers	42-67077	CG-Q	P-38H	127
Ayers	42-67277	CG-Q	P-38J	127
Carr	44-14068	CG-F	P-51D	129
Clark	44-72784	CG-N	P-51D	130
Clark	44-14296	CG-S	P-51D	131
Clemmons	44-15492	CG-U	P-51D	132
Clifton	44-13723	CG-T	P-51D	131
Coons	44-14068	CG-C	P-51D	129
Earls	44-13937	CG-N	P-51D	130
Elliott	44-13623	CG-K	P-51D	130
Fryer	44-13084	CG-Z	P-51D	133
Jenkins	42-67074	CG-J	P-38H	125
Jenkins	42-67825	CG-J	P-38J	126
Kreft	44-267904	CG-O	P-38J	127
Landers	44-13823	CG-O	P-51D	130
Lawrence	44-13701	CG-D	P-51D	129
Littlefield	44-13577	CG-U	P-51D	132
Penn	44-14451	CG-Q	P-51D	131
Sherman	44-13611	CG-U	P-51D	132
Shipman	42-67060	CG-A	P-38H	124
Shipman	42-67805	CG-A	P-38J	124
Sill	44-11370	CG-R	P-51K	131
Snell	44-13549	CG-A	P-51D	128
Thorsen	44-13747	CG-I	P-51D	129
Tipton	44-26971	CG-X	P-38J	128
Unknown	42-67064	CG-C	P-38H	125
Unknown	Unknown	CG-H	P-38J	125
Unknown	42-68132	CG-I	P-38J	125
Unknown	42-67199	CG-Y	P-38J	128
Trainer	43-12195	CG-1	P-51B	133
Trainer	Unknown	CG-3	P-51B	133

338th Fighter Squadron: CL

Pilot	Serial	Code	Type	Page
Black	44-11639	CL-L	P-51K	139
Blount	42-67057	CL-X	P-38H	136
Cramer	44-14121	CL-Z	P-51D	141
Dargan	44-63225	CL-C	P-51D	137
Gevorkian	44-14156	CL-F	P-51D	137
Haworth	44-13642	CL-K	P-51D	138

Pilot	Serial	Code	Type	Page
Henry	44-63227	CL-G	P-51D	138
John	44-13642	CL-K	P-51D	139
Kelly	44-13607	CL-H	P-51D	138
Konantz	44-14278	CL-N	P-51D	139
Konantz	44-72296	CL-P	P-51D	141
Lashbrook	Unknown	CL-T	P-51D	141
McGill	44-13743	CL-X	P-51D	141
McGinn	44-13740	CL-P	P-51D	140
McGinn	44-13954	CL-P	P-51D	140
McGinn	44-14291	CL-P	P-51D	140
McGinn	44-72296	CL-P	P-51D	140
Mercurio	44-13743	CL-X	P-51D	141
Righetti	44-14223	CL-M	P-51D	139
Stroud	42-67704	CL-K̲	P-38J	134
Schank	42-104106	CL-T	P-38J	134
Schank	44-13668	CL-I	P-51D	138
White	Unknown	CL-V	P-38J	135
White	42-67030	CL-Y	P-38H	136
Unknown	44-14223	CL-A	P-51D	137
Unknown	44-14112	CL-A	P-51D	137
Unknown	42-67042	CL-L	P-38H	134
Unknown	Unknown	CL-X̲	P-38J	136

343rd Fighter Squadron: CY

Pilot	Serial	Code	Type	Page
Abel	44-64159	CY-H	P-51D	149
Allen	42-67966	CY-V	P-38J	145
Allen	44-14049	CY-J	P-51D	149
Bartlett	44-14140	CY-O	P-51D	150
Bebaeff	44-15246	CY-Y	P-51D	153
Birtciel	42-67872	CY-D̲	P-38J	142
Birtciel	44-13350	CY-A	P-51D	146
Birtciel	44-14561	CY-D̲	P-51D	147
Brown	44-14135	CY-V	P-51D	153
Buttke	44-15025	CY-F	P-51D	148
Coggeshall	44-15608	CY-T	P-51D	152

Pilot	Serial	Code	Type	Page
Dvorak	Unknown	CY-A	P-51D	146
Eichhorn	44-15060	CY-H	P-51D	148
Erb	42-68095	CY-H	P-38J	142
Erby	44-15025	CY-F	P-51D	148
Erickson	Unknown	CY-E	P-51D	147
Fry	44-13374	CY-D	P-51D	147
Geary	Unknown	CY-K	P-51D	149
Gibbs	44-14175	CY-Q	P-51D	151
Gilbride	42-67053	CY-L	P-38H	143
Giller	44-14985	CY-G	P-51D	148
Giller	44-63204	CY-G	P-51D	148
Gordon	44-14348	CY-P	P-51D	150
Hoeper	44-15060	CY-H	P-51D	148
Hoeper	44-64159	CY-H	P-51D	149
Hoffman	44-14608	CY-T	P-51D	152
Krambo	Unknown	CY-U	P-51D	153
Lewis	44-13907	CY-S	P-51D	151
Lewis	44-14907	CY-S	P-51D	152
Maxwell	44-14384	CY-B	P-51D	146
May	43-28285	CY-J	P-38J	143
McCabe	Unknown	CY-K	P-51D	149
Mercier	44-14384	CY-B	P-51D	146
Mix	44-13837	CY-M	P-51D	150
Morris	44-14235	CY-Y	P-51D	153
Ozinga	44-13837	CY-M	P-51D	150
Parker	44-14885	CY-D	P-51D	147
Ryan	Unknown	CY-R	P-38J	144
Ryan	44-63231	CY-R	P-51D	151
Sorace	42-67058	CY-S	P-38H	144
Webb	Unknown	CY-W	P-38J	145
Welch	44-14140	CY-O	P-51D	150
Welch	44-72138	CY-Z	P-51D	154
Unknown	42-66718	CY-T	P-38H	144
Unknown	Unknown	CY-T	P-38J	145
Unknown	44-72242	CY-R	P-51D	151
Trainer	43-6928	CY-9	P-51D	154
Trainer	Unknown	CY-10	P-51C	154

Left: P-51Ds of the 55th FS, 20th FG at their base at Kingscliffe shortly before starting the next mission. The canopies are open in case the pilot has to make a quick exit in the event of an engine fire. Nearest aircraft is believed to be 44-11161, KI-X, flown by Capt. Mont J. Ryan. This machine was originally assigned to Lt. Feibelkorn of the 77th FS and was passed on to the 55th FS when Feibelkorn completed his tour in early December 1944. The date is therefore probably early 1945. See colour profiles 267 and 291.